A Suicide Note

of Hope

For Alexis

Hank K McGovern

5/23/19

A Suicide Note

of Hope

MORE THAN A MEMOIR

Hank McGovern

Peaceful Moon Press

Published by Peaceful Moon Press

ISBN: 1517529646
ISBN 13: 9781517529642

Printed in the United States of America ISBN-13: 978-0-692-56898-9
Library of Congress Control Number: 2015916625
CreateSpace Independent Publishing Platform
North Charleston, South Carolina

About the Author

Hank McGovern has practiced psychology in North Carolina and Delaware since 1983 when he earned his Master of Arts Degree in Clinical Psychology. He has run 10 marathons including the Boston Marathon, completed 28 triathlons including an Ironman on Cape Cod and was an English Channel aspirant, having trained for it for three years. Hank fashions his life on his values and growing from adversity.

He states, "I live for my philosophy so my philosophy can help me live." His mission is to reduce suicide by promulgating a new, unique perspective about the meaning of suicidal ideation.

About "A Suicide Note of Hope, More than a Memoir"
In *A Suicide Note of Hope*, I document an adventurous and traumatic memoir characterized by empowerment, inspiration, transformation, and humor. In "Goodbye", I begin the note and describe the precipitator, a spurious charge of sexual harassment made against me that was published in the Washington Post. In "Early Years: Chaos, Trauma, and Adventure", I describe a childhood fraught with pain, beginning at age 3 when my mother "fell" down the steps, broke her neck and died. Subsequently,

I had repeated rejections, being moved around so often that I lived in 10 different homes with that many sets of parental figures. A soft humor can be felt in my embrace of these younger years. In "Death Kisses and Transformations", I reflect on numerous times when I came close to death and quote William Blake, "When one kisses death, life becomes infinitely sweet." I ultimately conclude poetically, "Death is my best friend. It reminds me to enjoy life more each day." The reader can learn about a number of self-help skills from meditation and assertive behavior to cognitive skills and self-hypnosis that I have used to struggle through an adult life with a flimsy childhood foundation. My accomplishments in marathon running and triathlons and one about my evolution in religion and spirituality top off efforts to empower and transform myself in order to transcend the vestiges from childhood. The reader can learn useful skills and receive inspirational ideas for transformations.

A salient feature of this work includes the potentially lifesaving reframe of suicidal thoughts as a good thing and not a bad thing; they are signals that something in one's life does need to die. It's just not the person who needs to do so. With the death a new and beautiful life can be born. Please read it with love.

Dedication

This book is dedicated to the memory of my heroes: BF Skinner, Albert Ellis, and Milton H. Erickson.

A note of thanks is given to my friends Mike Hughes, Jayne Arrowood, Amelia Bland-Waller, Stan Dzimitrowicz, Bob Hensley, Denny Fernald, and cousin, Lou Stackler, who all have kept me alive.

CHAPTER 1

"I take it that no man is educated who has never dallied with the thought of suicide."

WILLIAM JAMES

PSYCHOLOGIST AND PHILOSOPHER

IT WOULD ONLY BE POLITE for me to introduce myself and provide a bit of an explanation before murdering myself.

My name is Hank, and I am a 42-year-old, single psychologist with a masters degree. I mention my profession and degree because they relate to my last and final crisis of injustice, a wrongful termination from a mental health center. The last nail in the coffin, if you will excuse the pun.

I have frequently enjoyed drama, and I mostly agree with the Shakespearean line, "All life is but a stage..." Therefore, I will create a dramatic display of suicide to satisfy your appetite for theater, with blood-stained walls, overdose vomit, and a deference to gravity from my tenth story apartment window. The media will love it. The combination of overdose with pills and throat slitting reflects my androgynous style, as you might be aware that it's more effeminate to overdose and more masculine to use violence. An androgynous suicide seems more balanced and complete. Also, the balanced act will serve as a farewell to both God the Father and Mother Nature, kind of cosmic and beautiful. Of course the violence will be my eternal bon voyage to the bitches and bastards of this world, hypocritical automatons who have helped me reach this decision. Do not misunderstand me; I am not blaming the automatons for my act of suicide. I own the responsibility for the act and believe each person is ultimately responsible for the act of suicide. I refuse to give anyone power by blaming them for my exit. I am willing to hold them as precipitating factors, though, as they created events that awakened my internal Grim Reaper who lies dormant in all of us. The decision to depart, however, is mine.

It is 1:00 a.m. on this cool October night, and with my window slightly open, I can hear the gentle reaction of trees to a whispering wind that makes the candlelight dance playfully on the moonlit-shad- owed walls of my room. The peacefulness of this moment speaks the language of death. She invites me, and the pain will be gone as soon as I accept her invitation. The violence will begin soon after sunrise and by 7:00 a.m., the squad cars will have arrived and a few curious onlookers will capture a brief glance at my mangled corpse.

You might wonder why I've reached this decision, and I am acutely aware of its' importance. After all, the philosopher, Albert Camus, once articulated the only truly important philosophical question is whether to end one's life. All else is moonshine. Certainly my suicide will be the ulti- mate act of control over my life and death cycle, my cosmic existence, and how many people choose to exert this kind of control over their destiny? In all honesty, though, I do have to question, am I taking control or am I allowing the bitches and bastards to control my fate? Am I giving into them? It doesn't matter so much now. I can't stand the intolerable pain that just goes on and on. Freedom from the pain will be my reward. Never mind that I won't exist to enjoy the reward. I don't have time for logic. Nevertheless, Nietzsche does make sense: " The final reward to the dead is to die no more."

I am reminded of my last suicide attempt nearly 23 years ago during the midst of a severe depression. I had just returned to the home of my cousin, Jack, after my first semester at High Point College, where the depression invaded me. I missed the first semester of that Freshman year because I was recovering from a car accident that occurred in August of '72. When I moved to college for the Spring quarter, I had trouble making friends and concentrating on my studies and became severely depressed. At any rate, Jack had no clue as to how to relate to a depressed 19 year old who he had just taken into his home three years earlier. He acted like I should have been able to function much better than I was able and even did me the dubious favor of getting me a construction job. If you are familiar with the fatigue and weakness experienced by someone who is severely depressed, you can imagine how I functioned on a construction job. I usually got away with sitting in a corner of an apartment we were building. The suicide attempt occurred when I awakened in the middle of the night, as I dreaded four more hours of agonized tossing and turning before sunrise. There had been too many of those nights. The solution? Cancel the agony forever with 19 sleeping pills. Anticipating my death within an hour or so, I laid in bed with a peaceful sadness, allowing memories of Mary, Cindy, and a few other ex-girlfriends to drift through my mind. Mary, on more than one occasion, informed me that her mother had talked of adopting me. Cindy was one of the most beautiful girls in the sophomore class and my first girlfriend. And then the sun rose and despite my groggy state, I struggled out of bed to the cacophony of an oblivious Jack, who was giving me orders to do some yard work. I failed in my first attempt at that young age, but I was only a light- weight. I'll succeed this time.

Why am I bothering to write you a long note since I intend to kill myself? I don't know. Maybe I don't need to know.

You may be familiar with the problem of sexual harassment in the workplace. You may also be aware of how it is exploited as a weapon by corrupt employers. Well, I received a false charge of sexual harassment in April 1996 when I worked at the Cluckland Mental Health Center in South Carolina, and the charge was an example of the hysteria with which that problem is often treated. The charge was based on me lightheartedly telling a coy female worker that I was going to "flirt with" her on two occasions. The Center's Administrators, Dr. Brenner, Dr. Stone, and Dr. Wilson wanted to fire me for unrelated reasons. I think the problem should be called sexual hysteriament in cases like mine. To be fired for telling a woman that I was going to flirt with her? I didn't even subsequently flirt with her. I wish you could know more details of the situation so you could understand my decision to exit. Maybe you could forgive me. It would take too much energy to explain.

Please forgive me for anything I've done to hurt or harm anyone. I never meant to cause you pain. I hope you will understand my intention now is to avoid any further trouble I might cause on this planet by just getting out of the way.

While I am aware of my anger, I am also aware of a little sadness. I have a few good memories about people, times, and places. I have to admit, I will miss them, unless of course I become dust in which case there will be no I. If there's no I, there won't be an absence of pain because there has to be something to miss the pain. Of course without an I, the dust of my being blends into an ocean of life-dust where you will join me one day.

The sun arose sometime ago, and my pills and razor blade are still where they were at 1:00 a.m. I feel a bit weary albeit a bit motivated to finish this explanation to you before my commission of a final exit. Allow me forty winks, and I will continue.

CHAPTER 2

Early Years: Chaos, Trauma, and Adventure

"When I look back on my childhood I wonder how I managed to survive at all. It was, of course, a miserable childhood... worse yet is the miserable Irish-Catholic childhood."

FRANK MCCOURT,
ANGELA'S ASHES

I NOTICED THAT INSTEAD OF completing my suicide as planned, I dreamed about my childhood. Most people didn't believe I would survive it.

In my exoneration process, I told you immediate reasons for my execution, but I believe this note will be more complete if I include some remote reasons from those early haunting years.

I recently spoke to an old friend, Cindy, who lives in Wilmington, Delaware, about the bogus sexual harassment charge and other job debacles. Cindy has known me since I was 17, and she responded without hesitation to my descriptions, "That sounds like something that would happen to you" and giggled a bit. Perhaps sensing I did not take her remark as a compliment, she qualified that I was not deserving of misfortune; bad luck just seemed to follow me along my path in life.

However, I know Cindy was politely telling me I have responsibility in creating my misfortune, and I am aware of some truth in that perspective. This bag of bones called "Hank McGovern" has often said things to piss people off, particularly authority figures who abuse their power and show disrespect to their subordinates–this pattern has continued since my youth. The particular history that has shaped my personality style is not one I requested, and I will provide a description of it as an excuse for my suicide. It will serve as a mitigating factor in the judgment for my hereafter, if there is one. Perhaps my expression will also fire me up enough to complete my final act according to the promise in the beginning of this note. I would hate to disappoint you.

My Mother   *Father/War Hero*

My father was an alcoholic airplane pilot in 1953 when he met my mother who was a waitress in the restaurant he frequented. Relatives say his alcoholism began in India and China during World War II where he routinely "took shots" before flying over the Himalayas, known as "the hump," transporting wounded and dead soldiers. He became captain, was awarded medals, and apparently my mother was impressed; she got pregnant with him.

Since they were Roman Catholic, they were most likely opposed to abortion and chose to get married instead. As a consequence, I was born

March 15, 1954, and according to stories from aunts and uncles as well as from facial expressions in some pictures, both of my parents enjoyed and loved me–when they were sober. They fought physically and verbally when they were drunk, and I am certain the Guillain- Barre Syndrome, a childhood disease of the nervous system, that I developed when I was two or three was brought on by their violence.

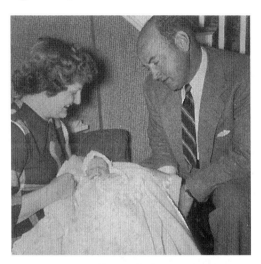

Parents loving

My memory of Guillain-Barre syndrome is limited. I was playing with a green, battery-operated car on the living room floor after supper. I attempted to stand up but immediately fell down with each attempt. I took each fall quite matter-of-factly. After several of them, I crawled to the kitchen doorway to demonstrate my newly acquired failure to my parents who were sitting and talking at the kitchen table. Do you remember a toothpaste commercial in which a child says, "Look mom, dad, no cavities!" after a dental visit? Well, my presentation was something like that commercial–"Look mom, dad, I can't stand up!" That is all I remember. I've been told that Guillain-Barre Syndrome was similar to polio, that the fear was that I would not walk again, and that since doctors were afraid I could be starting an epidemic, I was kept in isolation. I do not know if the problem was traumatic. I may have even benefited from the isolation; it gave me a time-out from the drunken violence.

My mother fell down the flight of stairs from the second floor of our two-story house, broke her neck and died when I was three. The incident happened at night, and many years later I learned my father was suspected of pushing her; the position in which she was found suggested force had been used in her fall. He also slept on the couch that night and had been drunk. Since he reportedly passed a lie detector test, no charges were brought against him. I believe because he was drunk, he pushed her down the steps but did not mean to kill her.

Mother holds me on steps where she was killed

During the next four years I lived with my father in that house on McGovern Terrace, the street being named after my grandfather and his family. He owned a construction company and coal business and was known for a legal case in which he fought against price fixing set by FDR–my grandfather won the case, representing himself as his own attorney. We were fortunate to have two other McGovern families including uncles, aunts, and cousins, on McGovern Terrace, as they minimized the extreme neglect of me from my father's worsening alcoholism. How could he take care of me and the bottle? I recall, for instance, walking to my

A Suicide Note of Hope

Aunt Nancy's house to request her to tie my shoelaces and to Aunt Betty's house to occasionally get lunch. I also recall nuns from St. Elizabeth's Elementary School that I attended in the first grade feeding me bananas as they were familiar with the neglect.

The irresponsibility resulting from Daddy's alcoholism was not without some fun. When the electricity was turned off from not paying the bill, my abode became the popular haunted house with friends like Billy Romanski. We could hide out in the cold, dank basement only to escape into the upstairs living and dining rooms that were dark and not much different than the basement. Knowing my mother broke her neck there added to the eerie feeling as Billy reminded me. Good ol' Billy.

I loved my father, and I am thankful he never abused me physically or sexually. I do remember being locked out of the house one night and was glad when he finally stumbled home in his drunken condition. He had trouble unlocking the door and uttered the phrase "son of a bitch," only for me to take it personally. Quick to retort, even as a five-year-old, I replied, "If I'm a son of a bitch, you must be a bitch—I'm your son." If he was prone to physical abuse, he would have done it then I suppose. Another memory includes our ride in the car one evening while he was driving drunk. When the officer stopped us, I asserted a plea, "Please officer, don't do anything to my daddy!" He spent the night in jail, and I spent the night at my neighbor, Billy Lukowski's house.

I vividly recall waving good-bye to my father from the airplane window just before takeoff when I was seven. With pride, I informed the man in the seat next to me, "See that bald man down there? That's my dad." It was the last day I lived with him. Since he did not have his driving license, my Uncle Charles drove us to the airport. My father told me I was flying to my Aunt Marge and Uncle Ray's home in Arlington, Virginia for a summer visit, when, in fact, I was being sent there to stay; he was unable to take care of me because the bottle was taking care of him.

So I spent my second grade attending McKinley School and lived with my aunt, uncle, and their daughter, Belinda, who went by the nickname Blin. Ray was a kind, generous man and a commander with the

U.S. Navy. He had a law degree, worked with the appellate court and later went on to become a judge on the court. He encouraged me to read, and I became acquainted with The Adventures of Tom Sawyer and Huckleberry Finn. I thought Tom was so cool pulling off the trick of getting his friends to whitewash the fence, and I identified with Huck whose mother died, leaving him to live with his alcoholic father. I also read Abe Lincoln, Frontier Boy and still remember the first page which stated he was born twelve miles from Knob Creek, in Hodgenville, Kentucky. Uncle Ray took me to historic sites in the D.C. area including Civil War battlefields and monuments, and I clearly remember the view from atop the Washington Monument after an exhausting climb up those stairs. My Aunt Marge, my mother's older sister, was a devout Roman Catholic and made certain I attended a religion class after Catholic mass on Sundays. Marge relied heavily on her faith to manage a seemingly endless stream of worry and physical complaints, a pattern that would continue for the duration of her long life. In general, Blin was unhappy that I was living there, and I was too, missing my father and occasionally requesting to be returned to him. I recall Blin telling me I was a "spoiled brat" and did not sense that she was simply attempting to enrich my vocabulary. In fairness to her, she did give me a transistor radio for my birthday that introduced me to the world of pop. "Johnny Angel" was a hit, and though it was tailored more to female tastes, I felt enamored by the sensuality of Shelley Fabares. Some years later my aunt told me Blin pressured her into sending me back to my father, and despite his incapacity to take care of me, she attempted to return me to him.

Subsequent to completion of second grade, Ray and Marge drove me to my Aunt Gerry's home in Wilmington, Delaware. Gerry was my father's sister so it made sense to Marge to drop me off at Gerry's so that she could take responsibility for delivering me to my father. The harsh words between Gerry and Marge was the beginning of their enmity that would last into their octogenarian years (at the time they were in their late 40s). Gerry was aware my father could not take care of me, and she drove me to Virginia Beach where her son, Jason, and his wife, Maria, and their two sons, Patch and Jackmer, were vacationing. Gerry asked Jason and Maria if they would take me into their home in Charlottesville, Virginia, and I then had my third grade home set. Many memories of that year bring a smile to my face. Maria once said she was going to faint when Patch and Jackmer, two and three years younger than me, and I "cleaned" our supper plates. And so each time we ate all of our food we'd request her to faint–perhaps as a means of satisfying her penchant for drama while appeasing us, she would "faint." When Patch and I were getting into mischief one night at supper, Maria yelled, "Patrick! Henry!" (my given name) and having a sense of humor, managed to disrupt her own annoyance by yelling "George Washington! Thomas Jefferson!" In the Fall, Patch and I and a few other kids were playing in the leaves, and we had Patch buried in them so that only his head was visible. We were excited to see ourselves photographed in the Charlottesville newspaper with the headline "A Small Patch in Leaves."

Despite some pleasant memories, I continued to feel sad and hurt that I was not with my father. I heard he lost his job as a commercial pilot, lost the house on McGovern Terrace and was living in a room on Market Street in Wilmington, but, of course, that eight-year-old heart simply wanted to be with him, regardless of the circumstances. Apparently Maria was fed up with me, as I recall her slapping my face when I did something so simple as say goodnight in a sing- songy voice. Consequently, I began to evince other misbehaviors. A conspicuous example involved a walk down a neighborhood sidewalk that began innocently enough on a hot, dry summer day. I was with a friend who had a book of matches, and as we struck them one at a time and threw them into the field beside us, we knew each one would go out before landing in the field. Of course it only took one to fail to extinguish such that the field was ablaze while our fun quickly transformed into fear. We ran to the nearest house which was just 15 yards or so away and alerted the home dwellers to our "discovery" that the field was "on fire." They called the fire department and we were heroes! The consequence of the fire engine, the siren, and the sight of the men putting out our creation was not sufficiently positive, however, for us to continue that particular activity. Fear drowned our excitement.

Although Maria never knew about the incident, she did take exception to a number of less flagrant acts.

Adding to my knowledge of Abe Lincoln, Paul Revere, and Daniel Boone from the many books I was encouraged to read, Charlottesville was a wonderful area in which to learn about and appreciate some of Virginia's most historical figures. For instance, each morning on my way to the school bus stop, I could see Monticello, Thomas Jefferson's home, on a hill in the distance. It was a kind of mystical experience for an eight-year-old mind to read about our third President and to then regularly see his famous dwelling at the beginning of each day. The memories almost touch a soft spot and elicit a wistful nostalgia. I am also aware my suicide will destroy those memories—except now you have them.

I was making friends and beginning to adapt to life in Charlottesville. Then Aunt Marge and Uncle Ray took me for what was supposed to be a two day visit at Christmas. I went with them to Arlington, attended the Roman Catholic St. Ann's church on Sunday and waited patiently on a bench outside an office where they had a conference with a couple of nuns. When they exited the meeting, the nun told me lovingly, "We'll see you in school on Monday." Shocked beyond disbelief you might say I was—I expected to be returned to Jason and Maria, not to be kidnapped by the one Holy and Catholic Apostolic Church! Technically, my aunt and uncle were kidnapping me, and the nuns were only accessories, but my anger didn't care who was mostly to blame. When we arrived back at the house, I pitched a royal fit until I "persuaded" them to return me to Charlottesville. It was not one of the Ten Commandments that a child could not refuse to be kidnapped.

I want to relate another relevant memory from Charlottesville before moving on to my fourth grade home—a memory involving what might be labeled in our hysterical era as "childhood sexual harassment." Karen, Nancy, and one or two other girls were all about my age, and since they thought I was "cute", they invited me into Karen's basement for a surprise. They hid behind a wall while they had me sit on the other side to wait for the excitement. I recall feeling both a little con- fused and a little flattered when they each danced out from the wall in training bras with their shirts off. Little did they know they were teasing a boy who would one day be charged with sexual harassment even though his charge was not nearly as egregious as theirs!

Apparently I was too unpleasant for Maria and Jason so they sent me to my Aunt Gerry's home in Wilmington under the pretense of a brief summer vacation visit. I can hear Gerry informing me while we were riding in the car to get Breyer's ice cream one night that I would not be returning to Charlottesville but would live with her, her 21 year-old daughter, Merrilee, and Merrilee's husband, Fred, in their house in Woodcrest, a suburb of Wilmington. I was glad to know I would be living in the area close to my father, as he was still living in his hotel room in downtown Wilmington. It would be arranged for me to visit him on Sundays by catching the bus from Woodcrest. Despite my eagerness to see my father more often, though, I felt confused and hurt that I was being shuffled from one home to another, especially under the guise of traveling to them for "vacation." I'd miss my new friends and, especially, those dancing girls. And now I'd never be able to get up the courage to burn down Charlottesville completely. During that fourth grade year, I attended St. Matthew's Parochial School with nuns as teachers and disciplinarians and lived with the strictness of Merrilee who was often punitive. I did not understand how the penguin, Sister Roberta, could get away with banging a student's head against a brick wall to emphasize her point. I do not believe Jesus Christ, who she was allegedly representing, would have condoned her disciplinary method. Neither was I pleased with Merrilee's technique of teaching me how to use a knife and fork–she made me cut dried sponges that were actually too hard to cut. She also used an object, I forget exactly what it was, for whipping, an experience that was more severe than a mere spanking. And when I forgot to wear my shoe rubbers one rainy day, Merrilee decided to make me wear rubbers to school every day thereafter, rain or sunshine. You might imagine the embarrassment I felt on the sunny days. Merrilee the sadist. Fred was a little more pleasant, teaching me how to throw and catch a baseball, to root for the Los Angeles Dodgers, and how to swim and shoot a rifle. My Aunt Gerry worked as a secretary for DuPont, and I don't recall much about her from that year, probably because she was too tired to do much after her workday. All in all, I was tense and scared most of that year.

Perhaps the anxiety was exacerbated by my Sunday visits to my father. As a routine, I would obediently go to St. Matthew's Roman Catholic Church, always by myself, on Sunday morning. I would, in good faith, pray to God that my father would be sober that day. Most of the time he was drunk, and I could tell whether or not he was from the window of the bus as it approached him waiting outside his hotel for my arrival. I began to question the value of praying to an entity called God; I was holding up my end of the deal, saying my prayers, going to confessions, mass, doing the rosary and what about Him? In my pathetic and desperate effort to make my father stop drinking, I recall taking one of his bottles of Seagram's from his medicine cabinet in his bathroom and began pouring it into the sink. As though it were an emergency, he bounded from his bed and snatched it from me before the bottle was empty, but did not hit me. Again, if he was prone to physical abuse he would have likely whacked me a good one. You see, his lack of physical abuse of me is one reason I do not believe he intended to kill my mother. In fact, he was a kind man, a good man. Often he would take me to a movie, and I remember seeing "The Incredible Journey," "101 Dalmatians," and "South Pacific." (His judgment may have been impaired in taking a nine-year-old to see "South Pacific"). On occasion he left me alone in the movie theater and would get me afterward; at those times, I felt like a burden. He probably was leaving me at the theater alone so he could drink his whiskey which he seemed to care for a lot more than me. During his sober Sundays, we did have some pleasant times, walking down to Brandywine Creek where we'd gingerly step from one stone in the rushing water to another and having submarine sandwiches at Sam's Sub Shop or steak and potatoes at the Bonfire. We also would go to the airport where he flew before he lost his job, and one of his ex-coworkers might take us for a short flight or up in the control tower. I always felt uptight and anxious catching the bus at the end of those visits because it meant returning to the hostility of Merrilee, and I also felt sad about leaving my father another time. Maybe one day good ol' God would hear my prayers and make Dad stop drinking so I could live with him.

Certainly no one was happy with my living situation, and my Uncle Bill would serendipitously discover a solution through an acquaintance, John Groff, at his job as an accountant. John had attended the Milton Hershey School in Hershey, Pennsylvania, an orphanage for boys started by the chocolate mogul, Milton Hershey. One lonely day I was standing at the dining room window feeling a little down, looking out at the snow, when Merrilee announced she had something to tell me. I was certain I had committed another sin, probably as bad as not wearing my rubbers and she had decided to beat me and lock me in a closet for a month. Instead, she informed me I would be interviewed for acceptance into Milton Hershey in the next month. If I was accepted, I would live there. I would escape Merrilee! I effortfully controlled the alacrity in my heart as exciting thoughts raced through my nine-year-old mind. Might Milton Hershey give me a happy home?

Chocolate Years

In 1909 Milton S. Hershey and his wife Catherine began an industrial school for four orphan boys. In 1918 he endowed the school with his fortune he had acquired from the chocolate industry. Food, shelter, clothing, education, medical and dental needs were provided for free. Set in a pastoral atmosphere of rolling hills and verdant landscape, the idyllic homelife appeared almost dreamlike and certainly was an answer for many boys and widowed parents.

On June 15, 1964, my Aunt Gerry drove me to the student home Revere (named after Paul, how cool!), the junior home cottage in which I'd live for the fifth grade. I was on a roll–five different homes with five different parental figures for each of my first five grades! Mr and Mrs. Miller ("mom" and "pop") were house parents at Revere, and they were both warm, friendly people. I suddenly had 11 "brothers" as each of the homes housed a certain number of boys. We had our share of chores, responsibility, and discipline. Paddling was in vogue, and my buttocks were black and blue on more than one occasion. Extramural sports programs were organized, participation was encouraged, and I conscientiously played goalie for Sherman and Revere's soccer team, feeling wondrous pride in winning the championship that year. Implanted in my memory bank is the chocolate soccer field cake Pop and Mr. Siler bought for a party celebration. My sense of pride was also enhanced when I was elected President of our fifth grade class and made the Distinguished Honor Roll. Life was getting better.

Still I missed my father and even entertained the fantasy that we might live together one day. I recall attempting to get my father to like me more by borrowing some humor from <u>Huckleberry Finn</u>. I stated in a letter, "I am learning my multiplication tables and am all the way up to 7x5=36," although when Huck made the remark I believe he was being serious and thought his arithmetic was correct. My likeability was not the issue, though, and certainly was not sufficient to maintain Dad's sobriety, and I could only look forward to seeing him on holiday vacations during which I stayed with Aunt Gerry.

Subsequent to fifth grade, the boys transferred to Intermediate Division homes where they would live for three years before being transferred to the Senior Division. I went to Stiegel, named after a Pennsylvania glassmaker, and lived with Mr. and Mrs. Akers and 15 other boys. Stiegel was my sixth household in my first six grades, and it seems the excessive number of personalities with whom I lived would be a prescription for me to develop multiple personality disorder as an adult. As far as I know I just have one, but that's just Hank talking.

Just a week or so after my transfer, I was wrestling on the mat with a couple of fellows, Jake Polonkey and Dwayne Poppe, in the basement. Another boy entered the room with a somber expression and summoned me to go upstairs as I had some unexpected visitors. My Aunt Gerry, Uncle Bob, and Aunt Mary were in the office with Mr. and Mrs. Akers, and they all were eerily solemn. Aunt Gerry had me sit on the couch beside her and, with a gentle firmness, informed me my father was found dead two nights ago, about 2:00 a.m., on a city street. He had been drinking and choked to death on his vomit.

Words cannot fully describe the intensity of my reaction. I can say I cried uncontrollably while experiencing a sense of disbelief and betrayal, not only from my father but from God. I attended the funeral at Mealey's Funeral Home in Wilmington and recall the immense sadness I felt while looking at my father in the casket as well as the panic when it was lowered into the ground at All Saints Cathedral Cemetery the next morning. He was buried beside my mother, and my imagination found serenity in the superstition that my parents could now peacefully coexist in heaven. Interestingly I clung to that belief despite my earlier discoveries about the nonexistence of Santa Claus, the Easter bunny, and fairy godmother. Ah, the fantasies born by the mental tricks of childhood. The following poem written about ten years after my father's death reflected my experience at the funeral:

Leaving

Cased in polished walnut, lying in soft white satin,

With a final black suit fitting tight on cold stiffness,

He says goodbye in silence to trickling tear faces

That once wore the anger they now must forget.

It's a sad affair of flowers,

too late prayers drip from lips,

a prelude to marble stones, neatly rowed,

beautiful nametags for all the someones not seen.

Dust, ashes, and water are a holy farewell;

the lowered last home disappears into cool, dark earth,

freezing frantic mourners, branding their memories.

During the sixth grade, I was fortunate enough to make a friendship with Mike Hughes who encouraged me to try out for the swim team, coached by Dick Thieler, our geography teacher. Swimming became an effective antidepressant in helping me cope with the trauma of my father's death. I also joined the choir as a diversion from my feelings of pain, and the early morning practice helped me escape a bit of housework. I suppose the singing was an antidepressant of sorts, and I enjoyed traditional songs such as "Come to the Church in the Wildwood" and "Copenhagen." Music began acquiring a celestial quality for me, and its biological and psychological rewards were icing on the cake. Perhaps it is the gift of music for which I can be eternally grateful. Choir boys, however, were teased, the director called "Happy Harry" due to his alleged gay orientation, and I decided to quit on March 15 as a birthday present to myself. Swimming was a more rein- forcing challenge, though, and especially because I liked the coach, I persisted with it.

For the first time since I began school, I lived in the same house, Stiegel, with the same authority figures (it is almost nauseating to consider them parental figures), the Akers, for more than one year. Mrs. Akers was the worst of the two as she was characteristically overbearing. She'd routinely take one of us boys, frequently me, and give long, tedious lectures, sitting in the stairwell. They were probably more painful than corporal punishment. To her, my attitude was the problem, and when I was on the kitchen crew drying dishes, she'd often say, "Wipe that look off your face and smile Henry." I, on a couple of occasions, wiped my hand across my mouth, producing a ridiculous phoney smile to literally comply with her order, and she would then scold me further for being a smart aleck. Of course my attitude was not the most chipper when I was 11 and 12, and I seldom smiled when I was struggling with the death of my father. Mrs. Akers did not seem to understand that simple reality.

6th Grade Spelling Champ

Considering the authority figures over me as a child, it seems only natural I'd have problems with authority figures as an adult, doesn't it? There were times at Stiegle that could be described as pleasant as well as adventurous and exciting. We lived in a bucolic setting situated in a peaceful valley with nearby hills that provided an opportunity for our exploratory hikes. I continued to progress in swimming, won championships in wrestling tournaments, a trophy for foul shooting in basketball and was proud to be elected the Secretary of the Student Senate. My housemates Bill McConnell, Gary Weiss, Jon Haines and I would catch mice in a field on Saturdays and take them to Dick Thieler, who by that time, was our science teacher, on Mondays. Dick had a boa constrictor, and the class would form a circle around the aquarium in which it resided, to watch it kill and eat the mice. Jon constructed a "guillotine" for a history project which consisted of a board for a body to lie on as well as one shaped to form a blade, and, of course, a hole cut into a board for a neck. Although it most likely would not have broken a neck, and certainly would not have cut a head off, the blade was heavy enough that it would have done some damage to a neck if used appropriately. As eighth graders, we had bullying rights, and we dragged a screaming fifth grader, John, to the guillotine and forced him onto it. We managed to maneuver his neck into the correct position for an "execution," although we were not violent or crazy enough to pull the rope. We did scare him to say the least. Even though we had no intention of actually hurting him physically, Mrs. Akers walked into the room at the moment of the "execution." Shortly thereafter, her lectures seemed to decrease in frequency as did her directives for me to "smile." We had shocked her into speechlessness which, until the execution, was impossible.

While I developed a sense of pride with my athletic and academic achievements, our typing teacher, Mr. Francis, good-naturedly gave me a nickname that arrested my momentum for taking myself too seriously. During a class discussion one day, the word "udders" was mentioned, and I ingenuously asked the meaning of it. I had not milked a cow yet, and I simply had no experience with the word. Mr. Francis, and most of the class, found my question hilarious, subsequently calling me "udders" on a fairly regular basis. In an attempt to join his humor, I chose the definition and description of "udders" as a typing assignment; in the process of typing the paper, I learned another vocabulary word–protrusion.

The worst of Milton Hershey School had not been experienced until I was transferred to the senior division home, Cloverdale, when I was 14. Mr. and Mrs. Simmons were the house parents, and she was the harshest and most punitive of the 19 caretakers I had during my childhood and adolescence. As an example of her sadism, the kitchen floor in Cloverdale was large; she once made a boy scrub the damn thing with a toothbrush. I learned to fear and hate her quickly and knew some form of escape was essential.

Homeboys–a nickname we gave to ourselves–were known to occasionally run away, and the adventurous spirit of the 60s fostered such a plan for me as a means of escape. One night I packed a duffel bag of basic belongings and food, donned a denim jacket and jeans and quietly left Cloverdale at about 1:00 a.m. and began hitchhiking to Wilmington, Delaware. It was August 29, 1968. I remember writing the date on a sign along Highway 322. I really had no idea where I'd end up and fantasized landing in Florida and becoming a beach bum or hippie. The night was cool and quiet and provided a peacefulness never previously felt at such depth. I was superior to most living beings as they laid asleep, vulnerable and weak. I, on the other hand, stayed alert and aware, exploring various possibilities and was reminded of the story The Wolf Man. I was him.

My first ride was a man in a Volkswagen "bug." Almost too synchronous to be true, "Born to be Wild" by Steppenwolf came on the radio, "Hitchin' down the highway, lookin' for adventure...and whatever comes my way...". He only took me 20 miles or so, and I was glad to be let out after such a short distance; I could once again enjoy the fresh air and serenity of the clear sky, replete with twinkling stars. When Emerson once said, " The sky is the daily bread for the eyes," certainly he meant nightly too. As the night enveloped me with its mystery and tranquility, I felt very little, if any, fear. When one is so carefree and tuned into nature by his senses, there is no reason to fear. I had a new identity, a runaway, and went into a trance to fulfill the role.

As an aside, to speak the phrase "to fulfill the role"–is that not what we social beings do essentially? Whether we act politically, religiously, professionally, or romantically, do we honestly seek the truth and exercise our values or do we not immerse ourselves in a drama called life? And the news anchors and journalists love their jobs as narrators, dramatizing everyday events, absorbing our attention for gossip. Certainly, like Mick Jagger sings, "Every cop is a criminal... and all the sinners saints..." we change roles depending on conditions. Shakespeare summed it up too: "All the world's a stage and all the men and women merely players; they have their exits and their entrances and one man in his time plays many parts." If it were not for our dramatic nature, we would be bored even more than we already are. What we call "truth" in our judicial and religious institutions is usually just another theatrical tool.

I rolled into Wilmington at about 7:00 a.m. and had a breakfast of eggs, toast, bacon and juice at a dinette next to the movie theater where my father used to leave me on my Sunday visits to him. I decided to visit a friend, John Marioni, in Woodcrest but, tired from hitchhiking all night, first laid down on a city park bench and took a snooze like an experienced hobo. John was surprised and glad to see me, but since his mother would have qualms about letting a runaway spend the night, I had to sleep under a bush in a nearby yard. The bugs were unpleasant bed companions, but a runaway must be stoic about such things. Since I was concerned the next day that Aunt Gerry would be worried about me–Milton Hershey's administrators routinely informed the legal guardians about a runaway–I decided to call to inform her I was safe. She expressed only a little worry, sympathized a bit when I explained how intolerable Mrs. Simmons was, but then persuaded me to let her take me back to the school and for me to increase my effort to adjust. And so ended my three days of being "born to be wild."

Upon returning to Cloverdale and the Simmons', I was promptly delivered my punishment including two weeks of restrictions, consisting of no TV or any privileges, 10 swats with a paddle, which was a board with holes, and 10 hours of extra work. The label "10 hours" was nominal; Mrs. Simmons invariably would increase the duration of an hour by selecting unbearable, tedious jobs. For instance, one of my jobs included scrubbing to immaculacy each foot of 30 15-foot rafters in the carport, front and back, and the rest of the ceiling. I used a stepladder, scrub brush, and a bucket of hot, sudsy water and "accidentally" fell off the ladder onto the macadam in an attempt to have the task changed to something more reasonable. "Get back up there McGovern!" was the reaction of Simmons, who was polished at identifying victims foolish enough to try faking it to escape her sadism.

Later that year I received a stylish tie as a present from Aunt Gerry, and we had to get clothing approved by administrators if it was not issued by the school. It had wavy green and black stripes and was hip at the time. Before I had a chance to get my tie inspected, Mrs. Simmons cut it in half with a pair of scissors; I was stunned that even she could act so maliciously. I complained to the administrators, but they did nothing about her cruelty. She had no excuse for such heinous behavior, and the only explanation for it must have included some bitches and bastards from her childhood. Ah, I've caught myself providing a reason for her hate, using an understanding attitude. To not be hypocritical, I must use Jagger's "Sympathy for the Devil" occasionally even with her.

It is often difficult to harbor outrage when an understanding attitude and forgiveness creep into the picture and that applies to all people, the Administrators from Cluckland, Merrillee, and Millie Simmons. I have learned that people behave according to certain causes, that behavior is determined. The factors that cause behavior include the genes we have inherited, the learning experiences from our remote and recent past, and the rewarding and punishing consequences in the present. I have favored the humanistic statement by two psychologists, Henry and Ann Giaretto, "People meet their needs in ways they know how to meet them, and if they knew how to meet them differently, they would do so." Similarly, Einstein spoke, "Peace cannot be achieved through force; it can only be reached with under- standing." For me, quotes such as these serve as pearls of wisdom, and when they become integrated, it becomes less tempting to act with revenge. Indeed, how can we act with revenge when we accurately understand the causes of The Other? Maybe Millie Simmons was sexually and physically abused by a father or brother, and, who knows, maybe something about me reminded her of them. While I do not believe the past she experienced excuses her behavior, her trauma at least affords an explanation; understanding the explanation can be a step toward forgiveness.

Nevertheless, during the ninth grade year, I suppressed a volcanic anger that occasionally erupted in oozing seepages. I had not learned about forgiveness yet. During study hour one night, I sat at my desk in my room so incensed that I wrote at the top of a piece of paper "100 Ways to Spell Simmons" and proceeded to list the filthiest expletives imaginable. Maybe it was because I looked guilty or fearful when Mrs. Simmons walked by my room that she decided to walk in and right up to my desk. Attempting to appear calm, I closed the notebook. My effort did not stop her intrusiveness. She opened the notebook and began flipping through the pages, one at a time, while my heart beat rapidly with each resounding flip. A feint hope that she'd miss The Page accompanied my mounting anxiety. Suddenly a slap across my face sent me sprawling out of the chair and onto the carpeted floor. At that moment, I wanted to blend into the floor and become one with it, perhaps my first zen experience. No such luck. Millie said nothing after ordering me to bed for the night.

Mr. Brown, the senior division director, who weighed 300 pounds and stood 6'5", and who had been in the farm league for the Pittsburg Steelers, paid a visit the following morning at the request of Millie. I was summoned to the office. Brown looked mean enough to be on the offensive line. Millie looked like the female rendition of Satan. I was given a choice: 10 swats with the paddle or 10 hours extra work. Considering the 10 hours could easily transform into 20 to 30, depending on the intensity of Millie's sadism for that week, I felt for tunate to have the opportunity to have my buttocks decorated black and blue. As I left the office to join the other students for breakfast, a clowning Jay Rock looked up and made a face at me, triggering my nervous laugh–Millie's obnoxious shrill voice followed with, "O.K. McGovern, if it's so funny how about 10 more!"

I believe the emotional abuse at Cloverdale was responsible for some traumatic effects. I recall having difficulty urinating when I lived there. One thing that worked was to imagine Millie's face in the urinal, placed so that I could pee on it. It worked marvelously. To this day, if I have difficulty urinating in a men's room, or anywhere for that matter, I verbalize an expletive or two and imagine her face—the urine shoots directly into it. The bladder and kidneys do not forgive easily. There was a bit of a silver lining in the year of the Cloverdale cloud. I earned my first year letter on the varsity swim team, and I made a good friend, Dave Feese, who was a senior. Since seniors did not usually befriend freshmen, I felt especially pleased. Dave was on the varsity basketball team, despite his relatively short height at 5'9", and I thoroughly enjoyed our one-on-one competitions as well as just shooting on that outdoor court for fun with him. I can still picture myself covering him, hear the basketball bouncing as he dribbles, having difficulty with his quick movements.

It was in the musical arena, though, that I most relished his knowledge, skill, and zeal. I do not know how much the reader of this note is familiar with the music of the 60s and early 70s, but to me it seems like the golden era of rock for the century; the creative revolution sparked by that era was in the spirit of Dave Feese. He was a drummer in a group, The Stone Myth, and he taught me about the unique splendor of what each instrument had to offer. We discussed details of popular groups such as The Beatles, The Rolling Stones, The Supremes, Steppenwolf, Deep Purple, The Iron Butterfly, and Spirit. And when Dave and I listened to the albums together, whether in the office or basement, we were in a musical heaven of exploration, delight, and discovery. It was Dave who encouraged me to read The Beatles by Hunter Davies, and I identified much with the childhood and adolescence of John Lennon, abandoned by his parents and raised by an aunt. Many years later I thought of Dave when I wrote: "Music is God's sister, visiting the earth for an eternal moment." Dave wrote on the back of his senior picture that he gave to me, "Hank, to a good friend and a great guy. I will never forget you for letting me borrow your albums. If you ever want to get rid of them, look me up. Stay in good spirits and don't let the school get you down." I will never forget him for the gift of friendship he gave me. I may mention Dave Feese's death a little later in this note.

I was transferred from Cloverdale to Southfield at the end of my freshman year. I believe Millie arranged for the transfer since she could not stand me after reading the expletives I used to describe her. I gladly accepted the transfer. I felt a sense of relief at being able to escape her, and my friend and fellow swim team member, Mike Hughes, was at Southfield. However, I continued to feel restless and dissatisfied with life at Milton Hershey within a few days of the transfer. As did Cloverdale, Southfield had cows that we milked, milk that went to the Hershey factory for your chocolate bars, and I did not like cleaning and currying the cows, washing their tails, and you guessed it, their udder bags! I liked rooming with Mike, but a few other older boys did not seem to like me much and one of them, a varsity wrestler, let me know his feelings in what began as a friendly wrestling match; humiliation and soreness ached in my body for days. In general, life after Cloverdale was not as happy as I had hoped.

So, together with Paul Gale, one year my junior, I set out on another escape. We ran away at night and hitchhiked to Wilmington, taking the same route I took a year ago. The only difference in the experience from the last year was that I had to share the quiet night, cool, fresh breeze, the desolate highway and the star-speckled sky with another orphan. Our parental supervision was God the Father and Mother Nature. We were special.

When we reached Wilmington the next morning, Paul decided to go 30 miles north to Philadelphia, his hometown. I waited with him for his bus by the Kent Hotel, where my father used to wait for me six years earlier. I visited John Marioni again and called my Aunt Gerry after a day or so of keeping the adventurous runaway image. To my pleasant surprise, she said she'd take me out of the school since I seemed so miserable–her decision became a major transition in my life.

THE ILLUSION OF FREEDOM

The homeboys of Milton Hershey spoke of life outside of the school as the "free world," not understanding the meaning of freedom, and the responsibility in making the choices and decisions it requires. Freedom would mean being able to wear bell-bottom pants, not having a curfew and growing my hair a certain length. Easy Rider was at the movies and seeing it with Tom, Max, and Mike White, who had also been homeboys, was an exciting introduction to a distorted image of freedom. I no longer had to worry about a tyrant like Millie cutting up my cool ties, and if I felt like going to Dunkin' Donuts after school, I wouldn't have to finish an hour of chores first. I expected freedom would resemble heaven, unaware of how it could also lead to hell.

While I missed a few of my friends from Hershey, I anticipated attending a public high school, Mount Pleasant, with excitement. I would live with my aunt in an apartment and soon experienced a mild anxiety about my new freedom. How would I adjust to a lifestyle of attending school with girls, choosing who to try to make friends with, deciding the best clothes to buy to fit in, and when to study French and geometry. And how could my school subjects compete with mini- skirts for my attention and concentration? While my Aunt Gerry was pleasant and kind, she used a rather permissive approach with me, an approach, that of course, failed miserably.

Some say, "you are what you eat" or "you are…whatever," and much of my life seems like "you are what you read." Immediately after getting out of Milton Hershey, I read a book about a gang called Tomboy, and although the protagonist was a girl, I felt like I learned appropriate protocol from the behavior of the boys in the gang. In an effort to make friends and to simultaneously satisfy my appetite for rebellion and adventure, I began hanging out at night with a gang. We took pride in our name, "First State," wore black leather jackets, would usually spend evenings in the parking lot of a hamburger joint, used drugs (mostly just pot) and alcohol (my worst night was mixing several beers, a pint of cherry vodka, and a few diet pills), occasionally got into mischief and fights and welcomed our reputation as greasers. Several conspicuous events come to mind from my times with First State. Following a football game at William Penn High, a game that we won, I individually began taunting a group of tough guys from the other side in the parking lot. The lads reciprocated with their own aggressive language. The last thing I remembered was informing them that "we" (my cronies who were talking in friendlier language to other people about 20 yards from me and were completely unaware of my shenanigans) would drive across town, pick up some more of our tough guys and return for a sincere brawl. Suddenly I was supine after being knocked out, and as I opened my eyes, the world was spinning and rather hazy. My friends decided to come to my aid, but no gang fight ensued. I was obviously a lightweight and did not know when, where, how, and with whom to pick a fight. Dave Hunnings drove me to the hospital on his motorcycle, since my lip was bleeding profusely. I was uncertain as to whether I should feel stupid and embarrassed or cool and tough in school on Monday when the other students, particularly a few attractive girls, marveled at the stitches in my lip; of course the former, but not the latter, was appropriate. I discovered the fellow who sucker punched me was known as "Doodlebug Turko," and he was in the process of becoming a semi-professional boxer. I could certainly vouch for him.

I continued to maintain my athletic activities, mostly sandlot basketball and varsity swimming. In the fall and early winter of that sophomore year, I constructed an almost surreal schedule of playing basketball with a group of wholesome, law-abiding fellas in the early evening and dashed off after the games to the First State hangout. I was the only kid involved with both groups and in all honesty, only felt on the periphery of both, getting into a couple of fights with members of each group. With the basketball crew, there was Mike Stenapoulos, who was irritated as hell at me during one game for no apparent reason. When I knocked the ball out of his hands at one point, he sucker punched me in the face. For some reason, probably Catholic guilt, I never threw the first punch in a fight, but if the other guy hit me, that gave me the license to light into him, except, of course, in a case like Doodlebug. Being better in wrestling than boxing, I threw Mike to the concrete, got on his back and repeatedly punched the back of his head so that his face kept slamming into the concrete. I soon got off and despite his somewhat bloody and black-and-blue face, we reconciled and kept a bit of a friendship.

A similar skirmish happened at the First State hangout one night when Fran Butler and I were wrestling, initially just for fun. Franny had a reputation as a macho, violent fighter, and when I began "winning" I suddenly realized I had a tiger by the tail; he began taking it a little too seriously. We abruptly stood up. He pushed me against a wall and with his fists clenched and his temper bordering on rage, positioned his face an inch or so from mine and challenged, "Do you wanna fight mother-fucker?!" I just looked at him incredulously. He obviously had some hurt pride. "Say yes or no!" He had me trapped–if I said no I'd be a "chicken"

Recent runaway

and if I said yes I'd be in a pointless fight with a madman who might hurt me. "Say yes or no!!" Deciding to be the funny man at the inauspicious moment, I simply stared at him and yelled "Or!" After all, he gave me three words from which to choose–why not pick the one suggesting the least damage? As Fran reached to the ground and picked up a board with nails in it, I ran, and did so at what was probably a personal record pace. Fortunately, with his cumbersome weapon, he had a difficult task chasing me for about 50 yards before giving up. The following day he saw me in the school parking lot and ap-proached me with an intimidating gait and expression. When he got close enough to hit me, his terrifying facade dissolved into laughter and we shook hands. We maintained a friendly rapport thereafter. He probably had not met many people who could be as crazy as him and felt refreshed that someone would join him in his venue.

The swim team and its deadly 6:00 a.m. practices afforded me yet another opportunity for friendship and social acquaintance. Dave Tone, who rivaled me in the breaststroke, and I developed a friendship rather quickly, and he introduced me to his friends from Sigma Pi Alpha (ΣπΑ), Mount Pleasant High's only Greek fraternity. Supposedly a step up in sophistication from First State, I felt a greater sense of pride, or maybe it could more accurately be called hubris, associating with these cultured aristocrats. Soon it was rumored I would get a pledge to ΣπΑ, a reputable mark with some of the attractive girls of the upper echelon. And when a beautiful sophomore, Cindy Mason, asked me to the Sadie Hawkins dance, I was floating on a cloud. I can still smell the sweetness of that perfume. Happiness became a possibility.

Cindy and I genuinely liked each other–maybe it was love–and went together for a few months. We spent most of our time talking on the phone, walking to her home together after school where we'd make out in her den, and occasionally attending some event. She treated me to a rock concert at the high school featuring the group Chicago Transit Authority just after they released "25 or 6 to 4" and immediately prior to their becoming big time. However, I really had no idea about developing intimacy, and perhaps it was my anxiety about doing so that precipitated the end of my first romance.

It was during our Spring break that Cindy's parents sent her to Fort Lauderdale to visit her grandmother. I imagined her enjoying the ocean, the warmth, the sand and especially those other boys who would come on to her in her sexy bikini! Life is just not how it should be sometimes! Not to be defeated by my imagination, I called my friends Max and Mike White, who were two years older than me, and who also manipulated their mother into taking them out of Milton Hershey School. The partying in which we decided to participate presented me with a girl with whom I could cheat on Cindy as well as my first serious experience with the police.

Moderately intoxicated, we patronized a late night hamburger joint, The Charcoal Pit. While sitting in a booth with Jerry, the quarterback for Max's high school, Conrad, Jerry went to the restroom and stayed there for an interminable length of time. When the waitress gave me my check and asked the whereabouts of Jerry, I told her, honestly, I did not know–I barely knew my whereabouts! She informed me if he could not be found, I would be responsible for his bill since he'd been sitting with me. I adamantly refused on the grounds that I had not eaten his food and was surprised that she summoned an officer of the law from his booth to settle the matter. As he told me that I indeed was responsible for Jerry's bill, I blurted, "Ah fuck it! I'll pay it then!" I supposed the expletive would give me some power in a situation in which I otherwise felt powerless.

Instead of giving me the time to pay, however, the officer yanked me out of the booth, hand- cuffed me while pushing me out of the restaurant, and prophesied, " That's the last time you will ever lay an F in front of a waitress!"

My Aunt Gerry's permissiveness changed slightly after picking me up at the jail at 2:00 a.m. and taking me to see a probation officer shortly thereafter. She even grounded me or so she thought. I began cutting school, getting poor grades, and to top it off, I told Cindy I had cheated on her—that damn Roman Catholic guilt. As a consequence, she broke up with me. Gerry asserted she would not tolerate my masochistic demise and told me I'd either have to go to a reform school or live with my cousin Jack McGovern and his wife, Trisha, who lived in downtown Wilmington. I had always liked Jack who, with Trisha, had visited me at Hershey once, so the choice between his home and reform school was not a difficult one.

Jack worked as a city policeman, did a tour in Viet Nam, was somewhat bigger than me, and the implicit understanding among all parties was that he possessed the physical attributes necessary to shape my behavior properly. While he and Trisha were only 11 and 10 years older than me respectively, they were not emotionally prepared to raise an incorrigible 16 year old. They had only been married nine months and were continuing to make their adjustments. For example, Trisha was pregnant. Still, Jack's authority and sense of humor and Trisha's tolerance created a structure that made me focus more on the responsible enjoyment of high school in contrast to the destructive path I'd been taking at Aunt Gerry's.

At the time I was making the transition to Jack's home—the tenth of my childhood/adolescence—I met Scott Phillips at school who was to become my best friend. Scott was a year older than me, and having his license, he drove downtown to pick me up. While we indulged in our share of imbibing and smoking pot, we behaved a bit more tamely than I did with the First State gang. Typically, we'd pick up a couple of six packs of beer and drive to the Concord Mall where we'd drink in the parking lot and attempt to pick up girls inside the mall. Jack ruled drinking unacceptable, however, and upon observing my inebriated appearance a little later than my 12 o'clock curfew one weekend night, not only grounded me but prohibited me from getting my driver's license for a year. He was beginning to remind me of Millie Simmons in his inability to make the punishment fit the crime.

Nonetheless, I valued the acceptance I felt from Scott who was popular in school, humorous and clever, and an aficionado of the Beatles who had just disbanded. We listened to and discussed John Lennon pouring out a primal catharsis about his childhood of neglect and abandonment as well as soothing solace from his maternal partner, Yoko Ono, in his first solo album <u>Working Class Hero</u>. Certainly I could identify with the song, "Mother":"Mother…You had me…But I never had you.. . Father…You left me…But I never left you…Children don't do…what I have done…I couldn't walk…and I tried to run…" I also told Scott I found meaning in the song "God" in which Lennon intones "God is a concept…by which we measure…our pain…" And proceeds to bellow a litany of figures and concepts in which he does not believe, including "magic, I-Ching, Bible, Tarot, Hitler, Jesus, Kennedy, Buddha, mantra, Gita, Yoga, Kings, Elvis, Zimmerman, Beatles." He finally ends with a lonely, solipsistic perspective, "I just believe in me…Yoko and me…And that's reality." Maybe because I had been abused so much by authority during my childhood, I had trouble believing in authority figures, including many mentioned by Lennon. Ten years later, Mark David Chapman criticized Lennon for his self-pity in much of his music and murdered him, and I felt a loss with similar emotions to those I felt when my father died. John Lennon had changed my life, and he would be my immortal hero.

If one word were used to describe what John Lennon stood for, it would have to be peace. And if we were to take a few moments each day to practice peace, how much better would our world be? Can you <u>Imagine</u> it?

I continued to enjoy my friendships with Scott, Dave Tone and guys such as John Patterson from ΣπΑ, Julio and Jorge Don, and their cousin, Jose Perone who all escaped Castro's Cuba, and Mike Walters, from Archmere Academy who would almost kill me one day. I also developed a respect and appreciation for several members of the swim team who drove an extra half hour out of their way to pick me up from downtown for 6:00

a.m. practice. Downtown was outside of the school district which was an inconvenience that was tolerable, especially when I considered the alternative was reform school.

Unfortunately the inconvenience of living outside the school district became magnified into a trauma. Since swimming on a team had been a lifesaver for me since sixth grade, when it helped me escape the depression from my father's death, I valued it greatly. In addition to achieving a varsity letter in the ninth grade at Hershey, I also earned one in tenth grade at Mount Pleasant and anticipated becoming a four-year letterman by the end of high school. Maybe I could get a college scholarship for swimming. In good faith and with heightened expectation, I began practicing with the team in my junior year, looking forward to winning some first places in events such as the 100 yard butterfly and 200 yard individual medley and maybe breaking a school record. However, the monster of disappointment would once again raise its ugly head in my life. I was called into the guidance counselor's office on the day of our first swim meet. He informed me that although the school made an exception by allowing me to attend despite my residence outside the district, I would not be permitted to swim for the school. If I swam and another team discovered where I lived, our team could be disqualified for the year. The only swimming I experienced that afternoon was despair; doing the violent butterfly through my head, a painful backstroke through my veins and arteries; doing the hopeless breaststroke into my heart and a pathetic crawl along my spine. Despair won an undeniable victory in the individual medley throughout my very being that day.

How could I tolerate my sickening status as a nonswimmer? Swimming had become a substitute parent for me, one I could rely on, and taking it from me was entirely unacceptable. So I continued to awaken at 5:00 a.m., meet my rides to practice and swam with the team as permitted by a sympathetic coach, Lee Eldredge. And I swam in an exhibition lane in some of the meets; I could not earn points but could perform. My motivation was not as high as when I could compete, my performance not as good, and my spirit was far from sanguine. I swam simply for its intrinsic value and for the camaraderie of the team.

A bright spot came in the Spring of that year when John Patterson invited me to join him and a group of acquaintances in a camping trip to Myrtle Beach, South Carolina for Easter break. The excitement of driving to that beach from Delaware temporarily put me on top of the world. John and I drove overnight with Bob Serata in his car-truck, and the freedom inspired an intoxication by beer that would be long remembered; I passed out in the back of the truck and became punished with a Carolina sunburn that was not only painful but embarrassing. A still more memorable event during that trip was an introduction to Tim Hill which was nearly synonymous with the introduction to the psychedelic world of LSD, experiences I was to discover could range from bliss and ecstasy to panic and terror.

During the acid experience, I perceived the universe and reality in an alteration that transcends language and logical thinking. As I gazed peacefully at the moonlit ocean, a swim to Europe seemed not only achievable but enjoyable. After all, since Jack Morrison of the Doors sang, "Let's swim to the moon…Let's climb through the tide… On a moonlight ride" without having an ocean, then surely I could embark on a leisurely swim across the Atlantic and reach England by sunrise. And maybe I'd do some butterfly. Holding two pieces of popsicle in each of the appendages dangling from my wrists that were mundanely referred to as "hands," was at least as profoundly meaningful as a surgeon grasping a human heart in one hand and a liver in the other. And when I looked in the mirror and noticed how similar my face appeared to Paul McCartney's, all I needed to do was begin singing "Yesterday…And all my troubles seem so far away…" and abracadabra–there was Paul. Such the philosopher-magician was I, until about 2:00 a.m. which marked the time I had been told I would be "coming down." Well, I wasn't coming down, and my peculiar reality quickly began losing its charm and wonder. I grew uncomfortable, squirming in the tent, awakening other campers, and finally panicking after concluding I would either become crazy for- ever or die. The anxiety drained me; after about two hours of worry that seemed like two months, I drifted off into a light sleep. My brief sleep was soon greeted by a morning unlike any other, consisting of a splendid sunrise and the mystical singing of birds. The surrounding trees, with grateful branches and leaves growing into the sky, were more fresh and beautiful than ever. Nature was speaking to me, awakening me to its awe and beauty and reminding me of all for which I could be thankful. Breakfast by the fire and the companionship of my friends reminded me how wonderful the mundane world truly could be. There was no need to swim to Europe. I had come down from my trip and was at peace.

It was a refreshing change to live with Jack and Trisha after my junior year and into my senior year. That transition was a first for living with a relative for two consecutive years since living with my father in the first grade. Like many of the McGoverns, Jack evinced the Irish trait of alcoholism, but his problem was not severe enough to cause me any disasters. Of course I was often reminded of Dad. Jack compensated for occasional obnoxious behaviors with his charisma, humor, and good heart which manifested by doing such things as coaching the DeMolay basketball team on which I played. The stability of living in the same home for a year and a half made me feel an unusual sense of security. Every pleasant exception does, in fact, matter.

Mount Pleasant offered a few advanced courses to seniors as a means of stimulating intellectual interest as well as ideas for college pursuits. Scott had taken two of them, philosophy and psychology, and had discussed them with me since the previous year, even during our Friday and Saturday night adventures. Mixing Plato with Budweiser and girls was a bit odd, but Freud and hedonism provided a nice balance. As a consequence, I was primed for some new learnings that would create meaning in my life.

In philosophy class, the teacher, Jody Ambrossino, required us to read Beyond Freedom and Dignity by the famous psychologist, B.F. Skinner. Skinner was known as a controversial behaviorist because he proposed a technology of behavior that, if applied scientifically to human behavior (he experimented with white rats and pigeons) could alleviate the frightening problems threatening the world and survival of our species. Essentially, the behaviorism of Skinner postulated that all human behavior is caused by genetics and by conditions in our environment, conditions both remote and recent. Behavior occurred because it was determined, ruling the concept of free will as an invention. In other words, Skinner was saying that the idea of freedom was basically illusory and that, if our species wants to survive, we had better master a scientific analysis of behavior. This new philosophy provided a perspective to me that I could understand, accept, and articulate so that it served as an advent for years of argumentation. The perspective also clarified some of the chaos in my life, and I felt relieved to know my behavior had causes. It was a much better perspective than self-blame.

A concept frequently stated throughout <u>Beyond Freedom and Dignity</u> was the "contingencies of reinforcement" in a person's environment that shaped and controlled his or her behavior. I enjoyed learning a number of other behavioral terms. A positive reinforcer was any consequence following a behavior that increased the frequency of the behavior it followed. The term "reward" was the layman's word for reinforcer, although I learned that since many things described as rewards do not increase the preceding behaviors, they would not be deemed positive reinforcers. Money would be a positive reinforcer since the behavior preceding the delivery of money continues or increases; commissions tend to prompt more sales and paychecks usually maintain the continuation of labor. Negative reinforcers were consequences that increased any behavior that avoided, terminated, or escaped that consequence. A parent's threats to a child might increase to terminate the child's crying or nagging. If the crying temporarily stopped, the threatening would be strengthened. A parent's spanking of a child also increases when it has the immediate effect of terminating the child's misbehavior. A runner similarly might increase his running speed to escape a dangerous dog or other animal.

Many years later I described an incident to classes I taught in colleges whereby I was running on a path in the woods with one other fellow; we had been left behind by several of the faster runners. Suddenly we heard a growl among the trees that sounded exactly like a bear, and my speed increased abruptly, probably sprinting the fastest in my life, for about100 yards. When I eventually looked over my shoulder to determine how long I had to live, I observed the"bear" happened to be Bob Leonard, the negative reinforcer, who doubled over in a paroxysm of laughter.

Punishment had a converse relationship to reinforcement; instead of increasing behavior it decreased it. Punishment was the procedure Skinner criticized most for several reasons. For one, the punished behavior was often suppressed only temporarily, and in instances that it was eliminated altogether, other retaliatory behaviors would occur instead. Also, punishment was said to have a deleterious effect on other forms of performance-related behaviors, accounting for why a child might appear nervous when doing things he is learning to do. Together, each person's history of positive and negative reinforcement and punishment as well as his or her current schedule of reinforcement constituted the contingencies of reinforcement for that person. And if those contingencies were arranged and organized effectively, a person's or group's behavior would be better controlled than if the contingencies were allowed to occur haphazardly and accidentally.

Skinner's premise was that all of our behavior is controlled by our genes and by things external to us and that we delude ourselves by saying our behavior is controlled by a free will, by our feelings or by our thoughts. Determinism was the philosophy expressed by Skinner, although he was not saying that we must be victims to the controlling environment or passive recipients to stimuli impinging upon us. Determinism is not fatalism. In fact, he was saying the converse, that by arranging stimuli, events, reinforcers, and conditions, our species can take better control over its own behavior and thereby perpetuate its own survival. Many years later I read and valued the following quote by Skinner that nicely summed up his perspective "...We are all controlled by the world in which we live. The question is this: are we to be controlled by accidents, by tyrants, or by ourselves?" I have used that quote in regard to Stare, Brenner, and Wilson, and other tyrants of the employment world, as their behavior has prompted me to use self-control in resisting the urge to hurt them.

This new perspective held that the behavior of Millie Simmons, Merrilee, my father, and each disturbed person I knew could be explained and understood by these determining causes. Hence, if their behavior could be understood as a function of genetic and environmental factors, and not caused by evil forces, could they not be forgiven more easily?

These individuals in my life did not have control over their behavior because they, like the rest of us, did not have a technology of behavior scientifically applied in their environments. According to Skinner, such an application was not only possible, but important for the survival of our species. Most of us are unaware of what causes and maintains our behavior. In a sense, when Christ said, "Forgive them Father for they know not what they do" he was expressing an understanding for the misbehavior of his time that could be derived from determinism. Joining Christ's and Skinner's attitudes might seem like combining strange bedfellows (especially since Skinner was an atheist!), but they both, in their unique ways, one spiritually and one scientifically, emphasized the power of understanding human behavior. In his book Walden II, Skinner described at length how his principle of positive reinforcement could be applied to an entire community, and though his utopia fell short of heaven, it was characterized by peacefulness, creativity, happiness, and productivity along with less consumption, pollution, and politics.

A digression on the words of B.F. Skinner seems incongruent in a suicide note, doesn't it? Here's an explanation. Since my father neglected and abandoned me as a young child, I always looked and hoped for a father figure—someone to love, to admire, and to imitate. None of the male substitutes I had could reasonably be considered good father figures. A few of them were good in some ways, but there was no stability, no consistency, and I never had a place I could call home. Now, consistent with Anna Freud's (daughter of Sigmund) statement, "Creative minds have always been known to survive any kind of bad training," I have periodically created my own father figures based on what I have learned about them, their achievements, lifestyles, and their values. And what better person to admire and emulate than the behaviorist of the century, B.F. Skinner? I wonder if anyone else in the world has created both John Lennon and Skinner as their father figures. I had an advantage as an orphan.

I was fortunate enough in 1975 and 1989, a year before he died, to have interactions with Skinner, the first by phone and the second by letter. I called him on the phone in '75 and when his wife, Yvonne, answered, I asked for "Dr. Skinner." She yelled, "Frreedd!", and I thought, "Just like any other American household." I told him that I agreed with most of his writings but queried as to how he would square transcendental meditation, which I practiced regularly at the time, with his behavioral philosophy. "I wouldn't," he bluntly replied.

"But Dr. Skinner, TM is a part of the behavioral process."

"Well, everything is a part of the behavioral process," he returned. "In meditation you close your eyes and say a mantra. Since the consequence of saying the mantra is relaxation and its physiological effects, the mantra becomes a reinforcer," I cogently urged. "It sounds like something Jacobson did back in 1938."

"Oh," I said, a little disappointed I didn't get him to appreciate my explanation.

"But good luck with it though" he politely closed.

In 1989, I wrote to him and posed what I considered a challenging question. If behaviorists are scientists who do not believe in the value of examining inner experience, such as thoughts and feelings, should they not avoid references to inner experiences in their every- day language? For instance, instead of saying "I love you" a behaviorist should communicate in more measurable terms, such as "I want to be with you for intimate conversation, affectionate behavior, and sex as frequently as possible." I was excited and surprised to receive the following response from Skinner at his office in William James Hall, Department of Psychology, Harvard University:

"Dear Mr. McGovern:

Of course it would be better if everyone used scientific language, but that is not possible in casual discourse. The physicist uses ordinary language to talk to his machinist, and it has always been difficult for behaviorists to use the popular cognitive or lay vocabulary in similar situations without criticism. That was my point.

Sincerely,
B.F. Skinner

P.S. Why oh why do people not put their addresses on their letters? Envelopes get thrown away before the letters are answered, and I was lucky to be able to recapture yours."

I was especially pleased to read the P.S., imagining that he actually felt "lucky" to 'be able to recapture…" my letter.

One of the reasons for which Skinner's philosophy was so controversial was that <u>Beyond Freedom and Dignity</u> lent itself to misunderstanding so well. Most of the public, as well as much of academia, saw it as an affront to our individuality and a threat to the freedom for which our country strived since its inception. I felt I understood behaviorism well after reading and discussing it and especially liked it since it provided an opportunity to argue, to immerse myself in controversy, and of course, to know that I was right, all examples of positive reinforcement. Jack tended towards criticism, called me "stupid" or "weird" on occasion–finally I could be intellectually superior to him as an expert on behaviorism. A rebel with a cause.

Jack did provide aversive controls such as negative reinforcement and punishment in sufficient doses so as to modify my behavior from my sophomore year–prohibiting me from getting my driver's license for a year was one of his harsher measures. He also provided a good deal of positive reinforcement in the form of stories, humor, occasional praise, encouragement, and privileges. With his control I behaved more responsibly than I would have otherwise, and I was thankful to avoid reform school.

Many folks are curious about first sexual experiences, and perhaps I'd be remiss by not at least mentioning my compliance with Murphy's Law on two occasions, when I was 15 and 16. Reference to Murphy's Law is sufficient without going into embarrassing details.

Even in suicide one has some pride. A one-night stand in Georgetown when I drove there with my friend, Mike Walters, prevented me from graduating from high school as a virgin–a dubious achievement for an 18 year old. The one-night stand with this somewhat older woman was symbolic for my brief parental relationships that ended abruptly during the previous 15 years.

One Spring weekend, John Patterson, Dan Smith, Tom Hill and I drove to Rehoboth Beach where we pitched a tent at one of the campgrounds. Tim, the fellow who gave me the LSD at Myrtle Beach, bought another form of it called "White Sunshine" for our trip (pun unintended). We took it during the bright of the day and needed to stay in the tent until the sun came closer to setting since the bright- ness did not mix well with the ophthalmic effects of the acid. Well, sitting in a small tent with three other wise guys for three hours only amplified the paranoia that is often experienced during an acid trip. I don't think I ever disliked people laughing at me more, and, of course our mutual paranoia only made us laugh at each other even more. However, the laughter was pathetically transparent; the fears, anger, insecurities, and infantile silliness manifested on our faces as though we were caught with our emotional pants down. Finally, sunset was approaching. The flowers on the quilt I had brought began blossoming. Relief and beauty were on the way. When we walked to the beach, seagulls were flying over the ocean, in a southerly direction, and as they glided in slow motion, they were changing colors: oranges, blues, purples, a variety of pastels! The mystical sense of transcendence I experienced as I watched those colorific creatures calmly coasting along the skyway left a permanent, aesthetic impression in my consciousness. And yet, I would not recommend that anyone take LSD. The effects are too unpredictable.

I graduated from Mount Pleasant with average grades, plans of attending High Point College, and an interest in reading a few authors other than Skinner. The ominous nature of futuristic works such as George Orwell's 1984 and the macabre possibilities of abusing condi- tioning principles in Anthony Burgess's Clockwork Orange fascinated me. Aldous Huxley and Herman Hesse absorbed my attention, with the former providing more of a cerebral experience, and the latter more of a spiritual/ emotional journey, characterized by unconscious struggles between the sensual and the sublime. Certainly I could identify with the protagonist, a student in his teens, in Hesse's Beneath the Wheel, whose unhappiness, sense of isolation, and mental exhaustion drove him to suicide. I found it interesting Hesse had undergone psychotherapy with the renowned analyst and student of Sigmund Freud, Carl Jung, after attempting suicide. <u>Steppenwolf</u> depicted a man inclined to an ordered world of bourgeois life and tastes while simultaneously experiencing the wolf of the steppes–a world of dark rebellioun, creative imaginations, and fantasy that bordered on mad- ness. Together with the literary work, <u>The Fall</u>, by Albert Camus, <u>Steppenwolf</u> stimulated my memories and thoughts about my father. To the best of my recall, the middle-aged male protagonist in Camus' work had prospered well in the absurdity of contemporary society but eventually took a nosedive as the result of certain vicissitudes and ultimately had to confront the meaninglessness of life within the context of his own depressing demise. I believe these works also mirrored what were to be experiences in my adult life, perhaps even serving as forebodings in the outskirts of my consciousness.

My intellectual, literary life in the summer of '72 provided balance to the exciting stress of my first job as a salesman in one of Wilmington's well established clothing stores, Mullins, and making friends in a Polish neighborhood with guys who played basketball, drank beer and smoked pot, and used an old apartment in a rental house to party with the fairer sex. Seeing the Rolling Stones in Philadelphia–"Exile on Main Street" had just been released–with those fellows was a memorable experience. I do not know the eventual outcome of an obese girl flailing wildly on the floor of the coliseum as a result of her acid trip. However, the most memorable experience of the summer would happen with my friend, Mike Walters, in his green Volkswagen, as we drove hastily to the beach at Cape May, New Jersey on August 19, a Saturday night.

It was a consequence of that car accident with Mike that I first became acutely aware of the precariousness of life, and the sweetness of it was enhanced by the nearly fatal accident. Is it possible that sweetness that has forced me to resist my suicide so far? Let's see.

Before I end my life, let me tell you about Mike and me and our little mishap. After hearing about it as well as the suicidal depression and psychiatric hospitalization within the same year, you will conclude I have experienced sufficient pain, together with the pain described thus far, such that suicide is a reasonable choice.

I don't know why I've waited so long by writing so much. Sometimes I get a little verbose. "A little verbose" is an oxymoron, isn't it? Well that reminds me of my favorite oxymoron. A foxy moron. I made that joke up. Maybe it can be a part of my legacy.

Are you still with me?

CHAPTER 3

Death Kisses and Transformations

"When one kisses death, life becomes infinitely sweet."

WILLIAM BLAKE

BEFORE WE EMBARKED ON OUR evening drive to Stone Harbor, New Jersey, on August 19, 1972, Mike drove me to the liquor store to make "the run," the term we underage drinkers used to describe our illegal purchase. We would stay at Mike's friend's house at the beach, Mike would drive, and the least I could do to show my appreciation was to make the run. Two cases of beer would do, one to polish off during the drive and another to share with the others after our arrival.

During our drive, Mike was obviously in his optimal beer guzzling state. He had been spurned by his girlfriend earlier in the day, and what better way to escape hurt and anger than to drown it with Budweiser and head for the shore. Down they would go, one can after the other. In our teenage minds there was an additional factor to increase our consumption--the more cans we drank, the more macho we proved ourselves.

We were just about at our destination when Mike ran a stop sign, and the car that smashed into my side of the car was, fortunately, not much larger than Mike's VW. While I do not recall the experience, I have been told that I regained consciousness about an hour after arriving at Burdette Tomlin Hospital. I was still intoxicated while simultaneously in shock and began flailing my arms and screaming like a madman. Since my lung had collapsed, with lacerations to the liver, kidneys, and spleen, not to mention the entire right rib cage broken, the madman needed anaesthetizing so the operations could begin.

The operations were almost the beginning of the end. I did not regain consciousness after they were completed, and Dr. Koknar informed Jack and Teena that my chance for survival was questionable. A Catholic Priest gave me the Last Rites after three days and Roman Catholic relatives drove from Wilmington to watch me bite the dust. Always a bit on the stubborn side, though, I began to show signs of life, and after five days of unconsciousness, I awakened to an astounded audience of visitors and nurses. My stubbornness was a virtue.

I was certain I was not at the beach, and I did not feel like drinking anymore beer. I had no idea why I was in this bed with tubes sticking in me, however, and I was not pleased with the 100 or so sutures holding my right eye in its socket. A nurse grabbed my hand as it reached to pull an i.v. tube from my chest, and the facts leading up to this imbroglio slowly began sinking in as the nurse slowly explained them to me. I was lucky to be alive, and the beach party would have to be put on hold.

An old Cuban man in the bed beside me laid in agony mumbling "amigo" and yelling "agua!", teaching me the Spanish words for friend and water. I made a friend immediately as I poured him a bit in his paper cup, the gratitude on his face temporarily suppressing his agony and fear. I still recall his smile. I may have been the last human to give him water. He died that day. His stillness was so final. I felt sad because I'd miss my new friend and frightened because I knew I almost died too.

Dr. Koknar didn't expect I'd be ready to leave the hospital in only two weeks after regaining consciousness, but he also didn't expect for me to live in the first place. He told Jack I'd made a "miraculous recovery" and attributed it partly to my athletic conditioning. I felt lucky about having opted to swim unofficially during my last two years of school despite my ineligibility to score points. I had often wondered why in the hell I was doing it, and my question was answered. It saved my life. (Those were the days when I wanted to live).

Needless to say, Jack and Trisha were put through a traumatic experience by my accident and its aftermath. They were young and beginning a family with their first newborn, Damien. Certainly they were eager for me to depart for college in August of '72 so they could get on with their own lives; instead, I managed to almost get killed, thereby rendering myself a convalescent and unable to attend college on schedule. And although I had been a burden to them for two years, neither of them ever gave me the impression that they wished I had died. I simply became more than they bargained for.

So during that Fall of '72, my responsibilities included healing, introspection, and coping with isolation. We lived in an older section of Wilmington amidst miles of huge trees, parks, and the Brandywine Creek, not far from where my father would take me for Sunday strolls. I read much of Will Durant's History of Philosophy and other works a notch above my intellectual maturity, in hopes of getting a start on my college studies that would begin in February. I read about pantheism which seemed like a reasonable doctrine. Since the existence of God was dubious, depending on one's definition of It, Him, or Her (or it, him or her), why not define God as the force that is inherent in all of nature, actually in all existence? Certainly such a force existed since nature and the cosmos existed. If one labeled that force that was responsible for the existence of the cosmos as God, the existence of God would not only be indubitable, the existence of God must, by definition, be pervasive. Or so I told myself. During that idyllic period, I took long walks in the woods, fresh with its autumn colors and scents, and would sit on a blanket of leaves, experiencing and appreciating the omnipotence, omnipresence, and splendor of God. The experiences were both mystical and transcendental; being a part of nature, I was a part of God. As a part of God I felt both humble and important, and of course, eternal. I awakened from my near-death experience to a gift of a new perspective on life.

There were times during that convalescence that my anger flared, anger over having lived so stupidly. I developed the attitude that drunken drivers should get the death penalty, and my friendship with Mike ended abruptly when I told him my idea. It was an insensitive thing to say, but I was not tuned into his feelings. While he had not been seriously injured in our accident, he had been traumatized; he was frightened I'd die during the five days I was unconscious and felt guilty that he caused the accident by running the stop sign. We were both emotional wrecks.

Mike dealt with it by eventually becoming a personal injury lawyer.

Of course my anger was triggered by fear, the fear of death to be precise, and I gained an appreciation for the precariousness of life. Death was life's next door neighbor that could come knocking at any- time. The values we place on the superficialities of our social existence became conspicuously absurd. Most things are not as important as we make them. And so I scribbled the following little poem:

<u>Vanity in Vain</u>
Her vanity led her to purchase a gold-plated mirror,
A hairdo for the week, she then had it done.
Some lipstick, some blush, and rouge down the block;
But a Chevy kissed her roughly as the street became a crimson pool.

The precariousness of life also seemed, at times, like a blessing. It was a reminder to focus on and value something about each moment. There is no guarantee there will be a next. A story I read years later about a Buddhist monk sums it up well. The monk ran from a tiger that noticed him from a distance, and not having an option, the monk jumped off a cliff. He grabbed a vine from the cliff and was hanging onto it with the tiger growling ferociously above. The drop was too far to let go, and suddenly a mouse began gnawing on the vine. The monk then saw a strawberry growing beside the vine, picked it and began chewing it. Delighted, he exclaimed, "This strawberry is delicious!" The summon bonum, or good life, might be the development of a state of consciousness that enables one to continually savor the deliciousness of the present.

My physical healing was on schedule for me to begin the Spring semester at High Point College in High Point, NC. Aside from occasional mild pain in my right rib cage, I had mended well and felt confident that, with my recently acquired spiritual development, I was ready to tackle my first college semester. Jack drove me from Wilmington to my dorm, a building that surprisingly had not been condemned. Its drab, dreary, and dirty condition would be a test for my spiritual development, and I had doubts I'd be able to study in that hellhole. To make matters worse, the common escape for many students from the gloomy ambience happened to be drugs, alcohol, and loud music.

Jack helped me unpack, wished me well, but as he drove away I had to suppress a terrible uncertainty and a profound loneliness. I was beginning my adulthood, and its basis was an unstable, chaotic, painful childhood. I was a tree without any roots. It was time for me to rely on myself, but since I never lived with any particular parent figures for longer than two to three years, my "self" was a fragile identity. Was my introspective, spiritual period in the Fall sufficient to strengthen me for an independent adulthood? I had doubts.

I took Music Appreciation, American History, English, State and Local Government and P.E. that first semester, and I expected the course work to be relatively easy. The reason for that expectation, I must confess, was based upon a cultural and academic stereotype. The Civil War was still being fought by many whose Southern drawl made me feel I was from another planet. I was attending a small college in the South that didn't require high grades and SAT scores, and surely because of its' reputation for being easy, getting As and Bs would be a cinch. It wasn't like I was attending the University of Delaware. Yeah, right. That snobby attitude would be met with a few disappointing grades that one might say, served me right.

A few freshmen were from Mt. Pleasant High School where I had graduated. A touch of Wilmington, Delaware gave me an anchor to my chaotic foundation. Remember Tom Hill, the generous fellow who gave me LSD? He, Robby Gainey, Scott McClure, and Sharon Jones welcomed me with reserved friendliness and congratulated me on my car accident recovery. They introduced me to several other students from the northern contingent, and this group shared memories of the culture that gave birth to them. Since George McGovern had recently run for the Presidency against Richard Nixon, numerous students asked whether I was related to George. Since I, in fact, had an Uncle George McGovern as well as a grandfather with that name, I affirmed I was related, and soon students approached and said I even looked like him. Unfortunately, my "relationship" had no influence on my grade in State and Local Government class whatsoever.

One fellow I met was Butch Hanson, a lad from Philadelphia who often wore his hair in a pony-tail style. Butch was a master at playing the piano, and he majored in that specialty for his college degree. Butch's idols were Bob Dylan and Beethoven, and he crafted both his personality and musical performance upon both of them. His caustic verbal style and witty remarks both attracted and repulsed me, but it was his mellifluous tickling of the ivories that was most entrancing. In addition to the Beethoven sonatas, he introduced me to the ragtime of Scott Joplin, and while" The Entertainer" was the most popular at the time, it was the magical jocularity of the "Maple Leaf Rag" that most hypnotized me. I occasionally visited Butch at night while he practiced in a piano room in the music building; he seemed to delight in the powerful effects of his piano on a listener. Indeed, those moments were a temporary nirvana. I wrote "Music is God's sister visiting the Earth for an eternal moment" on a little piece of paper and taped it to the door of my dorm room.

It was about a month after arriving at High Point College that I began to feel isolated and deprived of the interpersonal closeness that I never knew I needed so much. The students from Delaware were into a partying scene I was trying to avoid. The groups of Southerners and Christians shared a lifestyle that was foreign to me. And I needed more of Butch's friendship than he was either willing or able to give. In fact his snipes and put-downs were just the opposite of what I wanted, and together with the marginal grades I was receiving in my classes, became the ingredients for a clinical depression.

The stressors I experienced also had an exacerbating effect on the soreness in my right rib cage that never healed entirely from the accident. I was unfamiliar with the phenomenon of psychosomatic disorder and thought the soreness in my chest was caused entirely by physical factors. I had no idea why it was returning after dissipating for two months. Additionally, I was not exercising, and since I had relied on swimming for the previous six years, I gained an uncomfortable amount of weight. Late night trips to the snack bar didn't help. I was becoming increasingly depressed, had difficulty sleeping, and felt sluggish as I walked aimlessly to classes, around campus, wherever. Life at High Point was becoming the low point of my life.

My next symptom seemed strange to me, and I never felt so men-tally out of control. I began having an obsession of the name "Butch" repeating itself in my mind. I had not yet learned the language of feelings and was unaware of how angry I was at him. He had the potential to be a good friend, as I liked his intelligence, humor, and passion for music, but instead he had become hurtful and a threat to my self esteem. My dismal social life, self-doubt, painful physical condition, obsession, and disappointing academic performances com- prised a vortex of pain and despair and hopelessness--the stuff of my suicidal ideation.

I was not getting much social attention through the healthy means of developing friendships and because I felt so miserable and anxious, I began getting attention through complaints to anyone who would listen--complaints of inadequate grades, complaints of soreness in my ribs, complaints of weight gain, complaints of insomnia, complaints of my worthlessness, complaints of hopelessness, and occasional talk of suicide. Eventually, I complained that I was complaining too much, a complaint with which my peers agreed. I felt like an insecure construction of blood and bones with a crazy, miserable childhood, expected to behave and perform normally as a young adult, and I was further from that role than a pimp was from the pope. If I was trying out for a role in a movie as a severely depressed young man, surely I would have gotten the part.

Of course most of the attention I received was in the form of shallow advice; "just don't worry so much" or sympathy, "if I'd been through what you've been through I would've done myself in by now." I wondered if the latter statement was an indirect suggestion. Nights and weekends often included, "here man, take a toke of this," and not knowing marijuana worsens depression, I sometimes would. Some students strategically avoided me, and I secretly respected their strategy. I wished I could avoid myself. One fellow, Ron, of the sympathetic variety, with a twist of Christian compassion, suggested I talk with his psychology professor, Dr. Britt. Ron said Dr. Britt was a clinical psychologist, and he admired him.

Dr. Britt appeared to listen intensely as I described my experiences of the recent past and present conditions to him. His eyes drilled through mine and into my psyche. After about 40 minutes, he asserted to me that I would probably end up in a fetal position locked in the back ward of a mental hospital if I did not get some exercise. He demonstrated the fetal position in his chair, and I realized it was possible for things to get worse. Britt's theatrics scared me to say the least. He recommended I jog at least a few hundred yards each day and to see him again in a few days.

When I returned to his office, I still felt the heaviness and lethargy so characteristic of depression despite my compliance with his jogging suggestion. These feelings were experienced as though chains of lead replaced my veins and arteries. I told Dr. Britt I'd awaken at 3 to 4 a.m., could not fall asleep again and would feel sluggish as I dragged myself to morning classes where my concentration was so wrecked the professors seemed like no more than babbling robots. He telephoned the college infirmary, suggested they give me some anti-anxiety medication and arranged for me to spend a couple of days and nights there. The quietness of the sterile infirmary and the attractive, caring nurse, per- haps a bit maternal at that, Mrs. Isenhour, was a nice reprieve from the noisy dormitory. I managed to make progress on my first term paper, a comparison of Herman Hesse's <u>Siddhartha</u> and <u>Steppenwolf</u>, in the peacefulness of my chamber of solitude. Perhaps because I was able to identify with the madness that characterized the protagonist in the latter and because I longed for the enlightenment that characterized the protagonist in the former, I became sufficiently energized to complete the paper. In two days I was ready for the dorm and classes again.

I struggled through the rest of that Spring semester with help from the aforementioned resources, several understanding professors who gave me Cs instead of Fs, and occasional glimmers of hope. One such glimmer was a book I purchased entitled <u>Science of Being and Art of Living</u> by the founder of Transcendental Meditation, Maharishi Mahesh Yogi. The happiness and tranquility it promised by the regular practice of transcendental meditation was appealing to me, and maybe one day I would regain enough energy and concentration to read the damn thing. After all, I achieved one miracle in the last year by surviving the car accident, so in the deeper recesses of my mind another miracle was possible.

I returned to Jack and Trisha's home for summer vacation, and my depression (depressions become possessions) was perplexing to them. Jack simply did not understand how "a good looking, intelligent young man" with so much potential to do well in life could be so miserable. He tried to help me in his own way by getting me a construction job as a laborer, and the boss was kind enough to keep me for several weeks before letting me go. The job necessitated a moderate level of energy and strength, which to me, in my state of lethargic feebleness, seemed like a Herculean requirement. Jack was displeased I lost the job and demanded I find another. It was time to come down a little harder. So I walked about one and a half miles to Cathedral Cemetery where my parents were buried and asked for a job doing the landscaping. Maybe hanging out with my dead parents would cheer me up.

I did not get the cemetery job, but I convinced Jack I needed to see a psychiatrist. Two nights before the scheduled visit, however, I became intolerant of awakening at 3 a.m. and not being able to fall asleep again. When I awakened that night I went to the bathroom, said " To hell with it!" and took 19 Sominex, believing they would terminate my life. I laid down in my bed and felt simultaneously sad and peaceful, experiencing memories of girlfriends and a few people who seemed to have cared a little during my 19 years. Though I'd miss them, I'd escape the unbearable pain and suffering.

"Get up and get your work clothes on!" Jack thundered at about 7 a.m. "I'm either not dead or I've gone to hell" I thought to myself. Jack directed me to do some yardwork, and while I was raking, I had a brief, auditory hallucination in the form of some undetectable voice. It lasted only a few seconds but was quite scary. I do not recall what the voice said, but I did know it was unfriendly. I continued to work but informed Jack later that day that I had taken an overdose the previous night. He panicked, which I interpreted as a sign that he cared about me, and he went to his mother's house to consult with her. He took me to see the shrink a day early.

The psychiatrist sat and listened for awhile but when I talked of the worthlessness of my meaningless life and the idea of ending it, he stood up, lit a cigarette and paced. He said he was not going to commit me, although he offered me the option of admitting myself to The Pennsylvania Institute--The Hospital, in Philadelphia. I did not think it could hurt and even if the possibility existed that it might, I didn't care. Probably the worst would be that I might become brain damaged for life from electroconvulsive therapy, and, heck, that wouldn't be so bad.

Jack drove me to the Institute at 49th and Market. If I hadn't been so depressed, I would've been impressed at its majestic, old buildings, towering trees, well-groomed lawns and tended gardens. I would learn five years later in a psychology class that the hospital was the first psychiatric setting in the U.S., begun in 1783 by Benjamin Rush. Jack advised me to be a good patient, wished me well and before he nervously departed the premises, I thanked him for his good intentions.

An attendant, Edward, whose beard and long hair reminded me of George Harrison, helped me unpack, oriented me to the ward and its rules and asked me some questions for assessment purposes. What kind of animal would I like to be? A fish. It was lunchtime, and I felt certain the other three patients at my table were of the committed variety; their behavior was definitely not that of the voluntary patient. The woman to my left appeared to be in her fifties, and her tremulousness, nonsensical chatter and fearful eyes told me I was not alone in my psychic pain. I finally felt, for the first time in I don't know how long, a sense of social superiority. And what an opportunity for me to be condescendingly compassionate!

I was under the care of Dr. Robert Jones, the medical director, who started me on an antidepressant medication, tofranil, 75 mg. a day. We also began daily psychotherapy sessions. He first listened to my narrative of events since the car accident, with most of my story involving the happenings at High Point College. I could not understand how Jones could sit so stoically as I sat in anguish, talking of my physical pain, frustrating insomnia, obsession with the name "Butch," and fear that I was crazy. I contended that I was crazy because I sometimes looked at trees and saw fire shoot out of the branches. Jones was unimpressed, and more frustratingly, unconvinced that I was clinically crazy. He merely sloughed off my dramatic symptom, saying, "Why you're not crazy! You just have a vivid imagination; and the fire you imagine symbolizes your anger." I couldn't win with Jones--he was an excellent therapist.

I had an active daily schedule to follow at the Institute, which began with a journal class shortly after breakfast. The teacher, Bob Behr, gave us daily assignments to make entries that would be reviewed the following day. One of my favorite entries was my identification with John Lennon's songs on his first solo album, a work that was painfully autobiographical. The song "Mother" depicted his agony regarding the abandonment by his parents, and "God" expressed, through a yelling litany of all the things in which he did not believe, a mournful, solipsistic isolation. Consistent with his aloneness, the song "Isolation" conveyed his sense of that existential reality. The lines in that piece, "You're not to blame...You're just a human...A victim of the insane!" were ones with which I could not only identify; they applied to my current residence! In that regard, I found some solace, a little redemption. I took a drama class and felt proud when the instructor, Mary, encouraged me to major in it at college. In occupational therapy I made an ashtray for Jack and Trisha and moccasins for their son, Damien, and enjoyed clowning with another comedic adolescent who had a somewhat sadistic sense of humor. For instance, we were aware of how sensitive a middle-aged woman happened to be about her status as a psychiatric patient. Consequently, we would look at each other when in proximity to her and assert belligerently, "You're crazy! You're crazy! Crazy! Crazy!" We had not yet received the sensitivity training that was so common in the 70s. Of course we were also covering our own hurt and embarrassment about our status. Perhaps my biggest surprise was the benefit offered to me by the swimming pool lifeguard, Matt. Since he had his Water Safety Instructor certificate, he told me he could renew my Senior Red Cross Lifesaving certificate. Fortunately, the tofranil, psychotherapy, and placebo effect had kicked in enough to give me the energy to read the Red Cross lifesaving book and swim laps again.

Jones and I were making progress in our talks, and I began to understand more clearly and deeply what I had known all along at a shallow level, namely that my unstable, chaotic childhood had shaped my personality to be a little too unique. I will never forget one particular therapeutic moment. I had complained again of my obsession when Jones smugly interpreted, "I think you loved Butch."

"No," I protested with anxiety that he was insinuating I had homosexual tendencies. His remark was also a perspective that seemed incredibly strange.

"What's wrong with that!" he yelled, sitting forward emphatically. I mumbled weakly that I did not know, and he then dealt me the coup de grace in a gentle voice, "And that love is something you've missed since your father."

I sat quietly, trying to integrate this new idea. I felt sad and relieved all at once. Certainly I missed my father--there was no denying that. The mystery to that frightening obsession was gone, just like the melting of the wicked witch in " The Wizard of Oz." Jones' interpretations had marked a kind of rebirth.

Dad's son drinking shots *Father and son*

During the next few days I reflected on my history of relationships with friends and relatives. I could see how I sought the kind of acceptance and affection from them that a child would receive from his parents. Of course I never received it but was continually rejected since I was 3. There had been a sense of desperation in my attempts, and now, perhaps, I could seek love in a healthier, more realistic way and maybe tolerate rejections better. I did not feel a homosexual attraction to Butch, nor anyone else for that matter, but I had often wanted approval and reassurance from older males that could usually be self-defeating. Perhaps I could grow up. I liked the idea that my misery had been a result of not receiving love, and I found a new meaning in the recent releases "My Love" by Paul McCartney and "Give Me Love" by George Harrison. Maybe The Beatles had a good point when they wrote, "All You Need is Love."

One evening several of us younger patients were sitting together at the end of the hallway, listening to LPs and passing around a marijuana joint. As I did not want to disturb the positive effects of the tofranil, I put the joint up to my lips but did not inhale. I wanted to be accepted by the group, though, and passed the joint while appearing to enjoy it. Suddenly a nosey attendant appeared, his nostrils working like a steam engine. He detected the smell of our peace medication and didn't take long to discover the evidence. Our little party and its festive mood terminated abruptly.

The following day, Saturday, I learned my privileges to leave the ward were canceled by the nursing staff. I pleaded, stating that I did not actually smoke the pot but had only feigned it while fitting in with the party ambience. "Yes, of course, Hank. And we still believe in the Easter Bunny. You can talk to Dr. Jones about it Monday." But Monday was unacceptable; I had a Red Cross Lifesaving lesson with Matt that afternoon. "Sorry Hank, you're restricted to the ward."

Blam! My fist smashed the plexiglass of the nurses' station door that safely locked and protected the staff from us loonies. A nurse quickly called other wards for additional male reinforcement while one attendant initiated the proscribed first step--he asked me to walk upstairs with him to ICU, the unit for violent patients. I decided since they treated me as if I were violent, I'd give them a little of what they asked for. Using a medium amount of resistance, I kicked and banged arms with five or six men who managed to carry me in the elevator until setting me in an isolation room on ICU. As if I was dangerous, they set me down on the floor and ran out the door, slamming and locking it. How dramatic.

I laid on the floor, staring at the ceiling and began counting the spots on it so I could concentrate on something. Then I was reminded of Papillon, a novel that was made into a movie about Henri Charriere, who was wrongfully accused of murdering a pimp. He was sentenced to prison on an island off South America, and after attempting to escape, was put in solitary confinement. Steve McQueen starred as Papillon, and he did a good job of portraying psychological and physical deterioration during his time in solitary. His hollow jaws and protruding eyes could have been the face of a skeleton if it hadn't been unshaven. Maybe the drama instructor was right--perhaps acting was my calling. As I put myself in a light trance staring at the spots, a part of me was saying the experience of isolation from other mental patients and staff in a psychiatric hospital was about as far down on the status ladder as one could go. Another part was saying "it's not so bad."

Things got a little worse, though, before they got better. I was allowed to go back to my ward after a few hours on the condition that I take some medication. Sure, why not, as I swallowed a little pill. The damn stuff was thorazine, that's why not. I was now the quintessential slug. If I had known I'd be in a groggy state for almost another day, stumbling and slurring in the middle of la la-land, I might have chosen 24 more hours of Papillon on ICU. At least I could think clearly in my cell.

The next day Dr. Jones transformed the experience into a therapeutic one. Rather than scold, he said, "Just look at all that anger!" making me own my feelings. His directive surprised me and pushed me along my journey of emotional awareness.

Being a bit of an opportunist, I decided since I wanted to pursue psychology as a career, I'd make an internship out of a portion of my hospital stay. One particular memory includes a middle-aged man in a wheelchair, Bennet, diagnosed with schizophrenia. He refused the medication the nurses were insisting he take one day, asserting he was God and didn't need the stuff. Observing their mounting frustration and his defiant intransigence, I asked the nurses if they would let me give it to him. How could it hurt? was their response. I held the plastic med cup up to a light, looked with amazement at Bennet (a good therapist knows how to be a good actor), and queried, "Are you God?!" Of course he nodded and mumbled affirmatively. I looked back at the cup and announced, "This reads 'For God only'." I extended the cup to him with a spirit of adulation. Without hesitation, he grabbed the cup and downed the drug. His crooked smile spoke his damaged but persistent pride. The most hostile nurse looked at me with resentment that soon changed to a stifled gratitude. Years later I'd learn my approach was called "joining the patient." It is a respectful way of encouraging cooperation from the most resistant clients.

I felt more hopeful as I gained energy, began sleeping better and took more control of my daily experiences. Jones was usually able to reassure me when I expressed doubts about my adequacies and potentials. I described how much I struggled with writing my term paper for English class during the last semester and doubted I could undertake such tasks throughout a college career.

"What do you mean? Look how verbal you are!" Jones retorted.

When I had doubts about completing term papers during the remainder of my college career, I'd remind myself of that simple fact. A term paper simply became a way of expressing my verbosity. My flaw became a resource.

The most important insight from therapy was that my desperate search for affection, acceptance, and approval was a compensation from what I never received from my parents or parent substitutes; there had been 19. Since I never had a home with the same parental figures for more than three years, my developmental needs were not met well. While everyone searches for approval and affection from others, my search appeared to be like a six year-old in a nineteen year-old body, not a particularly attractive social approach and one that is unlikely to succeed. I never learned the skills that people with families and more stable backgrounds had learned. I also had poor self-esteem from getting rejected repeatedly and was understandably insecure. In therapy with Jones, I became aware of my unmet needs and social deficits and how important it was to accept myself, despite those inadequacies. After all, I never asked for my chopped-up childhood-- why should I get down on myself?

Easier said than done.

After I was in the hospital four weeks, I was informed Jack would take me out for about a week for plastic surgery on two chest scars and eye scars sustained from the car accident. Other than a brief romance with a young woman who was a patient in a room close to mine--an increase in libido is a pleasant symptomatic recovery from depression--my operation in the general hospital was uneventful. The Institute was a hard act to follow! And the improvement in the scars was only slight. They would be conspicuous for the rest of my life. Interestingly, I looked forward to my return to the mental hospital; I wanted to experience my place of rebirth a bit more before cutting the cord.

Upon my return I chatted away in therapy sessions and was discomfited that Jones was becoming more distant. He said very little, especially when I attempted to elicit approval by mentioning my accomplishments or impressing him with my goals. He particularly was in disagreement with what I considered an exceedingly noble plan--to swim the English Channel one day! Instead he emphasized how much he wanted me to find love. I thought he was being unrealistic. One day he stated he had something for me in his car, and I felt so important walking through the halls with him, the Medical Director, to receive my surprise. When we reached his sports car in the parking lot, he tore out a cartoon from Time or Newsweek about TM, the well-known abbreviation at the time for transcendental meditation. I had told him about the TM book I was reading, and he had seemed amused. I actually cherished this gift and kept it safely in my journal for a long time. It was a gift from my therapist who had rescued me.

I was getting the message from Jones' silences in our sessions that it was time for me to leave the hospital. He wanted me to initiate the decision to leave, though, and I was running out of things to say to this stoic medical director staring at me, the patient-specimen. The anxiety that accompanies freedom began mounting. After five weeks my psychiatric sabbatical ended.

A touching note was made in my journal by Bob Behr, the instructor, during my last week. He wrote that I had qualities that were not immediately apparent upon first meeting me, and, I remember, several included my humor, creativity, and compassion. He also wrote that these qualities helped him to like me. I thought about expressing these qualities sooner to people, but I wasn't quite sure how. I did keep his note for many years.

As Jack drove us through Philadelphia and away from my hospital-womb, a shivering panic sliced through me. The hospital provided a climate of acceptance and understanding, and the staff helped me recover from a suicidal depression. I was experiencing their loss as we cruised down I-95 to Wilmington, the city of my first birth. I became calmer as I reminded myself of the treasures I discovered during my recent transformation--the insights about my childhood from therapy, an awareness of my feelings, the knowledge about TM and energy from the tofranil. Even though I was the same person, the changes I felt were incredible.

I decided to use my life saving certification I received from Matt and got a lifeguard job at a motel pool for the rest of the summer. I didn't know it would entail the disadvantage of mowing the lawn when no one was in the pool, but I didn't know I'd meet a blonde, Linda, who'd become my second sex partner either. She was an important, almost necessary, surprise, as she coached me in an area in which I had minimal confidence.

However, Linda dumped me within a few weeks, and I threw a tantrum at Jack and Trisha's house. How could she do such a thing to fragile me, who was recovering from a clinical depression, a severe one at that, and just out of a mental institution!? Obviously, quite easily.

It became apparent that if I were to survive and progress, I would have to use my recently acquired resources, not just think about them. The tofranil and insight about my father were relieving, but they were not enough. The reality that life can be a painful struggle on a regular basis confronted me. The challenge was to find a reliable resource that would endure despite the disappointments from other people.

So, even though I had no formal instruction, I began practicing transcendental meditation. I read about "contacting the Being" in Maharishi's book, and he described Being as the underlying essence of existence or the basis of life. I sat on my bed, the same bed on which I expected to die just two months ago, every morning for twenty minutes with my legs folded comfortably, and I simply looked at a spot on the floor for the duration. I reasoned that while I could not see the subtler forms of the spot, including the molecules, atoms, electrons, protons, and neutrons, I was aware of their existence; by sitting quietly and focusing on the spot, I was becoming one with the Being. By contacting the Being, I figured I was becoming one with life. I am not quite sure Maharishi would have agreed with me, but I know I did feel calmer and more peaceful with each practice. I decided I was on the path to enlightenment.

A particular illustration Maharishi used to describe levels of consciousness was what he called the "bubble diagram." He explained a thought began at the level of Being as tiny and imperceptible, and as it rose up through the layers of consciousness, just as a bubble does in the ocean, it changed from the subtle to the gross. The bubbles in the diagram became larger as they rose from the unconscious to the sub- conscious to the conscious layer. When it reaches consciousness, one is aware of it as a thought. The mind was characterized by Maharishi as an endless series of waves, and while they often become stormy and tempestuous, the goal of meditation was to create a sea of calm. The regular practice of TM purportedly brought about longer durations of this calm sea in the stormy weather of each person's everyday life.

I felt prepared to face college again. I was surprised by the experience of my rebirth in the hospital. And TM was a wonderful technique I could practice regularly. It reminded me a bit of the prayer ritual I once did in my Roman Catholic days. Since it was more secular and scientific, TM seemed more valid. As the Beatles had practiced with the Maharishi, I was even more enthused about it. Life at High Point College would be better.

I know, I know, I know. I've whetted your appetite for a delicious display of suicide, and it's been three nights now. Have patience. It's not like I've talked myself out of it. I have had a nostalgic time, though, sharing memories from my adventurous life. And I'm not sure I'm finished yet. I'm the one who decides when it is time to check out. After all, this is my note.

CHAPTER 4

The Gentle Power of Meditation

"The fact that the mind rules the body is, in spite of its neglect by biology and medicine, the most fundamental fact which we know about the process of life."

—FRANZ ALEXANDER, M.D.

"Nothing can bring you peace but yourself."

--RALPH WALDO EMERSON

IT SEEMED I WAS LOOKING at the world through a new set of lenses, with colors as splendid as the rainbow, upon my return to High Point College for the Fall Semester, 1974. Just a few months earlier, the only solution to my painful misery was death. Now I had the insight from therapy that my relationships with people in the present were affected by the deaths of my parents and my relatives and orphanage treating me like a hot potato during my first 13 years: I'd lived in ten different pseudo-family settings during the so-called formative years. The insights helped me become more understanding and forgiving of myself for the depression.

The energy I felt from the biochemical effects of the antidepressant medication made me feel like I could work, love, study, and play. Also, the tofranil experience was educational as I previously had no idea how much the quality of my life was affected by my physiological state. I was reminded of the miracle drug, Soma, taken by the inhabitants of Aldous Huxley's Brave New World, one of the futuresque novels I enjoyed in high school.

I felt most inspired and empowered, though, by my newly acquired tool, transcendental meditation, that I continued to practice two times a day according to my version of what Maharishi Mahesh Yogi described in his book as "contacting the Being." Each morning I'd sit in a comfortable, cross-legged position on my bed, in a quieter dorm room from last year, and focus my visual attention on a small white spot on the floor. I reminded myself the spot symbolized the field of Being, the essence of all existence. We are all a part of the Being, can contact or feel one with it, and originally exemplified it as fetuses, long before we had thoughts, emotions, motives, and personalities. I was cognizant of the symbolic value of the spot because it was comprised of atoms and molecules, the building blocks of all physical reality. As I would sit peacefully, simply focusing visually on the spot, I would experience a profound sense of contacting the Being which Maharishi described as "Absolute" since the atomic constituents are static and everywhere. My spot, I told myself, was a symbol for the omnipresence of the field of Being. I surmised the experience was called "transcendental" because you go beyond the experience of everyday concerns, remaining quietly still, aware and awake to the experience without having any particular thoughts, a state referred to as "no-mind." When in this state, you accept the experience of simply existing as valuable, existing just like the desk, the chair, the rug--all existence. You are at one with all existence and are in contact with the Being. It was most peaceful and serene. You might call it a cosmic time-out.

Maharishi taught The Beatles, Joe Namath, Mia Farrow, and The Beach Boys meditation. If someone was cool enough for The Beatles, he certainly had credibility in my eyes. It wasn't until years later that I learned their song "Fool on the Hill" was about him, and I discovered he was not as "cool" with them as I originally thought; they were less than impressed with his attraction to Mia Farrow. Lust is usually not becoming to a spiritual leader. Dr. Stone, one of the Administrators from Cluckland, who orchestrated my firing, was a TM instructor, and told me a funny anecdote about an interaction Maharishi had with Mick Jagger. Jagger was saying goodbye to Maharishi after a period of having received meditation instruction. With paternal jocularity, Maharishi intoned, "Now Mick, be a good boy" to which Jagger responded, "Maharishi, I have a reputation to live up to." At least Stare offered me one thing of value.

As I understood Maharishi, the Relative field included the variety of manifestations we observe in our changing world--clothes, cars, buildings, mountains, trees, and flowers and anything else physical and mutable. The Absolute field was the underlying, eternal static essence of the universe. He used the metaphor of H2O to describe the distinction between the Absolute and the Relative. The changing forms of liquid to ice to vapor is symbolic of the Relative field, and, it is the Relative field that we observe with our five senses in our everyday reality. Practicing meditation involved quieting and stilling the nervous systems of the body until the mind and body approximated the stillness of the Absolute. Regular practice of once in the morning before breakfast and once in the evening before supper facilitated my progress along the path to attaining this level of being that Maharishi described as cosmic consciousness.

So while I'd sit for twenty minutes, focusing my attention on my visual mantra (the spot), I would let my thoughts drift. Sometimes I imagined the thoughts as tree leaves, falling off branches hanging over a river, floating through the air and gently landing on the water, carried away in the current which brought me back to the current moment, which is always the most important one for one's full experience of life. The point was not to get caught up in the content of thoughts, and instead, to let them flow and return to the experience of my focus on the spot and becoming one with existence--the experience of just being, not becoming. In the practice of just noticing my thoughts, I would perceive them as all equally unimportant and without value. For instance, a thought about a test grade would have the same degree of importance as what I would have for supper that night. By practicing in this way I conditioned myself to worry less and sometimes

I transcended the world of everyday concerns. My breaths would become deeper and slower during each of those four five-minute intervals. If I became concerned as to whether I was practicing correctly, I reminded myself to let go of that concern, another leaf falling off the tree branch, dancing in its descending cadence before lighting upon the river's surface, carried away by the perpetual current. Subsequently I would find it easier to blend into the spot, the symbol of the Being, the Absolute, and I'd often feel a lightness throughout my body during those moments of peaceful relaxation.

In addition to the practice of relaxation, I developed a deeper appreciation for the experience of change, that eternal reality that permeates the universe. The river that would transport the leaf downstream was the current of life, the flow of change, telling me to be mindful of my temporary, fluctuating existence. And since life is so acutely temporary, I realized I had better focus my attention on what is most important during each moment of it--what better way to develop this skill than by the practice of meditation. My appreciation of change was emphasized in 500 B.C. by the philosopher Heraclitus who asserted that everything was in a state of flux and articulated, "You cannot step twice into the same river." More recently, the rock n' roller David Bowie scored a hit with his song Changes in which he reminds parents that children "...are immune to your consultations. They're quite aware of what they're going through...ch-ch-ch-ch- changes." Of course I was astonished at the changes I'd experienced in the last year, from a conviction that death was the only solution to another awakening and rebirth, and I thought it ironic that the one constant linking Heraclitus to David Bowie was the concept of change. Awake to change as inevitable, I felt hopeful meditating. I finally had a reliable tool to make my miserable life better.

I elected to pledge for Theta Chi fraternity, the chief reason being that I would live in a dormitory of significantly better quality than the rathole of the previous year. I particularly liked the fabric, texture, and design of the Theta Chi blanket I purchased, upon which I'd sit cross-legged on my bed while practicing the Hank-version of TM. Of course I de-pledged the fraternity shortly after being blindfolded, wrestled by several "brothers" into a car and dumped in an unfamiliar neighborhood in the middle of the night. Such silly shenanigans that were all a part of pledging were incongruent with my new spiritual lifestyle as a transcendental meditator. Besides, I had achieved my main goal; I was living in a better dormitory.

Instead of developing any relationships with girls oriented to the fraternity/sorority scene, I became friends with Carol, a thoroughly enjoyable and cheerful young woman, with a seemingly perpetual smile, who was able to get around campus quite well despite her cerebral palsy. Carol's laughter was infectious and conducive to my ego, as it seemed I was always able to elicit her paroxysms with my apparently humorous antics that I had never known could be so funny. With John Denver singing "Sunshine on my shoulders makes me happy…" blaring from a dorm room, I'd walk away from visiting Carol's suite, slapping my shoulders and fighting them to "get the sun the hell off!" Looking down at me fighting with myself from her dorm's balcony, Carol would howl, nearly to the point of convulsion. I felt happy making her laugh. Her interest in my life story served to cement our friendship which I valued greatly.

I kept a cool distance from Butch. I managed to appreciate a few things from that relationship: awareness of the beauty of Beethoven and Scott Joplin's music, insights about my expectations of people, and how love can be powerful. Butch once disclosed to me that he would have been "mentally insane" if he did not have his piano skills; that statement emphasized the importance to me to be passionate about something in life. All in all, the experience of our relationship had significant value.

Instead of trying hard to make people like me who showed little likelihood of doing so, I made a couple acquaintances with kind, humorous fellows, such as Rob Davis and Scott Scribner, who were both slightly my senior. Rob and I swapped most of the poems we had written and complimented each other accordingly. He had taken the formal course in transcendental meditation and joked about how arcane the instructors were about the meanings of mantras. "I'll tell you my mantra if you'll tell me yours" was one of our favorite exchanges. I also liked to hear Rob occasionally say one of his favorite injunctions for living that was congruent with the meditative experience--"Let it flow."

Scott, perhaps less aesthetic and poetic than Rob but incisive in a savvy, street-wise sense, sometimes said one of his favorite truisms that had particular import for me, a struggling, young man who never had a home. He would pontificate with wry humor, "Hank, home is where you hang your hat!" Damn right. "I'll hang it over there, go to bed, sleep well, and see ya bright and early Scott." I guess his pontification, which was rather trivial, was powerful to me because it moved me from the perspective of never having a home to always having a home, everywhere, as long as I had a hat and something to hang it on. I still felt insecure making the transition to adulthood from a childhood without a foundation; "always" having a home made it a little better. Having the world as a home felt right for me as a meditator too.

During Christmas vacation, 1973, I attended a psychiatric follow-up session with Dr. Jones in Philadelphia. He said very little during the 50 minutes but maintained his inimitable stare at me as I talked at length about my recent semester and my experience with meditation. I wanted his approval for my adjustment and improved college grades. Toward the end of the session he informed me I probably had a "Mendellian inheritance with a twist in a genetic molecule," meaning I had bipolar disorder or what traditionally had been called manic depression. My lengthy description of my college semester and my increased energy (he still had me on a low dose of tofranil) were apparently enough for him to give me this diagnostic impression. In essence, he was explaining my recent happiness and college adjustment as molecularly based, not to mention pathological, discounting my practice of meditation and self-discipline and hurting my pride. So much for craving approval.

In the winter of 1974, a notice was posted on campus advertising the TM course would be offered for $75.00 in Greensboro. Although I felt I benefitted from my version of transcendental meditation, I was aware I was not practicing the standardized style, complete with instructions from a certified teacher, ritual, and mantra. Consequently I considered the possibility I might benefit even more and interested Carol enough to take the course with me.

It was the use of the mantra that most differentiated my version from the correct practice of TM. The instructor explained that mantras were meaningless sounds, comprised of one or two syllables that originated in the Hindu Sanskrit language. The mantra was to be repeated mentally and effortlessly for 20 minutes and was assigned according to some unique features of the recipient--the arcane aspect joked about by Rob--and should not be discussed in everyday conversation as the mantras would lose their power. Also, if you used someone else's mantra or one that was not assigned to you, unpleasant effects would likely come your way. For example, the mantra OM, a fairly well-known sound, was purportedly practiced by people who subsequently showed increased introversion and seclusiveness. One instructor told me if I used it I would wind up in a cave, and though the experience of sitting among stalagmites and stalactites sounded appealing, the thought of pulling bats out of my hair discouraged me from using it.

While the secrecy of the mantra seemed disingenuous, the purpose of it made some sense. The instructor described the "science of sound" relevant to the mantra; this science simply asserted that sounds have physiological and emotional effects. Have you ever felt the physical sensations when someone scrapes their fingernails on the blackboard? That metaphor was used by the instructor to emphasize that sound indubitably has physical effects--not a soul argued with him. While that sound is conspicuous in its effects, all sound has some physical and/or emotional effects. Ocean waves, singing birds, rustling tree leaves, and Debussy's *Claire De Lune* are just as conspicuous albeit serene. The sound of the mantra was described as soothing, and as the practitioner repeats it internally to him or herself, the parasympathetic branch of the autonomic nervous system, that branch which dominates during relaxation, is activated. As the person experiences the dominance of the parasympathetic branch for longer periods with continued practice of meditation, he consequently will experience the psychological effect of peacefulness, tranquility, and calm. Those experiences were more than just a little inviting.

Although I did not realize it until years later, after studying psychology, the mantra had several other cognitive effects. For one, it strengthened my concentration. Simply repeating the sound over and over, despite the intrusion of various thoughts, was a fairly easy concentration exercise--what college sophomore could not benefit from increased concentration? The sound of the mantra also disrupted intrusive thoughts better than the visual mantra (the spot on the floor), and made concentration easier in that respect. Disrupting negative thoughts and worry with a pleasant sound was gentle yet empowering.

I have contended that our most important psychological need is control, control over our internal worlds as well as control over our external worlds, similar to our biological needs for sleep, food, and water. The mantra served as a resource for control over my internal world. As the meditator silently says the mantra in her mind, she is controlling her mind's experience and thus satisfying her need for internal control. The instructor tells the student to do all this "effortlessly," to not try to stop any thoughts, and to say the mantra whenever it comes to mind, and, paradoxically, he is instructing to give up control. This paradox of achieving better control of the mind's experience while effortlessly practicing and giving up control is a rather aesthetic way of satisfying that need for control. As the mantra continues to disrupt thoughts, it dampens them, rendering them less powerful. The mantra, then, becomes more powerful and the meditator gives it power simply by using it twice a day during meditation and keeping it private.

Although I am still planning to commit suicide, when I finish my verbose note, I am not going to tell you my mantra. I will selfishly take it into eternity with me instead of sharing it. It's my last vestige of control.

Once I met a guru-like gentleman from India at a health food store who said the mantra serves as a beginning and an end to the meditation experience, and as a consequence, satisfies our need for closure to experience. No matter where the mind strays and meanders it has the mantra to which it returns for closure, a form of security. It's kind of like having a home to return to no matter how lost you get on a journey. And I didn't even need a hat to hang on my mantra!

So I practiced TM correctly for 20 minutes, twice a day, once after waking up in the morning and once before supper, according to my new instructions. It wasn't necessary to sit cross-legged, and, instead, I'd sit in a comfortable chair with my hands in my lap and both feet on the floor. I would look at my watch, close my eyes and wait 30 seconds or so before saying the mantra, over and over and over. If my mind wandered with certain thoughts, I'd return to the mantra when I became aware of the wandering, without worrying or criticizing myself for imperfect concentration. I'd remind myself to "be here now" which made it easier to let go of thoughts, all of which related to the past and future. After about 20 minutes, I would open one eye to look at my watch to see if 20 minutes had elapsed and if they had not, I'd close my eye and continue until they had. Then I would keep my eyes closed without saying the mantra for a couple minutes to reorient and awaken. Invariably, I would feel more calm, relaxed, and, consequently, optimistic, and these effects carried over into my everyday life.

Of course I adapted my practice to a variety of situations. For instance, Rob and I went to Montreat Anderson College in the mountains one weekend to visit Harry and Marsha, two of Rob's friends. For my morning meditation, I walked down the hill from our cabin and sat cross-legged by a pure, gurgling stream, appreciating the cool autumn air, and the fresh scent of the multicolored leaves. Nature and its godlike beauty made it so easy to be here now. I was one with nature. The 20 minute Thoreavian solitude of peace and tranquility is one I deposited in my memory bank; I've made occasional withdrawals many times since.

Carol liked the experience of practicing TM, but I discovered she wanted our relationship to be more erotic than I; a few impulsive lapses in judgment on my part did not help matters. I was, however, somewhat interested in her 17 year-old sister, Karen, and she fell in love with me. I found her attractive and very bright, but being perfectionistic in my standards as an immature 20 year-old, I indirectly broke up with her by not answering her last correspondence. After a period, I finally called her, and she sent me a beautiful card with an ocean crashing against the rocks at twilight and this message inside:

Dear Hank,   10/29/79
It was good to hear from you, real good. I received your letter at
a time when I was feeling kind of blue...
Sometimes it seems as though I'll always
be searching for that "lifetime lover" as Jack Croce
puts it--but even if you'll never be that person, I don't know--you
were my first lover and I won't be able to forget that.
Be happy honey. Always remember what's
most important to you and never let anyone ever interfere with it.
I love you,
Karen

I have always cherished that card and its powerful messages and still have
it tucked away in a photo album. It was one of the few times in my life
that I could recall someone saying she loved me and meaning it. A couple
of years later after transferring to the University of North Carolina at
Charlotte, I wrote this poem while lost in a memory of Karen. Sanskrit,
the university's art magazine, published it.

<u>Regret</u>
Unfilled envelope
Whispers to his hands
For hers far away.
Warm weeping thoughts
Slide through a wobbly pen
to capture the feelings
that were lost in pursuit of
too much not there.
While breaths become deeper
and the sentences cripple,
only the wind sails his dream.
it melts in crisp coolness.

Rob suggested I transfer from High Point to UNC-Charlotte if I wanted to major in psychology because UNC-C had a reputable pro- gram. Having helped a few patients at the psychiatric institute and subsequently having done better academically, I was ready to make a career of psychology. I felt confident enough to apply, partly as a result of my meditation practice, and was accepted as a second semester sophomore. In the summer of '74, just before my first semester at UNC-C,

I read in a book about picking up women that Charlotte was the number one best city in the U.S. for it. Suddenly an elevated libido was begging for integration into a consciousness that had been filled with Catholicism, and more recently, with spirituality from TM. Fortunately, begging is often successful.

Not much begging was necessary, though, as I observed the sensual female scenery in various shorts and skirts of stimulating length and design around campus.

I met Jennifer, a beautiful and sexy girl of 4'11", with jet black hair, almond eyes, and an inviting smile, at a keg party. She was a skillful dancer, with all the right moves to manifest her desirable body, and she immediately accepted my request; we did a dance called "the bump." We began seeing each other over the next few days and sleeping together after a week or so, although Jennifer made sure we limited our sexual activity to everything but intercourse for almost a month; my affection for her was obvious by my frustration tolerance! Sleeping with her while accepting her restriction proved I was beginning to love her.

Something I especially liked about Jennifer was the interest she expressed about my life and recent tragedies with which I had grappled--she was intuitive enough to see that I was still grappling. She supported my practice of transcendental meditation and showed curiosity about it. TM was to come in handy for her in a rather phenomenal way during the following summer.

After we had seen each other for a couple of months, Jennifer became pregnant. The university's doctor explained I'd worn a condom too tightly, making it break, and instructed me next time to leave a tail at the end of it to catch the semen. He told me not to pull it on all the way. The simple truth was that no one had explained that little piece of useful information to me. So if there's any youth out there who might be reading this note and who have never been told that, I pass it on to you.

We talked about an abortion, and neither of us liked the idea, especially Jennifer. She wanted to get married and said she was in love with me and wanted my baby. I retrospected on the tragic consequences of my parents' forced marriage, prompted by the conception of yours truly. I did not want that to happen again. I had mixed feelings. I loved Jennifer but was uncertain about spending the rest of my life with her. I sometimes wondered what it would be like to go out with other women. I was a sophomore in college and felt marriage and family would thwart me from my goals. I felt too immature to get married. The ambivalence was a message to me--don't do something you're going to regret. Despite the irate reactions of her father, I felt my decision to not marry was the most honest and responsible one.

Jennifer decided to have the baby, and I believe she hoped I would change my mind about marriage during the next seven months. I suggested she receive instruction in transcendental meditation, a suggestion with which she complied and practiced regularly, hoping to help her with the stress of pregnancy. During the summer of '75, she became a resident of a home for unwed mothers where I visited her regularly. We began an adoption procedure and requested that the adoption liaison person encourage the adoptive parents to have our child receive transcendental meditation instruction; although presumptuous, I felt my request was the least I could do for my child. Jennifer reported her meditation practice helped her immensely during the labor and delivery on August 13, 1975, when she pushed a healthy 5 lb. baby girl into the world. We named her Angela Marie. The brief experience of seeing her was bitter sweet, bitter anticipation of giving her to unknown people and sweet knowing she was healthy and would live with reportedly stable adults. Despite the painful, sad experience, adoption still seemed like the best option.

Meditating helped me cope with the loss of my daughter and to put the experience in a positive perspective; we did create a healthy human being and gave a responsible couple joy and opportunity. I also read further about loss and found a verse by William Blake to be fitting:

He who binds himself a joy,
Does the winged life destroy.
But he who kisses the joy as it flies,
Lives in eternity's sunrise.

I have relied on that simple verse in many subsequent contexts involving loss and have just about always found it freeing. Remember it if you ever catch a butterfly.

Jennifer and I gradually stopped seeing each other. It seemed awkward to continue our relationship after I decided not to marry, a marriage that would have bound us to our child. The losses of Jennifer and my daughter were a continuation of losses that began when I was three, even though I had become the architect of the recent losses. I was alone again.

The bi-diurnal practice of TM continued to free my thinking as much as was possible. For awhile, that was just a little. Together with the advent of the Fall, practicing meditation lightened my being, and I began to feel a renewed sense of energy. Usually, I was able to perceive the losses like those leaves, falling off the overhanging tree branch and landing on the flowing river, floating away, far away, with the current. The lightness of energy and the freedom of thought stimulated my creativity, culminating in poems such as

And It Is Fall

Biting breeze, gently splashing across earth, life's rippling current pauses, leaves dance in the sky,
heat has slipped away but a drifting sun persists, setting evening horizon afire with tender traces of baby-blue,
while cool, tense people plant themselves with wools and cotton.
Winding brook splashes, bubbling laughter over stones with rush,
Nature's chorus singing to her delicate hearts.
A moon climbs slow and early, sprinkling tree tops with lighted design,
Death is speaking, as it has spoken, its glory since time.

While the experience of TM certainly elicited relaxation and energy, my belief in it often approximated that which might remind you of religious belief. I enthusiastically described my TM experience to my college adviser, Dr. Lawrence Calhoun, a clinical psychologist who was characteristically incisive. He was a scientist to the hilt and asserted the mantra and special instruction reminded him of the placebo affect and that one could get the same results by simply sitting quietly for 20 minutes. After I continued to argue about the importance of the mantra, he threw down the gauntlet by saying we'd do an experiment the following semester. Though I excitedly agreed to it, he later reneged, and I continued to do my proselytizing.

Next, I found a book, <u>The Relaxation Response</u>, by Herbert Benson of Harvard, who along with Robert Keith Wallace of UCLA Medical School, became the first American researchers to demonstrate the physiological benefits of TM. Benson and Wallace discovered during the practice of TM oxygen consumption and carbon dioxide exhalation both decreased, skin resistence to electricity increased, and blood lactate, which is associated with anxiety, decreased. Benson also challenged the notion that the Sanskrit mantra was necessary, although he did indicate a mental device for concentration was essential. He suggested the practitioner use the syllable "one", which was to be said mentally during each exhale. (I found my mantra was, without doubt, more aesthetically pleasing, perhaps supporting the importance of sound promulgated by the TM people).

Benson further reported the physiological changes mentioned, along with decreases in drug and alcohol abuse and blood pressure, occurred in a variety of relaxation techniques, as long as four components were included in the technique. It was the physiological changes that he specifically identified as "the relaxation response." When I got my first job as a psychologist in 1983 at a state psychiatric hospital, I described Benson's technique and related information in this booklet I typed for patients that you, my reader, are welcome to read and practice if you like:

The Relaxation Response

The relaxation technique you will be taught is simple to learn and practical since you can practice it by yourself at home. It is called "The Relaxation Response" and was developed by Dr. Herbert Benson of Harvard University. "The Relaxation Response" technique is similar to meditation, as Dr. Benson conducted research on a certain type of meditation when it was brought to this country from India. If you practice the technique on a regular basis, once a day for 20 minutes, it is likely you will gain a number of benefits. Most people find, in addition to general feelings of relaxation, calmness, and peacefulness, their muscles are less tense and they are able to think more clearly. These experiences often lead to wellness and better health as they relate to a decrease in blood pressure and headaches, less stomach problems, and more efficient breathing. As a consequence of improving physical health, mental health improves and people are less likely to be anxious and worry as much and are then able to relate better with others without becoming too angry. While the benefits cannot all be listed here, it should also be noted most individuals report they smoke cigarettes and drink alcohol less than before they practiced the relaxation technique.

Based on the advantages, one might wonder about the reason for which more people do not practice a simple technique for 20 minutes once a day. Probably, the most frequent reason offered for inconsistent practice is the inconvenience it causes in daily schedules. I usually respond in two ways. Once, after practicing the relaxation technique for a few months, individuals often report they are making more efficient use of their time and their schedules run more smoothly. Two, it is common knowledge we rarely, if ever, gain something for nothing. We nearly always need to make some small sacrifice if we are to benefit in some way.

Another reason given for discontinuing the practice of relaxation is some people are afraid to "let go," an experience that is an important part of meditation. By "letting go" one allows him or herself to think or feel anything without worrying about it. It is as if some people need to worry! Eventually, if you practice regularly, you will find you are able to "let go" and allow yourself to give up rigid control. This phenomenon will be addressed further in the directions on how to practice.

Here are the directions for practicing " The Relaxation Response":

1. It is first important to select a quiet place. While it is often difficult, if not impossible, to find a room with total silence, it is a good idea to use an environment with the least noise possible. Some noises that may not be possible to avoid include a whirring fan or the chirping of birds. If minor sounds like these are present, you will still be able to concentrate on the relaxation process.
2. Next, you should assume a comfortable position. It is best to sit in a chair that has a back, with both feet on the floor and your hands in your lap. Then, close your eyes and become aware of your breathing, how you breathe in and out, allowing yourself to do it naturally without controlling it.
3. You will then concentrate on a sound, which will be the syllable "one," each time you exhale or breathe out. At first, you may want to say it aloud in a quiet manner, about five times. Then you will say it to yourself, silently, in your own mind. As you progress with your 20-minute session, you may find yourself stretching the sound out more as you go along. As you say "one" more calmly, slowly, and soothingly to yourself, you will, in a sense, be proving to yourself that you are relaxing.
4. Perhaps most important of all, you should allow yourself to have any thoughts or images and let them pass through your mind. And, as everything in life changes, your thoughts, good and bad, will change or pass away. Your attitude, then, is to be carefree and not to worry about whether you are practicing correctly. If you forget to say "one" when you breathed out, just go back to it when

you remember to do so, without worrying. If you are wondering whether you've practiced for 20 minutes, open one eye to look at a watch or clock and then close your eyes until you are finished. Treat all thoughts as unimportant regarding whether they are pleasant or unpleasant, and just let them pass. You'll have plenty of time to worry during your daily routine, so worrying during relaxation practice would be pointless.

5. As you reach 20 minutes, stop saying "one" and let yourself sit quietly with your eyes closed for about another minute. Then, open your eyes slowly. You will probably feel more relaxed and may think that nothing can bother you. However, it can and it will! Just wait a couple of hours! But, after you have practiced this simple relaxation procedure for some period, you will find yourself better able to handle stress and may find yourself taking better control of your life. I hope you decide to do so.

Hank McGovern

The few psychiatric patients I succeeded in getting to practice reported they did feel more relaxed after practicing and even liked it, but I don't know that any of them practiced it on a long-term basis. Most of them felt like helpless victims to life's vicissitudes, were over- whelmed by hopeless- ness and did not expect that regular practice of the relaxation response would make a difference. They had also been taught by the psychiatry profession that the correct way to get better is to be a compliant patient, take the prescribed medication, accept the doctors' explanations for their "illness" (including the idea they were ill), and if they didn't get better, they were "resistant." After the months, and often years, of experience as psychiatric patients, the possibility that something so simple as meditation could significantly help them was too foreign an idea. As someone who had been on both sides of "the couch," I could sympathize and empathize with them.

Since this part of my note is about meditation, let me skip ahead some years to another type I've been interested in called mindfulness meditation, derived from Buddhism. My favorite two books on this subject are It's Easier

Than You Think, by Sylvia Boorstein, a meditation teacher and psychotherapist, and Wherever You Go, There You Are, by John Kabat-Zinn, Ph.D., the founder and director of the Stress Reduction Clinic of the University of Massachusetts Medical Center. Essentially, the practice of mindfulness meditation sounds simple; you sit and focus your attention on your breathing, each inhale and each exhale. Your natural breath is your mantra. As in TM, you let your thoughts drift without any criticism or judgment.

A person is not directed to practice for a specific time at first, and may begin meditating for just five minutes or so each session, but with continued practice and more experience, meditation can last 30 minutes or more, depending on the needs and skill of the meditator.

It is a state of consciousness, or perhaps state of being, called mindfulness that is created by the daily practice of meditation. Mindfulness is awareness, an awakening to one's experience in the present moment. When one is fully present in each moment, she is more attuned to her own thoughts, feelings, sensations, and intentions, as well as those of others with whom she may be communicating. You become better able to focus on what is happening when you are wherever you are, and you do not think about what happened yesterday or last week nor are you wrapped up in anticipations about wherever you will be tomorrow or whoever you will be with. You are here now. Hence the title Wherever You Go, There You Are. That title also posits as an undeniable truism; in a physical sense, of course you are wherever you go. How often, though, do people develop what are called monkey minds, minds that jump around from the past to the future and from one person to another when they could absorb themselves more meaningfully and enjoyably in the present? The practice of meditating on the breath can take you from monkey mind to mindfulness so you can truly be wherever you are.

A few Buddhist propositions relevant to the practice of meditation also seem true and useful. One is that pain is inevitable in life because pain happens when we experience loss. And we all experience loss whether through death, divorce, accident, firing or downsizing, or any number of other crises. Suffering, though, is a choice, and you choose to suffer when you cling to that which is lost. Suffering is also experienced when you crave that which you don't have. Of course, we all have experienced craving, and as a consequence, suffering. As I cling to the job of a "Staff Psychologist," a job from which I've been fired more than once, I choose to suffer. Simply put, clinging and craving cause suffering.

The good news is that there is an escape from suffering. Your choice of it is usually unconscious; who would consciously choose suffering? Although you unconsciously slip into it, you can consciously choose to move from it to pain which is less intense and often shorter in duration. A simple injunction I've made up for myself is: "Instead of clinging or craving, let go, let it flow, let it be." That injunction is just a reminder, though, as the freedom from suffering and acceptance of pain are better achieved by the experience of sitting quietly, with eyes closed, and listening to your natural breath, each inhale, each exhale. Mindfulness meditation is the key to the door, exiting from the room of suffering to the room of pain. And focusing on the breath is also the key to the door leading from the room of pain to the room of happiness. What more empowering idea is there than the fact we can practice happiness? As you begin to appreciate and practice awareness of the breath that gives you life, you give it more value, and the clinging and craving of people and things becomes easier to give up. Hence, Boorsteins's title <u>It's Easier Than You Think</u>. After all, you already have your breath; what else do you need besides water and enough food, clothing, and shelter to keep you alive and living in the here and now? I like to call this "your present of the present." Like Socrates (ironic that I should quote a man who committed suicide, isn't it) asserted, "Those who want the fewest things are nearest the Gods."

Zen Master and Buddhist monk, Thich Nhat Hanh, and meditation teachers, Sharon Salzberg and Jack Kornfield, are other experts on mindfulness who have written excellent books on it. One meditation I like from Thich Nhat Hanh involves breathing in and saying one line, then breathing out and saying the next, smiling when suggested. It goes: "Breathing in, I calm my body. Breathing out, I smile. Dwelling in the present moment. I know this is a wonderful moment." Salzberg and Kornfield write eloquently about lovingkindness, integrating it in mindfulness meditation and my favorite is: "May I be filled with lovingkindness, May I be well. May I be peaceful and at ease, May I be happy."

Just to go off on a tangent for a moment. Phil Jackson, the ex-coach of the Chicago Bulls, is a practitioner of mindfulness meditation and a Buddhist, and I feel sure that his Buddhist perspective and characteristic equanimity were keys to his excellence as a coach and assets to the Bulls' six NBA championships (O.K. Michael was the biggest asset but remember, Michael refused to play for anyone but Phil).

Paradoxically, I don't believe Jackson craved those championships, though he certainly wanted them.

Not long ago, I combined my knowledge of meditation, hypnosis and prayer into what I call "Values Meditation." The nine values I've incorporated in it are ones by which I'd live my life if I were to continue living. I think it's too late now. I won't explain the process of "Values Meditation" but I will leave you with the specific values: optimism, flexibility, humor, mindfulness, acceptance, compassion, passion, responsibility, and cooperation. Maybe you can make up your own meditation with them.

It's been four nights since I began describing my plan to end my life. I delay my suicide, getting wrapped up in the nostalgic angst from my memory bank and believing I have something worth leaving for you. While I procrastinate, remember, the best thing about procrastinating is that you always have something to look forward to. I have always enjoyed saying that because I like to think I'm witty. If you don't think it's witty, that's O.K. I will at least pass it on to you procrastinators so you can view your tendency with a little levity. Hope that's ok.

CHAPTER 5

The Politics of Assertive Behavior

"Let each man sweep in front of his own doorstep and the whole world will be clean."

JOHANN WOLFGANG VON GOETHE

"Never play another person's game. Play your own."

ANDREW SALTER

I AWAKENED THIS MORNING, DAY five from the night I decided to kill my-self, and felt confused about my plan. I want to visit a few more rooms in my memory mansion--when will I end my life then? I've decided to write until I have gotten as much as there is to be gotten out of my system, kind of like vomiting, and then I'll do the drama.

As I have survived five nights, I'm reminded of Nietzsche's macabre humor when he wrote, "It is always consoling to think of suicide: in that way one gets through many a bad night." I have experienced the meaning in that statement, and perhaps Nietzsche did not intend any humor whatsoever when he made it. The meaning of which I speak is the relief I have felt knowing suicide is my choice, an option to end the suffering. Yes, I have the freedom to begin my eternal rest in peace whenever I want.

I also have the choice to continue with my final note. Why rush death? If I kill myself now I won't be able to finish this thing. If I finish the note, I'll then be able to kill myself. I might as well continue the choice that doesn't preclude the other, at least for now. There's nothing wrong with being patient about suicide.

After the breakup with Jennifer, my life at UNC-Charlotte took on a newfound loneliness. I was discovering what would be a lifelong pattern with me and women; when relationships end, a long interval of solo existence follows. While I had enough confidence built up by my meditation practice and academic progress to believe that life was probably worth continuing, I did not have the social skills necessary to achieve rewarding relationships with other students. The loneliness I often felt was accompanied by an existential reality reflected by Sartre's comment, "If you are lonely when you are alone, you are in bad company." Although I sometimes was at peace while alone, I was too often in bad company. Slipping into dysphoria again, at least I was confident I could avoid a severe clinical depression like the one from the summer of '73. I would have the opportunity to see "One Flew Over the Cuckoo's Nest" instead of living it.

A similar existential reality, the fact that we are all ultimately alone, was not particularly consoling either. However, there was an element of that idea that I found a little comforting. Since we are all ultimately alone, paradoxically, we all have that reality in common and, therefore, we have it to share. And sharing involves togetherness. We are all always together, in that sense, in this mysterious universe. The next time you feel lonely you might remember how many other people feel similarly; essentially, we are all alone together.

You might also get a dog or cat.

Sitting alone in a room at my friend Bob's house in the mountains during sunset in the late Fall, I recalled the LSD experience from a few years earlier and imagined the experience happening again in my immediate situation. I suppose the memory of the acid trip was a somewhat rewarding alternative to being intimate with a woman. The depersonalized nature of my imagined experience was reflected in this short poem that Sanskrit published:

<u>6 p.m.</u>
letters slip off a repeated newspaper
and dribble through fingers that try to save them,
disappearing in the jungle-curls of a shadow-sunned carpet,
his eyes follow,
leaving deep, dark holes where they lived.

As you might guess, I became motivated to escape my psychic discomfort, preferably by connecting better with other people. Recalling LSD experiences is not a way of getting genuine satisfaction. So I saw a college counselor, Dale Wachowiak, who recommended a book, <u>The Helping Relationship</u>, by Gerard Egan, a treatise that described how to relate well to others. It was written for counselors and Dale, knowing I wanted to become a psychologist one day, believed I would absorb the information on both a personal and professional level.

Of the various interpersonal skills explained by Egan, the one that is most memorable, as far as giving me hope of relating better with others, was empathy. Basically, I gathered that empathy is the ability to understand what it's like to walk a mile in the other person's shoes and to then communicate your understanding to that person. Empathy is a nondefensive, warm way of helping the other to feel like you could put yourself in his place, without becoming enmeshed, which is more like sympathy. (Etymologically "sym" is the Latin for joining together). Sympathy may be appropriate to use with family or friends but empathy was what I wanted to learn so I could become a psychologist, so went my reasoning.

Perhaps one reason empathy struck a chord with me is that the use of it enhances trust. During my first 18 years I naturally learned to distrust, a quality that fuels anger and won't get you very far in life. My trust increased a bit when I used empathy, for by understanding other people's feelings and perspectives I learned they were not always out to get me or reject me. I found they had understandable reasons for their behaviors.

A situation in which empathy could very beneficially be employed, possibly in a lifesaving way, would be that of road rage. If someone cuts you off in traffic, instead of getting revenge, you might consider various understandable reasons for the driver's poor driving. Maybe medication is effecting his driving. Maybe old age is the culprit. Maybe the person just doesn't have very good driving skills. Maybe he intended to cut you off because his macho pride has repeatedly been hurt, and he compensates by aggressive driving. Granted his compensation is not an excuse; however, it is a reason. Of course none of those reasons mean that you must react in a destructive way. Reminds me of a psychiatrist with whom I worked who used to say in a quiet voice, while stroking his beard, "Don't ever let crazy people drive you crazy."

Yet another use of empathy was employed by yours truly when I conducted sex offender therapy groups at two mental health centers. Now not many people consider child sex offenders to be human beings, but they are and when one considers the emotional, physical and sexual abuse they've often experienced as children, it becomes possible to use empathy with them. After they feel you accept them, they are better able to develop empathy themselves, and I routinely gave them mandatory homework assignments such as the "Apology and Empathy Letter." In those letters, the offender wrote to their victims, expressing how they imagined the victims must have felt during the sexual abuse and its aftermath. They also had to communicate a sincere apology. These letters were not to be mailed unless they were requested by the victim. If I didn't think the empathy was accurate or sincere enough, I'd tell them to do it again for next week's group. (This is one example of why sex offender therapy lasts a long time, usually at least two years or more). Several offenders eventually admitted these letters were one of the most valuable group therapy components.

When I used empathy while the offender told about his own childhood of neglect and abuse, he would often take advantage of it and rationalize he wasn't responsible for his current sex offense. People from his past were responsible for it. At that point, I'd emphasize that while his past explained his behavior in the present, it was not an excuse. There was an important difference between a reason and an excuse, and if he continued to use the latter, he'd be more likely to re-offend. Those offenders gave me practice at balancing confrontation with empathy.

Another interpersonal skill related to empathy, that seemed simple, was reflective listening. It involved listening closely and summarizing the words and feelings of the speaker. If someone stated, "I'm so confused, I don't really know where to begin. And I can't stand this feeling of being so out of control!", the reflective listener might, in a calmer voice, say something like, "It sounds like you're feeling confused and you're not really sure about where to begin. You're having difficulty with feeling out of control." The use of reflective listening for a sustained period of time in a counseling situation gives the client the feeling of acceptance and being understood.

Both reflective listening and empathy are excellent communication skills, but I especially liked some of the implications about their use. They underscored the importance of understanding and forgiveness, two of the most important ingredients of love. If we understand the reasons, and even the excuses, for the behavior of the other, our understanding becomes the water that puts out the fire of anger. In regard to war, the ultimate expression of international anger, Einstein wrote, "Peace cannot be achieved by force. It can only be reached through understanding," and I've often thought of his statement in the context of family and couples' relationships. When we imagine what it's like to walk a mile in the other person's shoes, and therefore understand her better, the door of forgiveness is opened, and the room to which it opens can be a room of love. A nice formula might be compassion + understanding + forgiveness = love. I sometimes wonder if maybe The Beatles were not being too simplistic in 1967 when they wrote "All You Need is Love." When you awaken to the importance of having loved ones at your deathbed, you can appreciate another Beatles message:"And in the end, the love you take, is equal to the love you make." And you make it here and you make it now. So you can use my encouragement, regardless of whether I'll be around, to use empathy as much as you can, especially with your loved ones. Let my encouragement be a parting gift. I had much difficulty applying what I read to real world experiences. I frequented bars and discos in the 70s and most women did not like the feeling of being counseled. I felt frustrated during the two years after my breakup with Pam and the birth of my daughter. In particular my frustration was related to my failures to secure a romantic relationship with the fairer sex, and as was customary, I poured my feelings into poetry. This one captures the frustration:

Almost Warm

i can still remember her candlelit wine,
shadowed cautious smile,
and a secret told to no one
plunged into severe depths
voyaged by few in such a romantic style
slightly parted lips quivered
while the fire of her feeling scorched across our table,
settling at the edge of my sirloin.
not any closer.

I even wondered at times about my own sexuality. I had no desire for men, but was I good enough for women? As a consequence of my doubts, I dug up this doggerel from the depths of my unconscious:

Sexual Metamorphosis

an androgynous prodigy,
complained of the dichotomy
between the yin and the yang,
his tin and her tang.
Absolutely distraught
at what he'd been taught,
he retired one night
and woke up hermaphrodite.

Regarding the use of empathy and reflective listening in appropriate contexts, I should also note that I was awkward using the skills with many psychiatric patients, the very group that you would think would appreciate a good listener. A semester prior to graduating from UNC-Charlotte, I got a job as a health care technician at the new inpatient unit of the

Mecklenburg Mental Health Center. In doing the intake on a new patient, a physically strong young man of about 6'1" who had attended West Point, I used warm, empathic skills while getting his vital signs and brief history. He was quiet and cooperative and gave me no obvious reason to be concerned.

A few days after the intake, I was sitting alone in the nursing station when he appeared at the door asking for a light for his cigarette. I said, "Sure" and reached to the counter for a lighter. He walked calmly to where I was seated, seemed like he was going to get his cigarette lit when, "Blam!" His fist smashed into the right side of my head, knocking me out of the chair and crashing onto the floor. Shakened and dizzy, with dissonant chimes resounding in my normally empathic ear, I staggered halfway to my feet. As he jumped on my back, con tinuing his lunatic pummeling and screaming, "You red, Commie bastard! You red Commie bastard!" I galloped down the hall, giving him a piggy-back ride, yelling, "Help!" When two other technicians, Clarence and Keith, and a nurse eventually walked slowly out of the dayroom where they were watching tv, he abruptly dismounted and strode directly to the seclusion room--his one behavior indicating good judgment.

I shouted, "Why did you do that?!" His bland reply: "Because I felt like it."

I decided that in addition to learning good communication skills, it was time to learn the martial arts and enrolled in a nearby American Karate facility. I was a bit more successful fighting other karate students than I was defending myself against the violent psychotic patient, and I enjoyed learning a few skills. I praised myself for winning a couple matches with a green belt fellow when I only had my yellow belt. Nevertheless my karate lessons were to be short-lived. During a fight, an advanced student, a purple belt, delivered a vicious kick to my ribcage, the one that had been broken in my car accident five years earlier. They felt like they were broken again. I realized that the painful blow by the patient did not mean that I had to punish myself with more painful experiences and decided quitting karate would be the less masochistic thing to do.

In regard to masochistic behavior, I want to make a point for those of you who engage in self-destructive behavior, whether it be in the form of addictive habits or relationships. Those who are trained in childhood for the role of victim in this drama called "life" have no obligation to continue masochistic roles until the final curtain; one can extricate him or herself by learning new scripts anytime, like the script of the survivor. Such a script of empowerment can become your internal dialogue. It's never too late to begin from wherever you are. That idea may sound ironic coming from a suicidal person, but it's true.

The less hectic second shift, from 4 p.m. to 12:00 a.m. at the mental health hospital afforded me and my coworkers the opportunity to get to know each other, and I made a good friend, Dale, about 12 years my senior. Dale was exceptionally bright, had a masters degree in clinical psychology, and the entire staff found him enjoyable. He showed concern for anyone who brought their troubles to him. He often made us laugh with his stories and outrageous humor and delighted in calling me "George," George McGovern still being in the forefront of the nation's consciousness. Instead of the charge nurse, Dale was implicitly accepted as the shift leader; our work with severely disturbed psychiatric patients needed his levity much more than the sterility of a medical authority.

When we'd get off work after midnight, Dale, I, and one or two others usually frequented a tavern or restaurant where we could speak our minds while talking shop. The dramas we experienced while working with patients were sad, frightening, and hilarious, and our talks helped us relive the events from a distance, empowering us to be the directors of the evening's scenes. As directors, we could criticize, edit, and be outraged at the way the charge nurses, doctors, other coworkers and patients screwed up so badly in their acting. We also gave awards when they were due. For instance, a Dr. Nesbit had an inimitable, unorthodox way of relating to patients. One night we laughed about how he managed to communicate with a paranoid patient who stood in a corner of the t.v. room, arms folded tightly across his chest, eyes darting around the room and refusing to interact with others. He was, without a doubt, the paragon of distrust and fear. Everyone was a source of potential danger to him. His distrustful, odd behavior only served to make everyone else avoid him thereby reinforcing his view that others didn't like him. Nesbit slowly walked up to him, with a hint of caution in each step and an award-winning expression of feigned fear, put his arm around the patient's shoulder and enjoined, "We paranoids have got to stick together." For the first time since his admission, the patient showed signs of relief and relaxation and even smiled. Such entertaining episodes always helped our afterwork crowd lighten up.

When we finished a late night breakfast on one occasion, we continued our conversing while standing on the sidewalk outside the restaurant. A beautiful Samoyed with no collar suddenly joined us.

I was in disbelief this stunning creature that seemed like it could've been a champion show dog was walking the streets alone. His pure, white hair, intelligent, brown eyes, and strong, tapered body magnetized me to him immediately. Dale agreed it would be compassionate for me to take him home, and I did so with no hesitation.

Although I fed the dog a little that night, he walked around the apartment salivating continually the following morning. As a result of his incessant salivation, my roommate, Harris, jocularly flipped that I should name him Pavlov. With less humor, Harris, with his damned conscience, told me I had the moral obligation to advertise the dog in the newspaper's lost and found, which I reluctantly did.

Thankfully, no one responded to the ad for Pavlov, and I then had a faithful and magnificent companion.

I kept that companion for almost a year, but I will not go into the details of what the grim reaper did with a car to Pavlov. I missed him for a long time and sometimes still do. When I do, I often recall the profoundly helpful yet simple verse by the mystic, William Blake. Sometimes it helps to repeat these powerful messages, not unlike prayer. I think I mentioned it in a previous night but Pavlov makes me want to say it again.

He who binds himself a joy,
Does the winged life destroy,
But he who kisses the joy as it flies,
Lives in eternity's sunrise.

Of course that Buddhist-like message can be applied to any experience of loss when the griever feels the need to move on. The message is congruent with that "simple injunction" I mentioned to you the other night, "Instead of clinging, let go." And as you do, you truly can free yourself from suffering. Letting go of Pavlov was hard. Life is hard.

Dale encouraged me to further my education by emphasizing I had the potential to do well in graduate school and in the psychology profession. I'd discussed with him the publication of my first article, "Perceptions of Behavior and Humanistic Therapies" in the Journal of Community Psychology, with my two junior authors, Charles D. Fernald, Ph.D. and Lawrence Calhoun, Ph.D. In addition to my accomplishments theretofore, conquering the GRE was the next step, and Dale gently exhorted me to face up to it.

I digress in writing about Dale, not to bore you but to leave thanks for a friend I loved. Being older than me, he probably symbolized a father figure, something I never had in any stable form. Of course I never told him I loved him. We were too tough for that kind of exchange.

I continued to stumble and fumble in my persistent attempts to connect with women, usually in bars. But the arrow that hits the bull's-eye is the result of the previous 100 misses. A bull's-eye finally took a voluptuous form one night at a bar, "The Fogcutter," and my arrow was on target. Susan was pulchritudinous, with a sensual smile and brown eyes that invited me to come more than halfway. Both our homes were close to the bar so we walked to mine where we enjoyed each other and a dream or two before walking to hers the next morning. Bob Dylan's "New Morning" came to mind--it was one.

Susan became the fourth woman to genuinely love me. I was welcomed in her home, a simple, suburban ranch style, where she lived with her 14- and 8-year-old daughters, Karin and Rebecca. She helped me get a better job as a psychiatric technician at Charlotte Memorial Hospital where she worked as a secretary in the ER on day shift. When I got off work at midnight, she'd often cook one of my favorite treats, sauteed mushrooms, and I didn't even have to assert myself.

Working on that psychiatric floor provided me with an introduction to assertive behavior training, one of the most empowering self- help skills I've practiced, but never mastered, in my life. Maybe they could help me socially in case Susan didn't work out. The psychiatric techs who had some college education were expected to conduct assertive training sessions two nights a week with a group of patients, many of whom had been diagnosed with severe depressions. Dr. Reynolds, our unit psychologist, outlined a format that we followed to teach the differences between aggressive, assertive, and passive behaviors, and much of the teaching involved role-playing. The most conspicuous situation for role-playing the three behavioral styles still stands out in my mind: "How would y'all react if you went to a restaurant, ordered a steak, and the waitress brought it to you burnt?"

In addition to Egan's work I mentioned earlier, the assertive behavior training I did helped me, at least a bit, in relating to others. And at that time of my struggling youth, each little bit of skill I learned anything about that showed any potential of helping me relate better with others became a new chink of light shining in the dreary basement of my uncertainty. Sometimes it seemed like I could lead a satisfying life despite the absence of a childhood foundation if I could just master the right behaviors.

Prior to going to graduate school, I wrote a booklet on assertiveness for the hospital. I wrote it at Susan's kitchen table and enjoyed occasional interruptions by Rebecca and Karin, not to mention the delicious results of Susan's culinary skills. The year I went out with her resembled the temporary homes where I'd spend a year or so while growing up; however, Susan's involved a little more warmth and love. I gave a copy of the booklet to the psychiatric floor and years later refined it on my first job as a psychologist at John Umstead Hospital. Most of the patients at JUH were not motivated to learn assertive skills as they were conditioned to believe that the only important treatment was medication; many, especially the involuntary patients, didn't believe anything could help them. My booklet was seen by some of the staff as an honorable but laughable attempt to reach an unreachable population.

The idea of an "unreachable population" reminds me of the importance of joining the patient in his or her reality. People need to be reached and joined in their realities before they'll be ready for anything to be taught to them, and one of my most memorable experiences at John Umstead involved a relevant situation. A social worker, Mrs. Mann, asked me to talk to her most difficult patient who had shown hostility, resistance to treatment, and was offensive to ward personnel. Two of his diagnoses were Schizophrenia, Paranoid Type and Antisocial Disorder, and these labels reflected how he was perceived by his doctors. I approached the patient, Allen, in the hallway and the following dialogue ensued:

"Allen, Mrs. Mann mentioned you have had some problems on the ward the last couple nights and might benefit if I talked with you," I said.

"I can't talk. The techs down on the ward tore my insides out and I can't talk because I am dead."

"Well, O.K., how about if you come to my office anyhow and we can just sit and talk a bit," I countered, hoping my persistence would communicate that I cared enough to get him to sit down with me.

"I can't sit and talk. I told you I am dead. The techs tore my insides out, I'm dead and can't talk," he maintained, unconsciously insisting I had to join his reality before I'd get any cooperation from him.

"Well, you know Allen, before I became a psychologist, I seriously considered becoming a mortician. Since I have an interest in mortician work and since you're in the state you are in now, we could get along very well together."

He smiled, experienced me in his reality, and walked with me to my office where we had a chat. How did he experience me in his reality? He knew that I knew that he did not believe he was truly dead. I knew he didn't believe that I had actually considered mortuary work (even though I actually had!). I accepted him, and, as a result, he accepted me.

Writing this note is triggering a few golden memories to tumble from the recesses of the storage room of my mind. While these visitors are, admittedly, a bit pleasant, they are annoying; they're obstructing progress toward my death. Excuse me for getting sidetracked with that favorite anecdote from the hospital.

Even though the assertiveness booklet was not received very well over-all, it still had some useful information, and a minority benefitted. I knew the information had the potential to benefit depressed people who kept their feelings to themselves and rarely stood up for their rights. It was not a complete assertive training package but a kind of introduction. One of my references, Your Perfect Right, by Robert Alberti and Michael Emmons, was in its 5th edition. Considered "the assertiveness bible," it could serve as a complete package if read thoroughly and practiced consistently.

Maybe as one of my last parting gifts, I can whet your appetite for assertive training by leaving you with a copy of the booklet I wrote.

Here it is:

<u>Learning Assertive Behavior</u>
Hank McGovern, M.A.
Licensed Psychological Associate

"We are all controlled by the world in which we live...The question is this: are we to be controlled by accidents, by tyrants, or by ourselves?"

B.F. SKINNER

Introduction

Assertive behavior is an expression of your personal rights, feelings, opin-ions, and thoughts in a direct, honest manner that does not violate an-other person's rights or feelings. By assertively expressing yourself you can stand up for yourself while preventing others from taking advantage of you. You can also state how you feel with confidence, make and refuse requests, give and receive compliments, deal with criticisms, and carry on social conversations. People usually find that when they communicate in an assertive style they see themselves as taking better control of their personal lives. The techniques and approaches in this booklet may help you learn your assertive style if you practice them consistently and use the feedback you get from others.

It is important to know that other people will not always like your assertions, but the intent is not to hurt another person's feelings or infringe on their rights. In fact, it is a value of an assertive approach to respect and appreciate the other person's rights and feelings. Assertive communication is a way of respecting yourself by letting others know how you feel and what you want and expect while still respecting them.

You will also find you will not always get what you want when you are assertive although you will communicate what you want. This difference is important. You will not always be able to get what you want because you cannot control another person's actions and feelings. By asserting yourself, though, you will bein control of your own feelings and behaviors. At the same time, you may find yourself getting what you want more often than if you act aggressively or nonassertively. If you were a sailor on a boat at sea, you would not be able to change the direction of the wind, but you could always adjust your sails.

Assertive behavior has a greater chance of success if it is appropriate to the situation. For example, it would probably be inappropriate to tell a police officer who has stopped you for going 20 miles over the speed limit that traffic laws are applied erratically and that he should not give you a ticket. It would be more appropriate to assertively and politely request that he give you a warning by saying something like, "I realize I was going over the speed limit. I was in too much of a hurry. I will slow down and stay within the speed limit. Will you please give me a warning instead of a ticket?" Of course, as you can imagine, you may not get what you request! You would have a better chance, though, than if you were hostile or showed a "bad attitude."

It is also important to take responsibility for dealing with the consequences of assertive behaviors. When you get the response you like, it is easy to feel proud and satisfied with your assertive behavior. However, if another person continues to infringe on your rights and feelings, it is important to PERSIST with appropriate assertive behaviors. This kind of persistent assertive behavior takes practice and patience and should be kept in mind as you read further about the techniques and approaches.

Differences between Assertion, Aggression, and Nonassertion

Many people confuse assertion with aggression. For example you might hear someone say, "Oh she doesn't need assertive training. She will tell you where to go whenever she feels like it!" The woman being referred to is being aggressive when she tells people "where to go." When I did assertive training during my internship in prison, many of the prison employees said the inmates did not need assertive training because they were already "assertive enough." These inmates made many demands and often became hostile, so they were acting aggressively but not assertively. Aggression is a destructive expression of anger, at the expense of others, whereas assertion is a constructive expression of feelings, including anger. The woman and the inmates above very much needed assertive training.

It is more common for people to say nonassertive or passive people need assertive training. They are referring to people who frequently let others take advantage of them and who usually keep their feelings to themselves--the Doris Doormats. However, no one is totally passive or aggressive. It is also common for people who are often seen as passive to keep their anger to themselves until they finally start yelling and screaming, in other words, becoming aggressive. If you believe you are usually nonassertive in situations where you would like to stand up for your rights and express your feelings more effectively, assertive training may be for you.

The following are a few differences between aggressive, assertive, and nonassertive behaviors. If you learn the differences you can become more aware of when you are acting according to a certain style and then make a decision about changing your behavior.

Aggression--violates other person's rights and feelings, discounts other person's decisions and choices, often loud, demanding, hostile, using offensive language. Frequently blames and puts down others, beginning statements with "You" messages like "You really messed up...!" Body language involves staring or eye contact that intimidates, loud sarcastic tone of voice, con- descending, threatening. Destructive criticism is common. The basic message is "MY rights, demands, feelings count but yours do not." The goal of aggression is winning while forcing the other person to lose, often through humiliating or degrading. Sarcastic humor and cynicism are often directed at others.

Here are some examples of behavioral aggression:

Confronting an employer who gives too much work--"You are ridiculous for giving me all this work! You don't know how to be fair!"

Confronting someone who has criticized you--"Who the hell do you think you are!? Keep that kind of remark up and you'll be sorry!"

Refusing a request--"Can't you get it through your head? That's a stupid request. Quit bugging me."

Nonassertive--violates own rights by failing to express honest feelings and thoughts; allows others to take advantage of ("walk all over") them; overly apologetic, timid, self-effacing, and inhibited. Body language includes minimal eye contact, eyes usually looking down, voice is soft, meek, sing-songy, shoulders are hunched, gestures convey nervousness, anxiety, tension; speech is hesitant, filled with pauses, throat is cleared frequently; giggling and nervous laughter are common. The basic message is: "My opinions, feelings, and rights don't count but yours do." The goal is to appease others and avoid conflict at all cost.

Here are some examples of nonassertive behavior:

Responding to an employer who gives too much work—"I'll do as much as you want me to do and stay late whenever you want me to. I can always call my spouse or babysitter and tell them I'll be late or cancel my plans."

Reaction to a critical put-down-"C'mon now, heh, heh. You don't really want to hurt me do ya?" or agrees or says nothing but stews about it.

Responding to an unreasonable request--"Ah...Gee...Well...I guess I can do it. Since nobody else will do it I'll just fit it in my schedule somehow."

Communicating feelings in a relationship—"Whatever you say. I don't have any feelings about your complaints and opinions. I'll go along with whatever decision you make."

Assertive--stands up for one's rights by expressing feelings and thoughts in an honest and direct manner. Does not allow others to take advantage of oneself and does not try to take advantage of others. Self-confident, relaxed, expressive, satisfied with communicating feelings and opinions although does not try to force or control other people. Eye contact is made in a firm manner without staring down the other person. Voice is appropriately loud, body gestures convey strength and confidence, speech is fluent emphasizing key words and with few hesitancies. The goal of assertion is to communicate feelings, rights, opinions while still respecting the rights and feelings of others. Compromise, fair play, and mutual respect are employed. Uses "I" messages, beginning with "I want...", "I feel...", "I think...", "My opinion is..."

Here are some examples of assertion:

Responding to an employer who gives too much work—"I would have to put in extra hours to do all of this work. I'm willing to work an extra half hour to do some of it, but I will have to say no to the rest of it."

Reaction to a critical put-down—"I don't appreciate that put-down. I don't want you to do it anymore."

If person continues to show hostility—"It sounds like you are angry. I will not be the target of it. If you'd like to talk about the reasons you are angry, I will listen to them."

Communicating feelings in a relationship—"I'd like to talk about the anger and hurt we are both feeling. I'd like to under- stand the reasons behind your feelings and I want to express mine."

Given the above guidelines and structure, you will want to find your own assertive language and style. It will also be import- ant for you to BELIEVE YOU HAVE THE PERSONAL RIGHT to live an assertive lifestyle. Here is a list of your personal rights for you to refer to from time to time:

1. You have the right to express your feelings in an assertive manner.
2. You have the right to be your own judge of your behaviors, feelings, and thoughts.
3, You have the right to say, "I don't know."
4. You have the right to say, "I don't understand."
5. You have the right to say, "I don't care."
6. You have the right to dignity, respect, and feelings of freedom.

7. You have the right to accept yourself for your unique- ness, in- cluding your flaws, imperfections, strengths, undiscovered poten- tials, beliefs, and values.

The following types of assertion are guidelines you can use for devel- oping your own responses. They should not be seen as devices to use ON other people but rather to use with others:

BASIC ASSERTION

Basic assertion refers to a simple style of expressing your rights, feelings, beliefs, and opinions. Some examples have been included in the above descriptions of assertion. Here are some others:

When being interrupted—"Excuse me, I'd like to finish what I'm saying."

When being asked an important question for which you are unpre- pared–"I'd like to have some time to think about my answer."

Expressing affection–"I really like you and value your friend- ship." "You are special to me, and I like getting close to you."

Expressing appreciation–"I really appreciate what you have done for me." (As an aside, I know much of this booklet sounds elementary, but what seems elementary often escapes us).

Here is a basic assertive format for expressing emotion. It begins with an "I" message owning a feeling, then stating the behavior of the other person that is leading to your feeling, and finally with a statement about what you want or expect. This format can be applied with both positive or negative emotional experiences. Here are two examples:

(negative) "I feel angry (part 1) when you put me down like you are right now (part 2). I want you to stop the name calling and call me by my name (part 3).
(positive) "I really feel close to you (part 1) when you share your feelings and memories of the past (part 2). I hope you will keep trusting me." (part 3.)

EMPATHIC ASSERTION

Empathic assertion refers to a sensitive communication that you understand and appreciate the other person's situation and feelings. Empathy has been referred to as a way of letting the other person know that you know what it's like to "walk a mile in his or her shoes." The first statement in this kind of assertion communicates your understanding and the second statement expresses what you want or prefer. Here are some examples:

When someone is persisting in making a request that you have already refused–"I realize it is very important to you that I do this for you. However, I stand by my decision."

When being criticized by an angry lover or spouse–"I know you are feeling hurt and angry and after what we've been through I understand how you're feeling this way, but I will not put up with your putdowns."

ESCALATING ASSERTION

This kind of assertion involves making a simple, straight- forward response to someone and then becoming increasingly firmer if the person continues to violate your rights. Here is an example:

When two people are having a conversation and a third person tries to butt in: "My friend and I would like to talk with each other privately." outsider persists: "I realize you really want to talk, but like I said, we want to have a two-person discussion without anyone else." outsider persists:" This is the third and last time I will tell you that we do not want you present. Please leave!"

CONFRONTIVE ASSERTION

This kind of assertion can be used when the other person's words do not match up with what he does. As an example, he may routinely break promises or fail to comply with agreements.

The formula involves stating objectively what the other person said he would do, what he actually did, and then stating what you expect.

Here is an example: You and your partner have agreed to call each other instead of coming over to each other's residence unannounced, but he comes to your place at 10 p.m. without calling. "You and I agreed to call each other before coming over to each other's places, but now you are coming here without calling me. I'd like for you to leave and stick to our agreement from now on."

Dealing With Criticism

Frequently when people are criticized they feel anxious or insulted and then assume a defensive position which results in a hostile argument. Sometimes people don't say anything at all, keep their feelings of anxiety or anger inside and then criticize themselves. Either way, aggressive and unassertive responses to criticism leaves one feeling dissatisfied with himself and resentful of others.

One thing to realize is that people who are overly critical are often dissatisfied with themselves. To take a break from putting themselves down they put others down instead. It might he helpful to know that other peoples' criticisms may be more a reflection of their feelings about themselves rather than a reflection of your abilities, competence, or worth.

Still, it is usually helpful to let critics know that you are not willing to put up with put-downs. "Fogging" is a technique developed by Manuel Smith to use when the critic is manipulating you into feeling "down on" yourself. Instead of becoming defensive you can agree that there might be a degree of truth in what the other person is saying, assuming that you believe there actually could be a grain of truth in the criticism. For instance, the critic might say, "You really dressed sloppy when you got up this morning" to which you could fog, "Yes, I didn't dress as well as I could have." If the critic continues, "Yeah, your pants don't match and your shoes are ugly!" you can persistently fog with "I know my pants could match better and my shoes really aren't the most attractive." Usually the criticism stops but if it still continues you can ask, "What's your point? I don't like your put downs and I want to know the reason you are criticizing me."

There are a couple of other statements that were suggested to me by Dr. Paul Watzlawick, a psychologist from Palo Alto. Simply, you might say, "You know, from your perspective, what you are saying is true." Your statement will be undeniably true because from the other's perspective, their statements are always true! When I've used that statement, it has left the critic stuttering and confused. Another one suggested by Dr. Watzlawick: " The statements you are making are really not as rude as you might think they are." Not stuttering but usually confused. You've just said something that sounds understanding and empathic while letting the other know he is being rude. If these techniques sound manipulative, I will agree with your criticism, but instead of seeing them as fighting fire with fire, I see them as fighting fire with water.

"Negative inquiry," another technique attributed to Manuel Smith, is a way of dealing with criticism. This technique can be used when you want more information behind the criticisms. If there is useful information in the criticism, the other person may be helpful to you. By using negative inquiry you can usually tell if the other is giving you some useful information in the criticism or if he is trying to manipulate or hurt you. In this approach you ask the person what he or she means by the criticism or complaint to get more specific information. Here is an example: The critic may say, "People really don't like your personality" to which the assertor could inquire, "What is it about my personality they don't like?" Critic continues, "You have a harsh tone of voice," Assertor, "My voice is harsh. Is there anything else that comes across badly about the way I talk to people?" "Yeah, you're too wishy-washy." "O.K. It would be helpful to me if you could tell me specifically what I do or say that seems wishy-washy. Please tell me." By not getting defensive and obtaining feedback about the way you come across to people you can learn some useful information that could help you improve your communications. If the person's intent is to be mean, he won't give you useful information, but at least negative inquiry will make that intent clear.

Sometimes people may try to put others down in an indirect way. A critic might say, "Oh you're dressed so lovely today! It gives you a kind of cutesy look." The recipient of this remark may feel confused or frustrated. It could be helpful to ask, "What do you mean?" By asking the critic to clarify his statement, you might prompt him to focus more on the intention behind his statement. Of course the person may not become more honest, but either way at least you can get more information from his response after you simply ask, "I'm not sure I understand what you mean. Could you tell me?"

It might also be helpful to think of yourself as becoming more tolerant when having to deal with a critic. After hearing criticisms, you may remind yourself about becoming more tolerant by saying to the critic, " Thank you. You just made me stronger." He might be confused but that won't be your problem.

To summarize, we do not have to put up with put downs. You can let people know your position on this matter. You might also improve the quality of the relationship by letting the critic know that you are interested in understanding the reason for the emotion (usually anger) behind the criticism. You could just say, "I would like to know why you're upset with me." Whatever you decide in particular situations, you will likely find yourself gaining confidence and better feelings about yourself as you refuse to put up with put-downs.

One more word about anger. The more tender feelings of fear or hurt nearly always underlie it. We are taught, both directly and indirectly, that lashing out is more acceptable than expressing hurt or fear because it shows we are tough. Expressing tender emotions may make us feel vulnerable. Can you muster the courage to allow yourself to be vulnerable?

Social Communication

Assertiveness also refers to the way people converse socially. People who are shy and anxious and avoid attempts to interact with others have an unassertive style. Frequently these individuals say they just don't know what to say when they are in the presence of others, feel uncomfortable and then leave the situation.

Aggressive styles try to control the social situation by a loud, domineering approach, frequent rambling, and showing irritation if his self-absorbed rambling is interrupted. Although this style is not usually enjoyed by others, people with an unassertive style will tolerate it and even feel comfortable with it since little effort is required from them when they are in the presence of the aggressor.

Several assertive skills can be used in social conversations. One is called FREE INFORMATION and involves following up on information that is freely offered by the speaker. During the course of conversation people communicate bits of information about themselves including their activities, experiences, feelings, and beliefs. To keep the conversation going you can follow up on small bits of information that are offered. For instance, if you ask someone how their day has been and they say something like, "Oh it's been boring. I really haven't done much except read a few pages of a book," you could follow up on the FREE INFORMATION about their reading by saying, "What book have you been reading? Fiction or nonfiction?" Of course you may be able to think of ways of using FREE INFORMATION with nearly anything someone says by focusing on any small bit of information they give you and following up with a question.

Another skill to use in social conversations is SELF- DISCLOSURE. It involves offering information about yourself to the other. The information could include your likes and dislikes, hobbies or interests, how you have recently spent your time, your opinions and beliefs, experiences from the past, goals for your future and anything else about yourself you would like the other person to know. A self-disclosure might be as simple as saying to someone, "I really didn't do a whole lot today, just took a short walk and watched a little t.v." to a more meaningful statement about your values and beliefs like, "I'm really for pro- choice. And I don't feel pro-choice is opposed to pro-life. I feel that the quality of life matters most, including the quality of the woman's life who may be contemplating an abortion."

It is also emphasized that nonverbal behaviors like voice tone and inflexion, good eye contact, and relaxed body posture are important for assertive social communication. If you use a lively voice, that is appropriately loud, while maintaining eye contact without staring, along with a posture that shows you are comfortable then you have a good chance of enjoying a conversation. The verbal as well as the nonverbal forms of assertive social communication can be practiced in a group setting or individually with a trainer. In fact, the only way you can really learn these skills effectively is through practice.

Another way of assertively communicating socially involves giving and receiving compliments. Unassertive ways of dealing with compliments include shy denial (Oh gosh, who me?), or rejecting ("You like this rag, I've had it for ages and it's way out of style.") Some negative ways of giving a compliment would be self-depreciation ("I'm pretty much of a flop at baking, but wow, you're terrific!"), or crooked ("Most people don't like you but I do.") A couple of examples of assertively receiving a compliment would be:" Thank you. I am proud of my performance too." And "I appreciate your compliment." Note that these examples of self-pride are different from egotism such as "Of course I did a good job on the speech. I always do well" which tries to impress or be one-up on others. Giving a genuine compliment is also rewarding to both the complimenter and the person receiving the compliment since both people usually feel good as a result of the interaction. A simple, direct compliment would be: "I really liked the letter you wrote. It was clear and to the point."

A final note I would like to make for this booklet is the idea that you may already know many of the points that have been made but you may not know that you know the information. I hope this booklet will bring to your awareness information that you already know so that you can use it in situations with other people. It's also important to practice these skills, make mistakes, improve and eventually become a better communicator. I know I have a way to go before I am satisfied.

I'll leave you with a quote by Winston Churchill which fits the experiences of learning and practicing assertive behavior: "Never, never, never, never give up."

REFERENCES

Alberti, R.E. and Emmons, M.L. Your Perfect Right: A Guide to Assertive Behavior. San Luis Obispo, California: Impact Publishers, Inc., 1986.

Lange, Arthur J. And Jakubowski, Patricia. <u>Responsible Assertive Behavior</u>. Research Press, Champaign, Illinois, 1976.

Smith, Manuel, J. <u>When I Say No, I Feel Guilty</u>. New York: Dial Press, 1975.

A few more words on my use of assertiveness, particularly regarding anger. Recall that I wrote my booklet in the mid 80s, during the time of the fifth edition of <u>Your Perfect Right</u>. I was in the process of adjusting to an adult life for which self-help books were my primary resources. Most importantly, my clumsy management of anger has been a culprit in the loss of numerous jobs. Now, note the admission by Alberti and Emmons in a later edition of <u>Your Perfect Right</u>:

> "For a quarter of a century, we've taught and written about ways to spontaneously and assertively express anger. Recent research, however, indicates that expressing anger --assertively or otherwise--may not always be the way to go."

In August, 1989, I began working in Winston-Salem's' mental health center as a staff psychologist. I observed the director, Jody, a social worker, was nervous about her authority and, consequently, made impulsive decisions when she felt threatened. And it is easy, as I was about to find out, for a nervous authority figure to make hare- brained decisions when a subordinate is assertive with her.

One day I received a note from Jody informing me a five year old son of one of my female client's had been observed with a black eye by one of the center's social workers. The note directed me to discuss the procedure for reporting child abuse to the Department of Social Services with the social worker. Jody would be on vacation and would get back with me the next week. I talked with the social worker about her observation but since I did not see the child's black eye and did not have any reason to suspect abuse, I did not report it. I tried to call the client to ask her about the black eye, but her phone had been disconnected. I reasoned that children get black eyes for a variety of reasons other than child abuse and was hesitant to report it to DSS. I also reasoned that if anyone had reason to suspect abuse, it would be the social worker who made the observation. Since she observed it, she would be the witness. I felt confident my decision not to report was a sound one.

When Jody learned that I did not report my client upon her return, she went off the deep end. My reasoning that the person who made the observation should report, if anyone should, made no sense to her. However, when she blamed me for not showing the knee-jerk reaction she expected for dealing with the problem, I decided to assertively express my anger to her, a decision that became my ticket to unemployment.

"Are you blaming me for my decision not to report?", I asked her. "Yes I'm blaming you! I told you to discuss reporting to DSS with Rhonda!"

"See, that's what makes me angry! I did what made sense to me!", I retorted, certain she would accept my healthy, assertive response, she being a mental health professional and all.

When Jody informed me the next day that I was being fired, I decided to communicate the facts of what happened to the North Carolina Psychology Board. I made the decision to inform the Board because I only had the job for five months, had been out of the Board's jurisdiction, working in Delaware, during the previous year and did not want the Board to have questions about my erratic employment (interesting how my erratic employment mirrored my erratic child- hood residential life, isn't it?). I discussed the decision with a psychologist, Dr. Kerry Jacobson, who I had seen for psychotherapy some years earlier, and he encouraged me to"just be honest with the Board."

I recalled that honest, direct communication is characteristic of assertiveness and felt I'd be rewarded by the Psychology Board's response, perhaps vindicating me for my"reasonable" decision. In reply to my honest letter to the Board, detailing my termination, they wrote back requesting that I sign the appropriate forms giving the mental health center and Jody permission to forward their details for firing me. Shortly thereafter, the Board sent me its statement, charging I was in violation of the law because

I failed to report suspected child abuse. They informed me I was entitled to a hearing to save my license.

Based on the hearing that involved attorneys and witnesses, the Board, consisting mostly of psychologists, used its infinite wisdom in formulating an official Decision that since I did not have a reason to suspect child abuse, I was not in violation of the law for not reporting it to DSS. In other words, they confirmed my original decision.

While I won the hearing, I was also injured. I had been wrongfully fired by a nervous authority figure who had trouble thinking clearly; she could not stand an assertive subordinate. I had been needlessly put through the wringer by the Board. It would take awhile for me to recover professionally, emotionally, and financially.

Six years later (1995), Alberti and Emmons finished their seventh edition of <u>Your Perfect Right</u>, with two new chapters, "Dealing with Difficult People" and "Deciding when to Be Assertive," both of which may have benefitted me in 1989. In regard to "overly sensitive individuals," for example, they state, "On occasion, from our own observations, you may conclude that a certain person is unable to accept even the slightest assertion. When this is apparent, it is better to resign yourself to this fact rather than risk the consequences... sometimes the potential gain is not worth the price one must pay in personal pain." If I had read this information from their 1995 work in 1989 and applied it with Jody, I may not have been fired and would've avoided the imbroglio with the Board.

Of course I could not read the 1995 edition in 1989, and that's a problem with parenting yourself with self-help books.

I admit that since I began learning about assertive behavior, I've often been too quick to stand up for myself and assert my feelings, rights, and opinions. Unfortunately, much of my approach has come across as defensive and tactless and with a kind of "I'll show you--you can't take advantage of me" attitude. I've gauchely applied it with difficult people who've had power over me in work situations, including the one from the most recent mental health center. Because a few administrators could not stand my assertiveness they concocted the sexual harassment charge. In many situations, I've expressed anger in what I've considered to be an assertive style but was perceived as aggressive. I don't believe I've ever mastered a tone of voice that assertively and appropriately expresses anger.

As I document my errors in practicing an assertive style, a behavioral style that can actually be very effective, I'm reminded of this line from John Lennon's song Mother: "Children, don't do…what I have done…I couldn't walk…and I tried to run…so I…I just gotta tell you…Goodbye."

Ironically, suicide is both unassertive and an aggressive means of expressing anger. It's unassertive because it is not expressing feelings of hurt and anger to others. It's aggressive because it is violence to one's self. You may have heard suicide is an act of "anger turned inward", that is, an act of directing anger against yourself. This looks like it may be my last act of anger mismanagement, doesn't it?"

But just a moment. This elaborate note is an expression of my feelings, memories, and opinions I've said I'd like to leave as "gifts" for you. Maybe you can use meditation and assertive behavior more successfully in your life. Maybe this is also one of my better assertive responses. Maybe I am getting better at it! I'm not going to stop writing yet. Maybe I'm just getting warmed up.

CHAPTER 6

Cognitive Skills: Befriending Your Internal Dialogue

"A man's life is what his thoughts make of it."

MARCUS AURELIUS

"I know of no more encouraging fact than the unquestionable ability of man to elevate his life through a conscious endeavor."

HENRY DAVID THOREAU

"Men are disturbed not by things but by the views they take of them"

EPICTETUS

I'VE NOTICED A MENTAL TRANSFORMATION occurring during each of my five nights of writing. When I began, I experienced "monkey mind", as my thoughts and images jumped around from one branch of mind to another, with no direction or glue and quite content to waste time in a childish manner. Monkey mind can be tolerable, although it's usually unpleasant. When the thoughts are painful and out of control, however, they can be frightening, and while writing this note, I am aware the fear is about death.

During my expressions of memory, feeling, and knowledge, I've noticed I create the glue that gives meaning and cohesion to my thoughts, transforming monkey mind into a safer place of calm. The expression need not be coherent at first, but as I freely write, the resulting direction my thoughts take then helps my heart to slow down, my breathing to become slower and deeper and my muscles throughout my body, neck, and shoulders to relax. My thinking seems reasonable, and for a period, there is no need to end my life.

The state of peacefulness and tranquility that I reach seems like the escape from pain that is the goal of suicide. During those moments, I am aware I do not truly want to die; I want to escape the God-awful pain my extremely angry thoughts wreek on my being. It's also apparent that I've achieved this escape that is under my control and it is an internal process.

It is this peace from writing, I suppose, that prompts people to keep journals. Journaling creates the coherence that is the essence of meaning and purpose, both of which are necessary for a healthy identity. Most healthy people develop this identity during the years of a safe, secure childhood. Perhaps journaling is not such a bad substitute for the absence of such a foundation. Journals become parents. So it is not just the self-help books upon which I've raised myself, but the monkey mind drivel transformed into a degree of meaning and documented in my many notebooks that has fostered my growth into a fairly self-centered, socially awkward, struggling bag of bones-sounds like I haven't done such a good job of raising myself. It is, though, an example of accepting whatever one has and using it in a creative way. And while I am flawed, parenting myself has enabled me to survive better than people expected.

While I've not given up the idea of suicide, I have noticed the idea has weakened during the last five nights of retro- and introspection. On the first night I was at a 9.5 on a 10 point scale of suicidal intent. I've moved down to a five as I sit, by my window, here now, savoring an assortment of colors in a sunset of serenity.

A couple nights ago I wrote about the experience of contacting the Being, the part within us that is a part of all life, all existence. In contacting the Being one transcends the clutter of mind and experiences the purity of his essence, just breathing, sitting, aware of everything and nothing in particular all at once. In Zen, this transcendental state is called no-mind, and the diurnal practice of the meditative experience renews, refreshes and energizes. This energy is felt in our body as lightness. Perhaps it was a meditator to whom a Yaqui mystic referred when he said, " To be a man of knowledge, one needs to be light and fluid."

It is paradoxical that the regular practice of meditation disciplines the mind when, in fact, you experience no-mind during it. From this perspective, it seems the active mind is normally a burden to our being. The internal chatter we call thought so often makes us anxious and irritable, and to make the most effective use of the mind, we must periodically escape it.

Ideally, the more we can maintain no-mind during daily activity, the better. When one has practiced this skill sufficiently, he can behave effectively without thinking and the result is a calm mind. The greatest athletes and actors are thinking very little, if at all, during their performance, and Yogi Berra once said, "How can you think and hit at the same time?"

So we can appreciate the value of no-mind. Nevertheless, we still get stuck in our thoughts. They invade our mind as clutter, weigh us down at times, keep us up at night, confuse us and trigger anxiety, while at the same time, we cherish our dear thoughts. They help us solve problems, create and construct our world, and Descartes went so far as to conclude his existence depended on them, stating, "I think therefore I am." Life without thinking is unimaginable.

As long as we have thoughts, how can we increase the degree to which they help us adapt and enjoy life, and simultaneously, decrease the degree to which they make us miserable? One answer is by the practice of meditation. Another answer to that question leads me to the subject of cognition, one of the most important subjects of the psychology profession. The clinical intervention called cognitive therapy is one of the most effective in treating anxiety, anger, and depression and provides tools for managing and utilizing our thoughts.

I first came across the term cognition in my undergraduate years in the form of therapeutic language such as "cognitive relabeling" and "cognitive behavior modification". Cognition seemed like such an erudite word but simply referred to the natural process of thinking. This natural process is comprehensive and includes all mental activity: thoughts, images, ideas, beliefs, interpretations, assumptions, expectations, and more. Despite the erudite sound, cognition was actually quite simple considering the incredibly vast mental phenomena it represented.

Since we have this burden of a mind that so often interferes with the expression of our heart we might as well make constructive use of our cognitions. That is, we put ourselves in charge by taking a proactive approach to them by deciding how and what to think instead of simply reacting to our thoughts. So psychologists invented the aforementioned therapy terms, along with impressively effective procedures, to help people systematically change their cognitions and thereby change their emotions and behaviors. And, as empirical evidence has indicated, a skillful monitoring of our cognitive world has helped many have a healthy and compassionate heart.

The entire field of cognitive therapy would be impossible to elucidate in one note--maybe my final--but I'll provide the essentials that I've learned so that you might benefit by them, hopefully better than me.

My first personal experience with cognitive therapy involved one of its versions, Rational-Emotive Therapy, in the winter of '76. I anticipated graduating soon, knew I had no one to depend on financially if I didn't get a job, and felt it absolutely imperative I get hired at the first job for which I interviewed, as a health care technician at a community mental health hospital. I expressed my worry and sense of urgency to my advisor, Dr. Calhoun, who said I probably made a better impression on the interviewer than I realized and said I needed to use some RET to deal with my worry. He was quite right. Although I didn't follow up on his advice at the time, RET was to eventually become one of my favorite therapies, especially when it evolved into REBT; the B stood for behavior, the only psychological phenomena I've thought as important as cognition.

I eagerly anticipated learning more about cognitive therapy in graduate school at Appalachian State University but first struggled in detaching myself from Susan; ASU is located in the Blue Ridge Mountains, in Boone, NC, about three hours from her home. Long distance relationships are far from ideal to begin with, and I hoped to meet someone in graduate school with whom I'd share more similar beliefs and values. So it was good-bye time once again and a hello to the solo path, a journey undertaken with a mix of relief and uncertainty.

The brilliant, multicolored mountains of a refreshing autumn provided a resplendent heaven for the soothing of a young man's pain and sadness. Stimulated by this abundance of sensory richness, I increased my running to eight miles a day and further channeled my energies into studying and partying. It did not take long to focus my attention on other things other than my last girlfriend.

Having received a teaching assistantship, I shared an office in a time-worn building with another recipient, Adrian. A rugged, handsome man of 30, Adrian owned a collection of stories from a life filled with pain and pleasure, stories he recounted with absorbing eloquence. He was a practiced raconteur, and his popularity sometimes made me envious. As a Special Forces Green Beret, he was scheduled for a Vietnam tour that culminated with nine of 12 of the men on his team getting killed. It was an eerie synchronicity that Adrian's detour from that mission involved his father's fatal heart attack for which he was granted leave. Our family member, Death, helped us quickly become friends.

Adrian and I did our fair share of partying as well as intellectual discussion and, on more than one occasion, mixed the two. I'll never forget driving around the ascent of a mountain curve with him late one weekend night, both in an altered state of consciousness, arguing about whether the concept of "intelligence" can accurately be applied to animals. From my perspective, "intelligence" was a measurable attribute of humans, and it would be anthropomorphizing to ascribe it to animals. From his perspective, animals possessed intelligence regardless of whether it was measurable. We adhered tenaciously to our positions.

"Adrian, humans have a neocortex, a part of their brains that differentiates them from animals. Intelligence is a quality of the neocortex and distinguishes humans from animals. Intelligence ain't an animal thing," I asserted, as we were getting out of the car to relieve our bladders behind a tree.

"Animals have intelligence. They don't have to possess a neocortex and you don't have to measure it with an I.Q. test to call it intelligence."

"But the concept was invented by humans to describe..."

Plop. On top of my head landed the digested white droppings from a bird. I believe Adrian's laughter reverberated to the next mountain range and towns miles away. Despite being the target of said shit, even I couldn't inhibit a chuckle that eventually burst into a paroxysm. Talk about synchronicity! As I'm arguing about animals not having intelligence, a bird shits on my head. I can imagine the animal kingdom in chorus: "Serves him right." I guess that's why it is said, "truth is stranger than fiction."

I suppose, depending on how you define intelligence, in a general sense, it might be accurate to say animals have intelligence. (As I'm writing this, my cat is giving me this odd stare.)

My friendship with Adrian was special on different levels. Earlier in my note I've written about how difficult it is for men to express love to one another, and I was surprised when Adrian told me he loved me. There was no sexual intention, just compassion, and that compassion triggered a variety of emotions for me. Other than my cousin Jack, who I later found out did not mean it, Adrian was the only man to say that to me.

You might recall my best friend in high school, Scott Phillips, from my second night's note, who discussed the life and music of John Lennon with me. Adrian also talked about Lennon with me, and I specifically recall his interpretation of the line "I'm just sittin' here watchin' the wheels go round and round..." from "Watching the Wheels" on his latest album. He said John Lennon saw himself as getting off the wheels of karma, which meant being free from the cycle of birth-death-rebirth and from desire. According to Buddhist philosophy, that freedom is our ultimate goal and is called Nirvana.

Soon after we discussed Lennon's song, I was in my apartment at night, watching TV, when the shock came on that he had been shot and killed. Stunned, I floated to a local bar, just to encounter other fellow zombies. Paul McCartney was in this shock when he told the media, "It's a drag." Following their criticism of his coldness, he explained, "That was stunned talk." It would take awhile for much of the world to move from our stunned state, the first stage of grief, clinically termed disbelief.

If you have any doubt about McCartney's feeling toward John Lennon just listen to the words in his song, "Here Today". He sings, "...I still remember how it was before...And I am holding back the tears no more...I love you. What about the night we cried, because there wasn't any reason left to keep it all inside...Never understood a word, but you were always there with a smile...And if I say 'I really loved you and was glad you came along, if you were here today...For you were in my song...Here today." When you absorb those messages along with the mournful melody of the violins, you will experience tenderness that just might stream down a cheek or two.

For years after hearing Adrian's interpretation about Lennon getting off the wheels of karma, I hoped he was correct; achieving that goal would be worth the tragedy. It seemed uncanny he wrote that song just before his death.

Getting back to cognitions. I was disappointed in graduate school that we would not cover cognitive-behavior therapy. There was an entire chapter on the topic in the book we used for our Fall therapy course, but the professor said it would be covered in the Spring semester. In the Spring, the professor said the form of therapy was supposed to be covered during the Fall semester. I wondered if they were trying to piss me off or drive me crazy. Instead, I laughed. I also felt more motivated to learn about cognitive-behavior therapy, but before I'd get that opportunity, it would be necessary to get through a lot of useless crap, stuff I would never use. At least I had something to look forward to--getting out of graduate school so I could learn.

Aware of a limited amount of time on this earth, I'm reluctant to detail additional stories about graduate school that could be considered a waste of time The stories would needlessly prolong this note. Suffice it to say they would include: the loss of my friendship with Adrian during alcohol intoxication, working as an "Indian" at the Tweetsie Railroad Amusement Park, dating a wealthy girl whose father owned a chain of department stores, a brief interaction with Rod Stewart when he was playing soccer, dropping out at the 17th mile of my first marathon due to inelegant training, giving my first research presentation entitled "Attitudes Toward Female Masturbation" at a professional psychology meeting, and having a wonderfully terrible internship at the Department of Corrections As I list these events, I'm getting the urge to tell you their stories; I'll resist.

I read a landmark work, *Cognitive Therapy of Depression*, by Aaron Beck, M.D., considered by many to be the "father of cognitive therapy" and his colleagues, Doctors Rush, Shaw, and Emery shortly after I began working at John Umstead Hospital in 1983. One of the most conspicuous findings documented was what Dr. Beck called the cognitive triad of depression. It consists of a pattern of beliefs the depressed person maintains about him- or herself, everyday experiences in the world, and the future. The depressed person views himself as defective, deprived, inadequate or diseased. It is because of these views that the person becomes depressed, thinks he is worthless and incapable of being happy.

I could very well identify with this negative view of self. Reflecting upon my first 18 years, it was obvious that I'd been deprived of parents and a home, and logically, saw myself as deprived. As a result of a "weird" foundation of instability and chaos, I had become a person labeled as "weird", not only by a few social acquaintances but even by my last pseudo-father figure, Jack. This label of weird became the defect I perceived about myself. I was also hypersensitive to criticism, "knowing" that criticism meant someone didn't like me, confirming my view that I was unlovable and would be rejected. I had the very strong belief I would always be rejected. After all, I always had been, why should that change as I grew into an adult? These beliefs were so ingrained they affected all attempts at intimacy, romantic or platonic. Additionally, the psychiatrist, Dr. Jones, told me it was not my practice of meditation and the work from psychotherapy that accounted for my improved mood but that it was a

"Mendellian inheritance" that explained my energy; no credit was given to my efforts. Hence, my genes gave me the disease of bipolar disorder, according to Jones, and I saw myself as diseased. It seemed my negative view of self had more than enough substantiation.

Yet in practicing as a psychologist, I realized I had the responsibility to objectively apply cognitive therapy to myself. After all, before helping others, it is ethically essential to heal thyself, at least to the extent that the therapist can practice the dictum "Primum non nocere", first do no harm. I learned the process of becoming undepressed involved taking alternative views or making alternative explanations to the chronic schemas that maintain depression. So instead of seeing myself as weird, I'd tell myself that just because there was a good deal of instability in my childhood, that did not mean I was defective. In fact, the instability had made me resilient, as I had been trained to adapt to change, and determined, as I'd learned to fight for what I needed, and strong, as I'd survived more than a normal amount of trauma. Of course these experiences produced a person who was quite abnormal, but an abnormal amount of resilience, determination, and emotional strength could be termed "unique", a much less pejorative adjective than "weird".

I also recall thinking of a new way of seeing the loss of my parents, including the neglect by my father, while on a run, a productive form of exercise for changing one's thoughts. I was at a mental health conference in Los Angeles and toward the end of my six miles, a light came on. Instead of aborting me, my parents married. They did not do well together, and their marriage destroyed both of them. In essence, they died so that I could live. When I consider that shift in perspective, I question even more my decision to kill myself.

This shifting of perspective is called reframing in the cognitive therapy literature, and of all the specific psychotherapy ingredients, the research has indicated it as one of the most effective. Not only does the frame change with this shift; often the lenses change too. That is, the changing of one's view in a single situation can generalize to other situations. Consequently, the world looks much different, so much different it can mean the difference between life and death.

A favorite example of reframing is from Tom Sawyer when Tom is punished by Aunt Polly who makes him whitewash the fence on Saturday. Tom's friend sees him whitewashing, begins to taunt him, and Tom responds by reframing the whitewashing as enjoyable. After listening to Tom talk about it from that perspective for awhile, the friend begs Tom to let him whitewash. Tom initially resists but eventually allows him some "enjoyment" and soon other friends are white- washing the fence while Tom sits in the shade, munching on an apple. The cognitive perspective helped me realize that while we all are unique, it is our commonalities that foster compassion and under- standing. We are all fallible, flawed albeit forgivable human beings, searching in our own ways, for opportunities to love and to be loved and to feel worthwhile. Furthermore, we all meet our needs in the ways we've learned how to, and if we knew how to meet them in better ways, we would do so. This perspective is called universality, and thinking about it has helped me accept my place in the world. It is an elegant paradox, too, that we all have uniqueness in common.

The aspect I found most empowering about cognitive therapy was the control it afforded the individual. By changing our thinking we change the way we feel. We do not become upset, anxious, angry, or depressed *because* of the events and crises in the world around us. The emotional reactions, or feelings, we experience are caused primarily by our thoughts and interpretations about those events. We have more control over our thinking than we do external events and other people; hence, we are capable of helping ourselves to feel better whenever we choose what we think. By generating what and how we think, we can harness the power necessary to take control of our lives. I was impressed that the basis for cognitive therapy was ancient, derived from Buddhist and Stoic philosophies, both of which predate Christ. Marcus Aurelius and Epictetus, both quoted at the beginning of this part of my note, were Stoics. The Buddhists indicated people cause their own misery by rigidly insisting the world should conform to the peculiar notions they have for it. Of course it rarely does. More recently, in the early 17th century, Shakespeare's statement in Hamlet, "Nothing is good or bad but thinking makes it so" spoke to the essence of cognitive therapy. The historical foundation, combined with the fact that cognitive therapy had clinical research support from the last three decades, made it rate very highly in my truth arena.

I met the internationally renowned psychologist and Director of the Milton H. Erickson Foundation, Dr. Jeffrey K. Zeig, when he gave a presentation to psychotherapists about Ericksonian Hypnosis and Psychotherapy in Rehobeth Beach, Delaware in 1989. Neither Dr. Zeig nor Dr. Erickson were cognitive therapists, but Dr. Zeig passed these handouts to the attendees that seemed to me to be excellent introductions to cognitive therapy, for either students or patients.

The first two of the 10 examples on the handout looked like this:

LOVEISNOWHERE
THEYTOLDHIMTOBEATTHEFRONTDOOR

When Dr. Zeig asked attendees what the first statement said, most read it as "love is nowhere", although a few read it as "love is now here." Both could be "correct"; it was an exercise in flexible thinking. Flexible thinking, the ability to see "reality" in different ways was at the heart of mental health according to Dr. Zeig. Conversely, rigidity was the tendency to view situations and act in very limited ways and was the basis for depression. When people report they are "stuck", they are experiencing rigidity. The second run-on sentence could be read: "They told him to be at the front door" or " They told him to beat the front door."

I approached Dr. Zeig out on the balcony, overlooking the ocean, a cool Spring breeze accenting the moment. I ingenuously challenged him, "Isn't Ericksonian therapy really the same thing as cognitive therapy? I mean both try to get the patient to change their maladaptive thinking." Although he certainly wasn't obligated to do so, Dr. Zeig treated my question with the utmost dignity, respect, and seriousness. I vividly recall his deeply prolonged, contemplative gaze at the ocean before signing my book that he co-edited. He wrote:

"To Hank: So you can enjoy discovering ways to join cognitive and Ericksonian approaches..."

Best regards,
Jeff Zeig
Rehobeth Beach1989

During the fall of '89, when I was employed at the mental health center in Winston-Salem, with the supervisor and social worker, Jody (who fired me and mentioned in my fifth night's note), I trained for nine days in Ericksonian hypnosis with Reid Wilson, Ph.D., and when I was fired in late December (Merry Christmas!), I wanted to use that training in a therapy setting. In searching for a supervisor, I contacted Verne Schmickley, Ph.D., who directed the "Center for Cognitive Therapy" in Raleigh. He had worked with the father of cognitive therapy, Dr. Aaron Beck, and had research referenced in Dr. Beck's landmark book, *"Cognitive Therapy of Depression"*. I hoped I could practice cognitive therapy and hypnosis. A wave of luck came my way, and I rode it by starting the "Center for Cognitive Therapy", of Winston-Salem, a branch of Dr. Schmickley's. I'd have the opportunity to treat people with anxiety and depression with cognitive therapy and habit disorders and chronic pain with Ericksonian hypnosis. And it had just been seven months since Dr. Zeig had encouraged me in his message to "...enjoy discovering ways to join cognitive therapy and Ericksonian approaches"!

My Winston-Salem office was as unique in its format as I was as an individual. I had just been thrown out of the house by Patti, my girlfriend and desperately looked for a place to hang my hat, a home. Located on the third floor of a red brick, 19th century building in the downtown section, I had two adjacent rooms, one for the office and one for my living quarters. Hardwood floors, ceiling fans, and no one else on the third floor, I experienced a peaceful solitude in the midst of a bustling city, and I called myself "the metropolitan Thoreau". Some of my most tranquil moments were just after midnight, sit- ting by an open window, meditating on the city below, murmuring its energy with sleep peacefully approaching. Unlike Henry David, though, I did have bathroom facilities on the second floor, electricity, a lawyer for a landlord, a $300. monthly rent, and an attractive but gay female therapist on the second floor. I had even slept with her once, in another city, at a different period of our lives and, obviously, before she'd discovered her sexual orientation. I felt content with my distinctive office-home blend of rusticity. In retrospect, it was one of my favorite homes.

Although Patti had given me the boot, I was soon bestowed with a copious population of females with whom to work. In addition to my small therapy practice, I coached a cross-country team at a private girls' school in town, Salem Academy. They were an enjoyable and fun bunch, and I joked that I was working on a hospital ward, listening to a continual barrage of physical complaints: "Hank, my throat's sore today. I don't think I should run. Hank, I have a headache. I can't workout. Hank, my knee is too sore to practice..." Da da da da da, at least several complaints daily. Nonetheless, I couldn't ask for better memories, and I still have the cross country t-shirt they gave me with all our names on the back.

My other female group consisted of a psychology class I taught at night at a community college in Greensboro. It being a class of nursing students, about ninety percent were women, and I perceived that more than one was, at least a little, attracted to me. Toward the end of the semester, after grades had been established, I gave in to my animalistic lust and allowed myself to fall in love with the one to whom I felt attracted from the first class meeting.

The passion put us both in a trance.

I'm tempted to describe the details of our nine month relationship, but I hesitate for concern that it will needlessly bring back more pain. Suffice it to say the lovely lass forecasted we'd be together "forever"---after she extricated herself from her husband. She never did. She separated and returned to him, reportedly because of her kids. As I deceived myself that she was not deceiving me, I victimized myself and blamed her victimizing me. Due to my self-deception, I clung to the crippling relationship far too long and delivered another dose of depression to myself. I know why the Buddhists say the cause of all suffering is clinging and craving.

I managed to keep my depression at the mild level and avoided the hell of depression I experienced at High Point by using the cognitive skills I was learning to use with clients. I typed an introductory booklet for clients entitled "Basics of Cognitive Therapy", and I will include it here, partly as a reminder about how empowering this stuff can be.

BASICS OF COGNITIVE THERAPY

Automatic thoughts are mental processes (cognitions) including words, phrases, complete sentences, and mental images that you experience continually. These automatic thoughts are triggered by our experiences and situations, and sometimes, they seem to be out of control, like when you may have said, "A thought just popped into my mind". We always experience automatic thoughts, and as a result of their fleeting and changing nature, we are often unaware of their emotional impact. One of the goals of Cognitive Therapy is to train people to become aware of their automatic thoughts and to recognize the effect they have on their emotions. Once you learn the skill of recognizing and "catching" automatic thoughts, you can question their reasonableness and, when helpful, dispute them. When you have disputed the irrational automatic thoughts, you can think of an alternative, more rational thought, and as a consequence, help yourself feel better and act more effectively.

Cognitive distortions are maladaptive, irrational ways of thinking that cause people to experience undesirable emotions such as anxiety, anger, and depression. Whenever you are feeling these emotions to an intense, highly uncomfortable degree, you are undoubtedly experiencing at least one, maybe more, cognitive distortion (s). A list of 10 common ones is provided for you in this booklet. As you learn to become aware of your automatic thoughts or self-talk, you can identify the cognitive distortions in the thoughts. When you have identified the dis- tortion embedded in the unhealthy thoughts, it becomes easier to challenge the thoughts and arrive at better, healthier views.

The self-help tool you can use is called a Thought Record. It is a form for you to write down the unpleasant feelings, identify the event leading to the distress, and most importantly, to write down the automatic thoughts. The Record includes a column to record the cognitive distortions your thoughts include, and, with practice, you can become more adept at identifying these distortions in your everyday interactions. A column for "more adaptive thoughts" is included to write thoughts that counter the automatic, irrational ones. Once you have let the adaptive thoughts sink in a bit, you will feel a little better, and you can record this new feeling in the next column. A final column is for the adaptive, enjoyable, or productive behaviors in which you'll likely engage after you have helped yourself think and feel better. "Likely Behavior" is a prediction or expectation, and, by strongly imagining it, the behavior is more likely to occur.

Patience and persistence is required to learn how to use the Thought Record effectively. You can do it alone, but a lot of discipline is required to practice regularly. I recommend practicing several times a week at first, and each practice may take from twenty to thirty minutes. A cognitive therapist may also be helpful as a supportive guide and teacher.

You might see that the Cognitive Therapy process enhances an alteration of consciousness, from one that is negative and pessimistic to one that is positive and optimistic. You construct this altered state of consciousness by practicing different approaches such as the Thought Record. Some of the adaptive thoughts you can write on the TR are questions such as the following, which may become a part of your everyday internal dialogue: "What evidence do I have for this conclusion?" "What other way is there for me to look at this situation?" "If this situation is as I see it, is it really the end of the world?" and "Even if what I am telling myself is true, is it useful to keep dwelling on it?" In addition to those questions, these rational statements apply to everyone from time to time and can also be used in the adaptive thoughts column: "I don't like this problem, but I can stand it. And I can manage gracefully", " Things never have to work out the way I want them to. Tough if they don't", "Other people have flaws and are fallible but that doesn't make them bitches or bastards. Those negative labels just make me angrier, and there's no need to use them." "I can try to do the best that I can and accept what happens." These rational, adaptive thoughts counter cognitive distortions and can help you adjust to life demands and stressors.

As an example, take a man, Nick, who has just been unfairly fired from his job. He may have thoughts like "The world shouldn't be so unfair and must not be so unfair!", "This is terrible, horrible!", "I can't stand this!", "Now I'm never going to get a good job!". It is not the loss of the job that is causing Nick to feel depressed and angry, but it is his distorted thinking that is leading him to feel so upset and hopeless. You can refer to the list of cognitive distortions to see the above thoughts include "should thinking" (Albert Ellis tells people to stop shoulding on themselves), magnification (Ellis's term is "catastrophizing"), and jumping to conclusions. Once Nick identified the distortions in his thinking, he can dispute his internal babbling. He might say, "It's not a matter of how I think the world should be. Unfairness is common, and I had better accept it and deal with it." "Of course I can stand it. I don't like it, but I can stand it." " There's no evidence to conclude I'll never get a good job again. If I learn from my past experiences and persist, I can find a good job again. And maybe I can do a few things differently next time." As Nick experiences these more adaptive forms of thinking, he will likely feel better, and, consequently, he will more likely take effective action.

This process can also be used with other crises such as death, divorce, illness and injury, and various kinds of other losses, whether real or imaginary.

Another example would involve someone with an anxiety disorder like panic attacks. The person typically begins sensing a physical symptom such as racing heart, dizziness, or difficulty breathing and will begin thinking, "I'm having a heart attack", "I'm losing my mind" or "I'm going to die". The distortions in these thoughts include magnification and jumping to conclusions. The person does not have a heart attack, go crazy or die. When the person persistently engages in these thoughts for long periods of time, though, he definitely makes himself more anxious, worried, uptight, and hopeless. The physiological effects of anxiety become exacerbated, and the person has a full-blown panic attack. The good news is that cognitive-behavior therapy is very effective for panic disorder. When a person learns to catch their automatic thoughts and dispute them and also practices relaxation exercises, they frequently discover they can master panic.

Another way to combat and eradicate cognitive distortions that is often effective with panic patients involves what is called a paradoxical approach. Using this strategy, the patient is directed to intentionally think about and write down his cognitive distortions as if they are valid. He may write down things like "Yes, I am definitely going to die tomorrow", "Yes, I can't even breathe", "Yes, I'm going crazy and will probably wind up in the loony bin" for a half hour (or an hour for those with longstanding panic). He may also be directed to act out these thoughts as if they are true. By writing these distortions down or acting them out, he takes control over them, and, of course, finds they are not true. In taking control over his distorted thinking, he becomes a survivor rather than a victim to those thoughts.

I strongly recommend people with moderate to severe depression and panic disorder to seek out a supportive therapist who can, in addition to teaching cognitive skills, explore the origins of a person's worldviews she has acquired which usually begin in childhood.

Hopefully this booklet will give you enough information about the cognitive approach that you expect it will be helpful to you. It is intended to whet your appetite. If you don't expect it to be helpful, that's fine--you can test it out. Research in the last three decades has found it to be effective, particularly with depression and anxiety disorders, although Aaron Beck, M.D. published a book called Love Is Never Enough, that applies cognitive therapy to couples. Regardless of how much you decide to use Cognitive Therapy, keep in mind this pearl from Winston Churchhill: "Never, never, never, never give up." If what you are doing is not working, it may be time to do something different.

HankMcGovern, M.A.

COGNITIVE DISTORTIONS

The following lists of errors in thinking are common ways that people make themselves anxious, angry, and depressed. When these distortions are identified and challenged, more reasonable, adaptive ways of thinking can be used and healthier emotional states can be achieved. These distortions are based on the research done by leaders in the field of cognitive therapy such as Aaron Beck, M.D., David Burns, M.D., and Albert Ellis, Ph.D.

Examples of alternative, more reasonable thoughts are offered.

Magnification---situations are blown way out of proportion so the person views them as much worse than they are. "Catastrophizing" is another term for this irrational way of thinking. When people use expressions like "awful!", "terrible", and "horrible! and "I can't stand it!", they are engaging in this distortion. Instead of these irrational terms, one can modulate his/her emotions better by using more rational expressions such as "inconvenient", "unfortunate", "unpleasant", and, most importantly, "I can stand it." The resulting emotions are healthier ones like sadness and annoyance instead of the more maladaptive ones like depression and extreme anger. For instance, one might rationally say, "It's unfortunate she broke up with me, and I feel sad" instead of the irrational statement, "It's terrible she broke up with me, and I can't stand it!" My favorite rational statement can be applied to any, yes any, emotionally difficult situation: "I don't like this problem, but I can stand it."

Jumping to conclusions---interpretations are made without sufficient evidence. "Mind-reading" is one example in which conclusions are reached about what others are thinking and feeling without finding out from them exactly what they are thinking and feeling. "Fortune telling" is another in which one proclaims things will turn out badly, again without ample evidence. It often helps to ask oneself, "Where's the evidence...(that this person thinks or feels this way, that I will never have another better relationship, or that I will not get a better job)?" Usually, there's no such evidence! So when you begin to jump to conclusions either don't jump at all or let yourself land softly.

<u>Mental filter</u>---one dwells on or focuses on the negative qualities of a situation or person and ignores the positive. An example would be a couple who had an enjoyable weekend at the beach and, on the way home, they had an argument that lasted for 20 minutes of their three hour ride. When her fellow employee asks the wife how her weekend went, she laments, "Oh, the whole weekend was wrecked because we fought and that messed up everything!" Of course the more adaptive, rational response would be, "It was pretty good overall. We did have an argument, but we had lots of good times too." Mental filter is also termed "tunnel vision".

<u>All-or-none thinking</u>---things are seen in extremes or black and white categories. "My spouse is a great, totally wonderful person!", and if the person has a few flaws, "She/he is a terrible bitch/bastard! A no good louse!". There are no shades of gray in this kind of thinking. People see themselves as complete successes or complete failures. This distortion is the basis for perfectionism, and I tell people, "Perfectionism is a mistake." It's more rational to be aware of shortcomings as well as strengths in others and to appreciate events for their imperfections as well as their finer qualities. You hear highly competitive athletes assert, "Winning isn't everything. It's the only thing!"--a good example of this distortion. It's much healthier to tolerate and even appreciate the shades of gray that are so often characteristic of people and situations.

<u>Emotional reasoning</u>---one reasons from how he feels and expresses thoughts in terms of feelings. For example, "I feel like an idiot so I must be one" or "I feel like you don't like me so you must not". These are automatic thoughts that people identify as feelings, and unfortunately, many therapists encourage this kind of confusion by not helping the client differentiate thought from emotion. Another common example, "I feel stupid" confuses thought with feeling. "Stupid" is not a feeling; it's a label.

<u>"Should" and "must" statements</u>---one criticizes and complains about themselves, others, and the world by rigidly insisting their own rules are the right, correct, and/or true ways to be. Statements include: "shoulds and shouldn'ts", "musts and must nots", "ought and ought not", and "have tos" and "got tos". "She should have sex when I want her to...", "He must not go out with his friends...", "My boss should treat me with respect...",

"She ought to break up with him…", "I have got to make this sale…", "I must succeed…" are common examples. Guilt and anger are common emotions triggered by these irrational demands. Psychoanalyst Karen Horney described them as "the tyranny of the shoulds", and Albert Ellis reminds people to stop "shoulding" on themselves and others and to give up "musterbating". Usually it's more rational to use terms like "better" or "prefer". For example, "I prefer that she have sex with me, but she doesn't have to…" or "I had better succeed at this, but I don't have to…" or "I want him to stay at home but it's not true that he must."

Labeling---calling someone a "jerk", "loser", "fool", "bitch", "bastard", and many other names is an example of this distortion. People make mistakes and demonstrate their flaws regularly, but putting them down with these overly emotional terms doesn't help matters nor do the labels accurately describe the person or explain their behaviors. In fact, the research suggests the more one uses labels such as these, the angrier that person makes him- self. The one word that does accurately describe a person who commits blunders, even blunders against you, yes you, as far as I can tell, is "human".

Personalization and blame---similarly to the above, one blames oneself for something they were not entirely responsible for and consequently, burden themselves excessively for an outcome that can more accurately be explained by several factors. Conversely, one blames others excessively and does not look at ways he contributed to a problem. It helps to "re-attribute" the problem or outcome to several factors, so instead of saying, "If I was a more giving wife, he wouldn't have left me" one might say, "We both shared responsibility. While I had some flaws, he also was demanding and unfaithful."

To begin, identify one situation daily leading to your feelings of anxiety, anger, or depression. What automatic thoughts run through your mind about the situation? If you can't identify what they are, say your thoughts aloud to make yourself aware of them. What we say is also what we think. Write these automatic thoughts on the Thought Record. Can you identify what distortions most accurately describe the thoughts? Now write down more rational thoughts using the examples outlined above.

Complete the rest of the Thought Record. If you practice, you will most likely be able to make yourself feel better.

Albert Ellis, Ph.D., is the pioneer of a kind of cognitive therapy called Rational-Emotive Behavior Therapy an approach having a number of similarities and differences to that of Aaron Beck out- lined thus far. Dr. Ellis formulated what he calls the "ABC Theory of Emotional Disturbance", identifying the "A" as the activating event, the "B" as the beliefs (irrational), and the "C" as the emotional "consequences". He explains people get themselves emotionally disturbed by incorrectly thinking the activating event (A), whether it is divorce, job loss, death, or a less critical incident, directly causes their emotional consequence (C). The strongest cause of their emotional upset, how- ever, are the irrational beliefs (B) about the activating event.

The simplest, most common fact that supports the assertion by Ellis and other cognitive therapists is how everyone varies in their resilience to stressful events. Why does one person recover more quickly and show less severe reactions than another person regarding bad things? The adaptive person shows more rational and less irrational thinking.

One can overcome emotional upsets by moving to D, which stands for disputing the "nutty", (Ellis uses provocative language to motivate) irrational ideas and beliefs. By disputing the irrational ideas and creating rational beliefs at B one can achieve E, a new emotional consequence. Usually the new emotions include sadness instead of depression, mild instead of severe anxiety, and irritation or annoyance instead of hostility; REBT asserts it's natural and healthy to experience unpleasant emotions on occasion, albeit the intensity and duration of the emotion is necessary to modify for healthy functioning.

In regard to irrational beliefs (ibs), Ellis lists three main ones, and they all include the concept of "must", leading him to coin the term "musturbation". They are:

1. "I must perform well, and/or win approval of an important person or else I am an inadequate person."

2. "You must treat me fairly and considerately and not unduly frustrate me or else you are a rotten individual!
3. "My life conditions must give me the things I want and have to keep me from harm or else life is unbearable and I can't be happy at all!"

In my experience, when I have felt extreme negative emotions, particularly anger, anxiety, and depression, upon surveying my thoughts, they have included the musts. Examples include: "I must get what I rightly deserve", "I must be treated fairly and/or respectfully", " That authority figure (boss, professor, parent substitute) must be reasonable", "I must perform well sexually", "I must be accepted, recognized, or loved", "I must achieve and get approval or recognition", "Things have to work out the way I want them to", "I must have this woman", and the list goes on. It's not that these ideas are entirely irrational--it's the intensity of the must that is self-defeating. I've discovered substituting "want", "prefer", or "would like" for the "musts" and the "have tos" makes me feel a lot better.

Disputing (D) of my irrational beliefs involves writing down on paper specific statements countering the ibs. For example, regarding the first one, I would write, "It simply isn't true that I must get what I believe I "rightly deserve". I want to get many things and that's fine; I can work or make efforts to get those things. But if I don't get them, tough. I will still live! I counter the next belief with: "I prefer to be treated fairly and respectfully, but if some people treat me unfairly, I can stand it. I can manage. The world is often unfair. Tough. I can stand unfairness even though I don't like it." I would substitute more rational statements for the other beliefs, and by doing so on a regular basis, I'd experience E, the new emotional consequence, which, in these cases, would be less anger, maybe just annoyance.

In reflecting to the Buddhists again, I recall their perspective that clinging and craving cause suffering. It seems apparent that the demanding nature of the "musts" and "have tos" posited by Ellis is synonymous with clinging and craving. The beliefs cited above convey a clinging to the ideal of good performance, and a craving for approval, fair treatment, and safety. That this wisdom has withstood the challenges of centuries suggests to me that we have valid solutions to life's problems; our responsibility is to practice them. Taking the "musts" and "have tos" to another level, we don't have to survive. It is not true that we must live, even for another day! Each time I've come close to death, I've discovered that reality. At those moments, death becomes a natural experience to be accepted and even appreciated, as a part of the cosmic change process. Our decay is a simple blend into the universe. It is the demand that we must live that causes the fear of death. Paradoxically, the demand to live makes life less satisfying--it only amplifies desperation. Perhaps it would help to remind ourselves occasionally that we want to live, although we don't have to. The idea might calm us down a little.

The idea that we often demand that we live, a form of musturbation, is addressed by Existential Psychotherapy. Dr. Irvin Yalom, a noted researcher, author and practitioner of Existential Psychotherapy writes about the concept of death anxiety. Death anxiety, according to him, is the root of all other anxiety disorders; common obsessions, compulsions, panic, and other fears are surface manifestations of the universal fear of death. Indeed, death anxiety reflects the irrational idea that we absolutely must live. If we don't it's as if it's the end of the world! Although I have never read about a joining of Ellis's concept of musturbation and Yalom's concept of death anxiety, it makes logical sense to join them; I'll do it now.

I hypothesize that if a person with a hand washing compulsion, a fear of heights, or an obsession would say, perhaps 10 times each night and morning: "I want to live. Since I would like to keep living, I will do what I can to stay alive. However, I don't have to live. I can accept death whenever it happens", s(he) would notice a decrease in anxiety. Now, a hypothesis is an educated guess, not a certainty. Which is to say it is not true that the results of practicing the meditation above must happen the way we'd like. I don't believe it can hurt, though, so try it out and test the waters. To give yourself a way of testing whether the practice of these meditative statements decrease your anxiety, before saying them each time, rate your anxiety on a 10 point scale with 10 as the most anxiety and 1 as the least.

After you calmly say these statements 10 times, rate your anxiety again. Any decrease, even 1 point is good. My guess is that if you practice regularly, you will change your attitude that you must live to a more rational and healthier one; you will want to live but will not feel you must. As a consequence, you will decrease your anxiety.

Another irrational idea cited by Dr. Ellis includes the notion that people, situations, and the world *should* be different. Guilt and anger are the two most obvious emotions resulting from excessive "shoulding" on oneself. The irrational nature of these ideas is manifested by the absoluteness by which people adhere to arbitrary rules, commands, and beliefs. "He should have given me the job." "She shouldn't get so angry at me." "Someone should have stopped to help the poor child." "My boss should treat me fairly." "My spouse should be more understanding of my needs." It is not that it wouldn't be better if reality conformed to these statements. It would be better. There is an important difference, however, between insisting things should be a certain way and maintaining they'd be better that way. And people decrease their neuroticism substantially when they develop and maintain attitudes that things would be better instead of dogmatically insisting they absolutely *should* be different. Quite frequently the world simply doesn't conform to people's peculiar, arbitrary notions of the way it should be.

In regard to the "shoulds", I've often thought they served a useful purpose, and if people viewed them as guideposts rather than as rigid absolutes, they would not be a problem. It's the "musts" that cause the real problem because of their demandingness. At a world conference, in the midst of attendee's swarming Dr. Ellis to get him to sign their books, I posed my insight to him in a somewhat challenging manner. "Dr. Ellis, I have been thinking about your perspective on"shoulds".

"Yes, they cause people real problems", he quickly replied.

"Well, it doesn't seem like the shoulds cause the serious problems. People need shoulds as a part of their values and beliefs. It's the "musts" that really cause problems," and because I offered such a brilliant insight, I half expected him to give me his blessing. Perhaps I even thought he should!

He did not; he didn't say anything. He did look at me, however, from where he was seated, busily autographing, in such a way I'll never forget. It was the look in his eyes. I wondered if he had sized me up as contentious. Maybe my timing wasn't very considerate. When could I have enlightened him with my insight though?

To this day it seems I had a good point. I still don't think the "shoulds" cause as much emotional trouble as the "musts". Put in certain contexts as signals or guides, shoulds can be helpful. For instance, I believe we should not intentionally harm each other; of course there are varying degrees of this possibility. Some pose as stronger"shoulds" than others. One of the strongest "should nots" is that opposing child sexual abuse. There's no doubt in most of our minds that the prohibition against it is reasonable and practical. I've informed sex offenders that it is reasonable for them to feel moderate guilt, but it's unhealthy and unproductive for them to feel severe guilt for the rest of their lives, as that would only intensify their depression, thereby preventing their progress in therapy and becoming more responsible in their lives. An appropriate level of guilt, though, should be one of the factors in helping them resist future urges.

For some people, though, much of their everyday thought and language is replete with "shoulds", and these are individuals who feel anxious and worry that they aren't doing the right or best thing all the time. The baneful nature mentioned earlier of this pattern was described by the psychoanalyst, Karen Horney, as the "tyranny of the shoulds" because the mind becomes a tyrant, constantly criticizing, commanding, and coercing behavior in the name of some arbitrary set of rules. For example, many girls have been taught they should always be nice, a rule that prevents them from being honest with themselves about their feelings and that causes communication problems in relationships. In these cases, it seems the "shoulds" are about as problematic as the "musts"; the difference may be one of degree.

According to Ellis's REBT, after people tell themselves that others should or must behave differently than how they do behave, they often tell themselves it's "awful" or "terrible" that reality doesn't conform to their absolute standards. It is the "awfulizing" that elicits the intense feeling of depression, anxiety, and anger. To dispute the "awfuls", "terribles", and "horribles" one can substitute less emotionally evoking words such as "unfortunate" or "inconvenient". So instead of catastrophizing the breakup of a relationship with the self-statements, "It's terrible (or awful) that she broke up with me!", the man could more rationally say, "It's unfortunate she broke up with me. I don't like it, but I can stand it. Tough!" As a consequence of this disputing, he will more likely feel a manageable emotion like sadness or disappointment rather than the dysfunctional experiences of depression and hostility.

Of course emotional management is most effective by persisting in the use of rational self-talk. A semantic disputing of only a few thoughts is unlikely to make much of a difference, and a return to anxiety, depression, and anger is likely. To make a real, sustained emotional change, it is important to practice disputing repeatedly, to do homework regularly, and to understand the difference between the "shoulds" and "musts" vs. the healthier "wants", "prefers,", and "betters" and the "awfuls" and "terribles" vs. the "unfortunates" and "inconveniences". Rational self-talk is not just a word game, though, and it is important to feel the differences in the meanings of the words as well as the attitudes they convey.

One might argue certain forms of abuse, trauma, or crisis really are "awful or "terrible", that it's not just a matter of semantics and attitude. Rape, murder, torture, and permanent injury all fall in the category of "awful". The philosophy of REBT does not intend to invalidate the nature of trauma experienced by a victim. The point is that the "reality" of external situations can be modified by what we tell ourselves. If it seems realistic to describe a traumatic experience as awful, you can decide how long to describe it that way and whether to select another perspective that might help you feel better. You have that choice. By shortening the duration of suffering you can cope. It may be helpful to describe it in the past as "awful" (It was awful that…) and state your ability to manage it in the present (…But I can stand it.) Our internal dialogues are always potential sources of empowerment, not only to help us cope but to rise above painful experiences.

The last step of emotional upset in the irrational thinking process according to REBT, after one makes himself depressed or angry by musturbating or awfulizing, is when the person exacerbates his emotional distress by the attitude, "I can't stand it!" Not only is it "awful" or "terrible" that someone hasn't done what she "should" have done; he gets himself more upset by telling himself her behavior is absolutely intolerable, that he can't stand it! So in relation to a boss firing a woman, her first irrational idea might be, "Mr. Smith should've been fair to me, and he must not be unfair!" followed by, "And it's awful that he is not being fair as he must!" with the subsequent coup de grace, "I can't stand it!" Dr. Ellis calls this attitude "I can't stand it itis", and I've suggested to clients that if they catch a case of it they can cure it with strong doses of "I can stand it". In fact, of the many suggestions I've given to people, the one they say often helps them the most is the self statement "I can stand this problem. I don't like it, and it is unfair, but tough, can stand it!". Of course the exact words differ to fit each person and situation, and some of the derivatives include: "I can handle this", "I can tolerate this even though I don't like it", "I can manage this", and one I have adopted, "I don't like this problem, but I can stand it and manage gracefully." All of these statements characterize the position of the survivor in contrast to that of the victim, and it is empowering that we can survive any situation by what we tell ourselves.

In a workshop, Dr. Janet Wolfe, one of Dr. Ellis's colleagues, gave us a metaphor for the ABC theory that I liked because it's easy to remember. If you visualize a clock, picture the 12 as the event, whether it's a divorce, death, job loss, or a less critical one like an everyday frustration. The 3 is where the "shoulds" and "musts" occur. Reflect on an experience in your life and see if you can detect how you insisted it should have been different or must not have been the way it actually occurred. Moving down to the 6, notice how you declared the situation or person was "awful" or "terrible". Stay with that for a couple of minutes and notice if you bring back feelings of anger. The 9, as you might have guessed, includes the "I can't stand it" attitude. Do you recall having maintained this position? How long did you hold it? Now go around the clock again and apply the rational statements already mentioned to counter the irrational thoughts. Go around as many times as necessary or stay in one position long enough to effect a real change in your attitude and feelings. You can make yourself feel better!

Having the knowledge of how you can change your upset emotions by disputing your irrational ideas and beliefs, you can prevent yourself from having dysfunctional emotions, and if you do happen to forget to apply rational thinking, and you most likely will from time to time, and find yourself getting depressed, angry, or anxious, you can decrease the duration and intensity of these emotions by reminding yourself to dispute the irrational ideas as soon as possible. A profound change takes practice, patience, and persistence, and with those, it is highly possible you will experience it. As Dostoyevsky once said in this regard, "A new philosophy, a way of life, is not given for nothing. It has to be paid dearly for and only acquired with patience and great effort." Centuries earlier Epictetus would've agreed, and now a century later, you can too. Wisdom is timeless.

Perhaps the most important element Ellis emphasized included Unconditional Self Acceptance (USA) and Unconditional Other Acceptance (UOA). Unconditional Self Acceptance means regardless of what one has done, no matter what mistakes or flaws have been exhibited each person has a core that needs to be accepted and appreciated. Each person has the Human Right to love and accept themselves. Similarly, we can also accept each other unconditionally.

By retrospection, I can see how I engaged in a storm of irrational ideas on the first night of this note. Plugging the experience into the ABC format, the Activating Event (A) was my termination and the people who were to blame for it. I immediately focused on the emotional Consequence (C) which included anger to the point of suicidal rage. The people who fired me were the culprits. I would have managed my feelings better if I were more expedient at disputing my venomous, irrational beliefs (B) that I was screaming internally. A few salient ones were: "Those bastards should not have fired me! They should not have unfairly and unreasonably charged me with sexual harassment for saying 'I'm gonna flirt with ya,'. They must not get away with it! I must get revenge! This is terrible, and I can't stand it!" Certainly I felt justified in holding onto those self-statements since the conspirators had committed egregiously unfair acts. It was the irrationality of my thinking, though, that caused my extreme anger. And after transforming the anger into an enemy, I became an accessory to it, plotting my own murder.

Let's see what would have likely happened if I had disputed my irrational beliefs more quickly, persistently, and or forcefully, approaches strongly encouraged by Ellis. Upon feeling rage, I could have recognized it as a signal that I needed to settle down and do some active disputing. After calming myself by meditating or practicing a relaxation approach, my thoughts would decrease from boiling to hot, maybe a temperature I could tolerate enough to proceed. I'd then identify the shoulds, musts, awfuls, and 'I can't stand it' statements. Take the first one: "Those bastards should not have fired me!"

My disputation: "If I label them 'bastards', I just make myself angrier. Labeling others in this way serves no purpose, and by using these labels, that carry hostile overtones, I tend to exacerbate my anger. The individuals are fallible, flawed human beings, as we all are, and identifying them in such a way can devenomize me a bit. There's no commandment that they should not have fired me. I know they made a mistake, which makes sense, since they are fallible, and I can explore how to deal with their mistake. I can also look at my mistakes that exacerbated their mistakes."

Regarding the irrational belief: "They should not have unfairly, unreasonably charged me with sexual harassment for saying 'I'm gonna flirt with ya', there's a significant difference between the irrational "should not" and "it would have been better if they had been more reasonable and not charged..." The rigidity of the should leads to and maintains anger, and it doesn't make sense for me to demand that individuals who showed a pattern of unfairness and unreasonableness to act differently in my situation. In fact, it makes sense they acted according to their pattern. The world is often unfair. Tough.

It is true my behavior did not meet the legal standard for sexual harassment. Specifically it was not persistent or severe. In the legal sense, they should not have charged me with sexual harassment. However, if I insist they should have complied with the law, I'll be insisting, actually musturbating, on the obvious; when things seem obvious, musturbation comes easily. Therefore, when it seems obvious to me that people should behave in a certain way, those times can be a signal for me to monitor my musts. It's not true the gang of administrators must comply with legal standards. I'll just consider the source.

Moving on, who says I must get revenge? Only I do, and by doing so, I again increase my tension and anger. I can dispute that irrational belief by: "I want to get some justice, but I don't have to get it. It's not the end of the world if I don't get what I want. Since I do want some justice, I can relax a bit and focus better on steps to take to get it. I will be better off emotionally, physically, and mentally when I persist and forcefully tell myself, 'I don't have to get what I want." A warrior doesn't demand what is uncertain. He remains light and fluid.

The one I like tackling the most is the "I can't stand it itis." When I realize I'm telling myself this, I begin to feel optimistic because I am confident I can stand it. I can stand it by telling myself I can, forcefully and persistently. "I don't like this problem, but I can stand it. I can manage gracefully." And if this tragedy follows the pattern characteristic of most tragedies, I will grow from it. An injustice was committed against me, but I can focus on my responsibility in the situation, and by doing so, I may learn to do things differently if I get into a similar situation again. Nietzsche's wisdom rings true that, "Whatever does not kill me will make me stronger." The transformation of "I can't stand it..." to "I can stand it..." is that of a victim to a survivor.

It is the perspective, "I can't stand it" that leads to suicide. To that statement the suicidal person adds a fatal, illogical conclusive clause, "Therefore, I must kill myself." Since I can, in fact, stand it, I can use my curiosity about what will happen as I hang around. Perhaps my curiosity will open a door.

The movie Papillon with Steve McQueen and Dustin Hoffman comes to mind again. Papillon played by McQueen, has been wrongfully sentenced for a murder and is held as prisoner on Devil's Island. After attempting to escape for decades, he finally succeeds by throwing a bag of coconuts off a cliff into turbulent ocean waves and jumping onto them from a cliff. As the movie ends, he is seen paddling out to sea, yelling, "Hey you bastards, I'm still here!" Each time I've identified with that scene, I've felt empowered.

Concerning the "I can't stand it itis", I'll always remember a surprising pronouncement by Dr. Ellis at an international mental health conference. He captured the audience's attention, stating, "There are two words that will cure all emotional distress." Since the audience consisted of psychotherapists highly motivated in curing their clients, they were on the edge of their seats to absorb these pearls. "Those two words: 'tough shit!" I reflected on my years of academic training, paying tens of thousands for tuition, struggling, studying and stumbling, testing and testing, laboring over term papers and dissertaton, and mused over his simple panacea. I paid for this conference and traveled across country to hear this glibness? As my irritation got hotter, a countering thought cooled it off. The thought? "Tough shit!!" I think one reason the "tough shit" mantra helps is that we all experience unfairness occasionally, maybe frequently. We complain of the unfairness, but paradoxically, at least it's fair that we all experience unfairness! None of us is singled out in having experienced it. Saying "tough shit" reminds us of the fair unfairness and toughens us to endure the shit.

When I take the time to dispute my irrational ideas and think more rationally, I nearly always make myself feel better. The physical changes include better health, and Dr. Redford Williams of Duke University has documented how sustained anger can result in coronary disease. The title of his book, Anger Kills, poignantly conveys the message. It is thinking that elicits the fatal anger, and it is thinking that leads to peace and acceptance. The process is the same, but it's the path that is different. Since we have this knowledge, we can take responsibility for choosing the path on which our thoughts can journey.

While cognitive solutions may seem simple, they are not simplistic, and to become skillful, it is necessary to practice using the Thought Record and/or the REBT disputing on a regular basis. Often, people deny they are "shoulding" on themselves, "catastrophizing", "musturbating", or catching a case of "I can't stand it itis" and incorrectly believe that inherent, terrible qualities of the events in the world cause their emotional distress. Since thoughts are so automatic and fleeting, it seems difficult to detect the irrational beliefs (ibs). And since these irrational beliefs operate at a subconscious level, it is frequently necessary to do some honest introspection (etymologically introspection is "seeing inward"), and when you do, you'll likely find the ibs. As Ellis directs, "Cherchez le shoulds, cherchez le musts!" Look for the shoulds.

Look for the musts!

I feel confident applying cognitive skills knowing the approaches of Doctors Beck and Ellis have four decades of solid foundation in the psychological research on emotional disorders. Such a foundation emphatically reminds me they can work if I put forth some effort. I also remind myself the philosophies underlying these therapies are derived from the Stoics and Buddhists. They've worked for more than a millenia! But only for those who apply them.

The wisdom continues to be passed down in various forms and flavors, and I'd be remiss if I did not mention the work of Martin Seligman, Ph.D., who discovered a phenomena called "learned helplessness", a concept that explains depression. In 1964, while a graduate student, Seligman did a series of experiments with dogs to demonstrate how animals and humans give up. After discussing his ethical problem with inflicting pain on animals with his philosophy professor, and developing a reasonable approach, he assigned dogs to three groups: one that received a mild shock and could escape from it by pushing a panel with its' nose, one that received shock from which it could not escape, and one that was left alone.

Subsequent to the first experience, Seligman placed the dogs in a shuttlebox that produced shock and had a barrier they could easily jump over to escape the shock. The group of dogs that were able to escape shock in the first experience quickly began to jump over the barrier, as did the dogs that were first left alone. However, the dogs that were first delivered inescapable shock made no effort to jump over the barrier, even though by doing so they would escape the shock. They simply laid down and accepted the pain, essentially having given up. Seligman concluded they had learned to be helpless.

In similar experiments with humans, with one of the exceptions being the use of loud noises instead of shocks, a Japanese graduate student, Donald Hiroto, produced comparable findings to Seligman's. Ensuing clinical research over the next few decades has supported learned helplessness as an explanatory concept for the etiology of depression. In teaching psychology classes, I've used it to explain why adults, usually women, remain in abusive relationships. As children they were helpless and dependent on parents simply by the nature of being children; they depended on them for food, shelter, and clothing. Parents, more so in the past than in the present, were able to physically, sexually, and emotionally abuse them, and the children literally had no avenues of escape. If they were available, most did not know how to go about using them, and as a result of their limited knowledge and resources, these "trapped" children learned to be helpless. As they experienced year after year of continued abuse, the victim mentality of learned helplessness was increasingly reinforced.

Having developed helplessness as a characteristic pattern by the time they get into abusive relationships as adults, they haven't a clue as to how to leave the relationship. They remain in relationships that are destructive emotionally, mentally, sexually, and physically, not unlike the dogs that learned they could not escape the painful shocks. Well meaning acquaintances advise them to "just leave", encouraging them for incredibly prolonged periods, only to get frustrated in their efforts, lamenting, "All she has to do is leave. She just won't do it." Unfortunately, the victims were never taught they could jump over the barrier of an abusive relationship.

Fortunately, there are learning opportunities in the form of psychotherapies, self-help approaches, support groups, and special friendships that can show them how to escape safely. After arguing his learned helplessness concept as cognitively based against the behavioral psychologists such as B.F. Skinner, Seligman realized since helplessness was learned, it could be unlearned. This discovery showed enormous potential for the arena of psychotherapy.

Not only could helplessness be unlearned, but optimism could be learned. In the research with human subjects, Seligman and his colleagues observed that a small percentage, the exceptions, never succumbed to helplessness. While initially at a loss for how to account for these exceptions, he eventually discovered the concept of explanatory style, or the way by which people explain the reasons for bad and good events. The explanatory style of optimists, he found, was significantly different from that of pessimists.

When bad things happen, pessimists say things to themselves that sound as though the bad things are permanent. Optimists, on the other hand, make self-statements suggesting the bad things are temporary, leaving room for positive possibilities. For example, a pessimist would say, "My wife is a bitch!" whereas an optimist would say, "My wife sometimes gets bitchy." The difference may seem trivial, but it's not; the effect is cumulative as the self-talk is regular and ongoing. Pessimists tend to blame themselves for bad events while optimists explain them by focusing on external causes. Thus, a pessimist would say "She's divorcing me, and it's all my fault", and the optimist might say, "She's divorcing me because her friends and family convinced her she can find better. I have flaws, but I'm not all to blame." Also, Seligman describes a dimension he calls "pervasiveness" which seems tantamount to the cognitive distortion "overgeneralization". Pervasiveness is exemplified when someone has had something bad happen and then, instead of looking at several good things that have happened on a particular day, will say the bad event contaminates the whole day.

The important point is that as, a result of his research, Seligman discovered optimism can be learned by changing one's explanatory style. In his book, Learned Optimism, he includes strategies for how to develop an optimistic explanatory style, and provides the ABC model of Albert Ellis as one of the main strategies. Learned Optimism, in addition to showing how one can create a buffer against depression, teaches how one can develop an explanatory style to facilitate athletic performance, improve physical health, and increase productivity and satisfaction in business organizations. Seligman has also focused on what he calls "authentic happiness", another cognitive-behavioral style that can be learned.

When I think of Seligman, I immediately recall the dogs that didn't jump over the barrier. They simply never learned that by doing so they could escape the shock. The question for us humans becomes, "Where is the barrier and how high do we have to jump? What skills have to be learned to jump over it?" The answer is in the search, and I guess that's what life is all about.

CHAPTER 7

Graceful Change by Acceptance and Utilization

"Happiness is the endowment with value of all the things you have."

MILTON H. ERICKSON, M.D.

"Problems are the roughage of life, and any soldier that has been on k-rations knows how important roughage is in a diet."

MILTON H. ERICKSON, M.D.

IT'S BEEN A LITTLE MORE than two weeks since my sixth night's writing which spilled over into a seventh day.

While each night of writing reduced my suicidal intention, I suppose the strongest prevention to killing myself was the change of attitude from "I can't stand it" to "I can stand it." Of course I can stand psychological pain, and as I tell myself I can, the pain diminishes. The more I tell myself "I can stand" pain, the more I establish the truth of that reality. This attitude change facilitates a transformation from the role of a victim to that of a survivor and empowers me to look forward to fighting my wrongful firing. As a consequence, I've dropped from a five to a three on my 10-point scale of suicide likelihood.

On night four, after some nights of describing my past, I began documenting skills and resources I've learned to use that helped me get this far in life, which is further than most people acquainted with my childhood expected me to get. Since I expected to die on the first six nights, I wanted to leave something that might be helpful to others. As a result, I've inadvertently helped myself so that I now experience only a residual of suicidal ideation.

In an effort to help us more, I feel it's necessary to tell you about the works of a phenomenal psychiatrist, Milton H. Erickson, considered to be the master of medical hypnosis. He is one of the few experts on human behavior I see as great enough to be a hero. His genius, generosity, and compassion, some of which I'll relate to you, is simply unmatched. Although I never met the man, his gifts have fulfilled a lifetime of Christmases for me.

I was living in Wilmington, Delaware in 1989, working as a Staff Psychologist at Delaware State Hospital. I'd been enticed by the promise of Dr. Colins, the Psychology Department Director, that he would help me get my Ph.D. if I took the job. After working there a few months and reminding him of his promise, he responded that he wouldn't be able to follow through on it. A series of other deceptions followed, and I discovered I couldn't trust Colins as far as I could throw him.

When I requested he assist me in getting hospital funding to attend a workshop on Ericksonian Hypnosis, he asked, "Are you talking about the works of Milton Erickson?" As I replied I was, he emphatically asserted he would not help. I got the impression from Colins, who was trained in forensic hypnosis, that I was not qualified to learn about Ericksonian Hypnosis, and I became even more motivated to get the money from alternative sources to make sure I could attend. If you tell me I can't, I will.

The workshop was the one I mentioned on night six involving Dr. Jeff Zeig, and in addition to the examples regarding flexibility, he related a bit about Dr. Erickson's life; it served as a model for accepting and utilizing pain. After contracting polio when he was 17 years old, the doctors did not expect Erickson to live, and I felt a kinship since doctors didn't expect me to live from my car accident when I was 18. I've also discovered the Guillain-Barre Syndrome I had when I was three was potentially fatal. Erickson overcame the crippling nature of the pain from his polio, though, by minimizing it through the use of his mind. He experimented with and practiced certain mental skills to the extent that he taught himself hypnosis.

He was willing to take risks and was characterized by a sense of adventure in grappling with problems. While his parents thought a companion was making the journey in a canoe with him, the friend canceled, and Erickson took the trip by himself from a lake by the University of Wisconsin, proceeded to the Mississippi River and continued south beyond St. Louis and returned home by the same route. In addition to strengthening his mental stamina, his physical health was much better, so much that he undertook college and medical school. He had learned a lot from his polio and years later remarked, "I have an advantage over others–I have polio."

To affect change in his patients, and frequently with anyone he encountered in everyday life, Erickson told stories and used analogies. By using this indirect approach, he facilitated immediate learning at the person's unconscious level. The first anecdote I heard was told by Jeff during that workshop. When he was a supervisee of Erickson's, Jeff was called by a defense attorney as an expert witness regarding the question of whether hypnosis had been applied properly in a murder case. As luck would have it for Jeff, Dr. Erickson was asked to testify by the prosecuting attorney. Since Jeff was nervous about going to court, Erickson told him the following story, prefacing it with the injunction, "Know the opposing attorney."

"Erickson said he was asked to testify in a child custody case on the behalf of a husband, agreeing to do so because the wife was potentially abusive. He sensed the wife's attorney was shrewd and thorough, and she proved that to be true by her challenging questions. She opened,'Dr. Erickson you say you're an expert in psychiatry. Who is your authority?' to which he replied, 'I'm my own authority', thereby defusing the power of her own list of experts.

The lawyer continued, 'Dr. Erickson, you say you are an expert in psychiatry. What is psychiatry?' Erickson responded 'I can give you this example. Anyone who is an expert in American History should know about Simon Girty, also called 'Dirty Girty'. Anyone who is not an expert on American History would not know about Simon Girty, also called 'Dirty Girty'. Any expert on American History should know about Simon Girty, also called 'Dirty Girty'.

When Erickson looked up, the judge's head was buried in his hands. The clerk of court was under the table looking for his pencil. The husband's lawyer was stifling his laughter.

Subsequent to his apparently benign answer, the lawyer put her papers aside, saying 'No further questions Dr. Erickson.' Erickson looked at Jeff and said, 'And the lawyer's name was… Gertie.' "

Jeff enjoyed the amusing anecdote, and more importantly, gained confidence. He would not have experienced much benefit if Erickson had simply advised "Don't be intimidated," as our unconscious mind often resists advice. We all like a humorous story, though, and hunger to learn from its messages.

From 1989 until 1994, I learned as much as I could about Ericksonian Therapy and Hypnosis. When I landed the job at the Cluckland Center, I was eager to practice my skills, and knowing my orientation was unfamiliar to much of the mental health profession, I decided to give a presentation to the staff. I was particularly concerned the doctoral level psychologist, Peg Strickland, Ed.D., who supervised me, was not receptive to my therapeutic approaches. Although she was a fledgling, and had gotten licensed about 10 years after I had gotten my license, she was exceedingly bossy with me. I had recently been certified in hypnosis and received training in Milwaukee in Solution- Focused Therapy, an offshoot from Ericksonian approaches, and she did not have training in these areas. I wanted my supervisor to learn about the therapy I was practicing, and my presentation would be my way of teaching her.

So about a month after beginning the job I gave my two-hour luncheon presentation entitled "Bits of Ericksonian Therapy," and to further introduce you to Erickson's' work, I'll give you the presentation. While a few of the stories are from my therapy work with clients, some are from the works of my favorite Ericksonian authors. They include: Stephen Gilligan, David Gordon and Mary Meyers-Anderson, Sidney Rosen, Paul Watzlawick, and Jeff Zeig. The self-hypnosis technique I call "See-Hear-Touch 54321," the story called "A Million Dollars," and "An Extramarital Ordeal," are therapy cases I conducted based on research done by Yvonne Dolan, Michael Yapko, and Jay Haley respectively.

Unlike psychotherapies that search for the causes of psycho- pathology, Erickson believed people had unconscious resources and strengths that, if elicited effectively, would solve the presenting problem(s). In that regard, he once wrote, "Each person is a unique individual. Hence, psychotherapy should be formulated to meet the uniqueness of the individual's needs, rather than tailoring the person to fit the Procrustean bed of a hypothetical theory of human behavior." He had faith in the unconscious as the source for answers if it was stimulated with stories, metaphors, and hypnosis. This first story I related was one Erickson originally told to a group of mental health professionals when telling them how to do psychotherapy.

"I was returning from high school one day and a runaway horse with a bridle on sped past a group of us into a farmer's yard…looking for a drink of water. The horse was perspiring heavily. And the farmer didn't recognize it, so we cornered it. I hopped on the horse's back… since it had a bridle on, I took hold of the reins and said, 'Giddy-up'…headed for the highway. I knew the horse would turn in the right direction…I didn't know what the right direction was. And the horse trotted and galloped along. Now and then he would forget he was on the highway and start into a field. So I would pull on him a bit and call his attention to the fact that the highway was where he was supposed to be. And finally about four miles from where I had boarded him he turned into a farm yard and the farmer said, 'So that's how that critter came back. Where did you find him?'

I said, 'About four miles from here.'

'How did you know he should come here?'

I said, 'I didn't know...the horse knew. All I did was keep him on the road.' ...And I think that's the way you do psychotherapy."

A graceful, even aesthetic feature I've liked about Erickson's therapy was his orientation of acceptance and utilization. That is, he accepted not only the obvious strengths and assets of patients but also their symptoms, delusions, and rigid behaviors. He even accepted their resistance! In addition to this acceptance, he creatively utilized whatever was expressed to the patient's advantage. I related the following story I called "The Carpenter" to convey this orientation:

"When working in a state hospital, Erickson discovered a patient who frequently expressed the delusion that he was Jesus Christ. That patient had not been doing anything constructive with his time. Instead of discounting the patient's reality, Erickson told the patient he understood he had experience as a carpenter. Since the patient knew Jesus helped his father, Joseph, who was a carpenter, the patient admitted he had. Erickson said he was aware the patient wanted to help others, and again, the patient agreed this was true. Certainly Jesus wanted to help others. Next, Erickson said the hospital needed help building some bookcases and would he offer to help. The patient agreed and participated in constructive behavior as a very pleasant carpenter. A snowball effect then occurred whereby the patient engaged in more socially appropriate behaviors and eventually was released from the hospital."

As my audience, consisting mostly of psychotherapists, had always thought the best way to treat delusions was with antipsychotic medication, Erickson's technique of putting the patient to work as a carpenter, consistent with his "delusion" of being Christ, was not only humorous but remarkable; it worked!

My next example of acceptance and utilization was a therapeutic intervention I employed two years earlier with an intoxicated man brought to the mental health center by his sister. Both were in their early 50s. I entitled the anecdote "Gatorade and Honey."

I asked a substance abuse counselor to join me and the alcoholic in my office to help with the intake assessment. As I began to ask the man basic questions, he frequently repeated that people were driving up and down the street in front of his sister's house planning to kill him. His sister disconfirmed his paranoia, but he was insistent "they" were out to get him. His fear prevented him from concentrating on the interview questions. The man did not pay attention to the counselor who advised he not touch another drop of alcohol and to drink Gatorade and honey to prevent a worsening of dts; they were in the beginning stage. After about a half hour of making minimal progress with the interview, I made eye contact with him and gravely stated, "You know people are driving up and down your street and are planning to get you, and now I know it. And you know and I know the best thing you can do is build up your defenses because you need to stop these people. Your life depends on it. And you can build up your defenses by not touching another drop of alcohol and drinking Gatorade and honey. You had better save your life." He'd finally become quiet and transfixed. He felt I had taken him seriously; I had joined him. When he returned to the Center the next day for the substance abuse outpatient treatment program, he was nearly sober. He participated in therapy activities and never mentioned another word about anyone planning to kill him. After a few days of outpatient treatment, he was detoxed enough to become involved in further counseling.

My audience's attention continued to pique, and I followed with a case of Erickson's that I called "Love at First Squirt," a case that originally appeared in Time magazine ("Svengali in Arizona," October 22, 1973). Again, notice the acceptance of the patient's limitation and the creative utilization of it.

"A woman came to psychotherapy as a last ditch effort. She was depressed, and planned to commit suicide because she felt a small gap in her front tooth disfigured her. She thought she was too ugly to attract a man, and would never marry and have children; as a consequence life was meaningless. Observing her unkempt appearance, Erickson told her to buy some outfits, to go to a beauty shop for a new hairstyle and to learn more about make-up and hygiene. He also told her to practice squirting water through the gap in her teeth while she was in the shower until she was accurate from a distance of seven to eight feet.

During their long interview, Erickson had the impression from a few questions that a young man at work was attracted to her. Each time she'd go to the water fountain, he was there, but since she didn't appreciate his attraction, she'd immediately return to her desk. After several sessions, Erickson got her to agree to dress up in her nicest clothes and fix her hair and make-up before work. When the man appeared at the water fountain, she was to get a mouth full of water and squirt it at him through the gap in her teeth. She was directed to take one step toward him, then turn around and run like hell.

While the woman was initially reluctant to comply with his strange request, Erickson told her since she didn't seem to have any good memories, and as long as she was planning to die, she should die with at least one good memory. Consequently, she followed through and was surprised the young man ran after her, caught her, spun her around and kissed her. The next day he met her at the fountain with a water pistol, she responded with a squirt and some flirtation and dating followed. She came out of the depression, related more to others and eventually married."

Most of the staff were hearing about this unorthodox therapy for the first time, and I could see the intrigue in most of their expressions. Dr. Strickland had walked out awhile earlier, and her departure signaled to me that I was doing well. I felt certain she attended, hoping she would see me flop, as she had previously criticized my therapy style. So I continued with a well known case of Erickson's called the "African Violet Queen."

"Erickson was asked by a physician colleague to visit his severely depressed mother during Erickson's upcoming trip to Milwaukee. She lived alone and isolated herself in her home. The physician feared his mother might commit suicide.

Erickson visited the woman in her home and asked her to give him a tour. He noticed some beautiful African violets, plants that require meticulous care. He also learned the woman ventured out of her home once a week to attend church, something to which she showed commitment.

Applying acceptance and utilization, Erickson got the woman to agree to grow more African violets and to stay up-to-date with important events, such as births, illnesses, marriages, and deaths of the church members. She was to give a plant to members for each event, and after doing so, she was invited to more social events. She soon came out of her depression and continued to send her gifts and became well-liked.

When she died many years later, a Milwaukee newspaper headline read 'African Violet Queen of Milwaukee dies, thousands mourn!'"

A primary culprit of psychological dysfunction, according to Erickson, was rigidity. People create their own misery by often doing the same thing repeatedly despite the attempted solution's utter failure in achieving its goal. Many believe if they try harder at doing the same thing, over and over, they'll eventually succeed; rarely they do.

This brief anecdote called "The Lost Key" I presented next crystallized the absurdity of rigidity:

"A drunk was standing under a streetlight searching intently. A policeman observed him and asked what he was looking for to which the man replied, 'My key.' The policeman joined the man and began looking for them. Eventually after no success, the policeman asked if he was sure he lost his key 'here?', and the man responded, 'No, not here, over there—but there it is much too dark.'"

To facilitate flexibility, the healthy antidote to rigidity, Erickson would shock, surprise, and confuse the patients. By doing so, he'd help them experience new perspectives, on both a cognitive and emotional level, in the immediacy of the therapy office. I told this anecdote exemplifying flexibility that I used with a client.

"I worked with a 40-year old woman who complained she could not get her husband to openly communicate his feelings to her. She'd been frustrated about this problem for many years and had tried hard to get him to talk more about their children, money issues, and their relationship. After listening to her complaints regarding his inadequate communication during numerous therapy sessions, I interrupted her one day by requesting she give me a million dollars. Nonplussed that her psychologist would say something so obviously inappropriate, she appeared dumbfounded before saying,'I don't have a million dollars.'

' That doesn't matter. I want you to give me a million dollars.' She more quickly repeated,'I don't have a million dollars.'

'I know. I know. But I want you to give me a million dollars.' I insisted.

With slight irritation she continued,' ' I don't have a million dollars!' Matching her irritation I maintained,' Give me the million dollars!'

Obviously disconcerted, partly because this seemed like a waste of her valuable therapy time (and money), she retorted, 'I don't have a million dollars!'

'Give me a million dollars.'

'I don't …Do you mean I'm asking my husband to give me something he just doesn't have?'

I gave a slight nod, watched her begin sobbing and after about 30 seconds of quiet said, 'You've done well to realize this. And you can take this experience with you.'" The woman wept for several minutes. In a matter of weeks she told her husband she wanted a divorce.

I ended the story by rhetorically asking the audience how many people they knew who expected something from another person that the other person just did not have to give them. It could be sex, money, sharing feelings, understanding, fairness, clear communication, generosity or any of dozens of other things the other person simply may not have to give. Frequently that possibility never dawns on people, and as they demand to have what they can't get, they become extremely frustrated. Erickson spoke to this when he said, "Into each life some confusion should come… also some enlightenment." He occasionally would shock or confuse people to get messages to sink in. My audience of psychotherapists was shocked and confused when I next announced I used acceptance and utilization of suicidal ideation with a 34-year old client, Lisa.

"She initially came to therapy reporting she felt moderately to severely depressed and that her difficulties stemmed from a childhood history of sexual abuse by her stepfather. As she was of above average intelligence, I thought a cognitive therapy approach might be effective, but after several sessions I obviously was getting nowhere with it. She insisted suicide was her only option despite my assertions that she might feel better if she considered alternative views of herself and her future. After hearing her repeated statement, "I just need to commit suicide," I eventually countered, "I agree. Suicide is something you should consider."

She was shocked and appeared anxious as she made eye contact. I continued, "I don't want to take the idea of suicide away from you, but I do want to give you something. I want to give you patience. Now when you consider eternity and how short your life is in the context of eternity, you can see that your life is like a tiny grain of sand on a huge beach. Maybe smaller. Since our life is so short, certainly you can wait until you're 85 or a little older before you commit suicide. In the context of eternity, that's really only a little patience; I do want to give that to you."

She never brought up the idea of suicide again, and though we continued to work in therapy for a few months, she did not attain the satisfaction that she had originally hoped for. However, when she decided to discontinue therapy with me, I asked her what benefits she had gained and she named two or three. Later that evening I received a message from her on my answering machine that she had thought of one more benefit: "You kept me alive."

The next therapy case I presented was one I was attempting to publish that I entitled "An Extramarital Ordeal." It was based on Erickson's approach he called a "benevolent ordeal" whereby he'd elicit a commitment from a client who wanting to overcome a problem, or eliminate a symptom, to engage in a specific behavioral process (the ordeal) that would be more discomforting than giving up the symptom. As a consequence, the client would overcome the problem instead of having to experience the ordeal.

"My client, Johnny, a 56-year old administrator of a national organization, had been married for 38 years when he sought treatment for his 'addiction' to extramarital sex. Although he did this about once a month and had been for the duration of his marriage, he reported feeling guilty because it hurt his wife. He'd seen two other therapists but to no avail–not a good prognostic sign. I wondered about his motivation and what he really wanted.

Johnny described a typical situation in which he'd pick up women. As he frequently made business trips, he'd usually go to bars where he and his friends would talk with prospective women. When Johnny would go to the restroom, his friends would tell the woman to whom Johnny had been speaking that his wife had recently died and to further induce her sympathy, would add that Johnny was very lonely. Upon his return, Johnny would engage in more small talk before disclosing his 'painful crisis.' Then he'd escort her to his quarters. Johnny smiled as he described his methods and admitted enjoying the control and manipulation these situations afforded.

I asked him if, in addition to relinquishing his extramarital escapades, he'd like to be more honest with women. Well, yes, of course he'd like to be more honest. I got his agreement that we could work on both goals.

I asked what advantages he hoped to gain by resolving his problem. After 38 years of extramarital sex why quit now? He said he'd be more certain his wife would remain married to him, would have less fear of getting AIDS, would rebuild a better reputation, and would have more energy to perform his job.

He required a little more effort and time to admit the only disadvantage–giving up his conquests–was a highly rewarding experience for him.

I informed Johnny I'd help him resolve his problem if he'd agree to do something I asked him to do that would be good for him. He asked me to tell him first what exactly he'd be expected to do, but I told him he first had to agree by verbal contract to do what he would be requested to do. I guaranteed it would be helpful to him. He asked if I was going to insist he be castrated, and I replied that would probably be unethical. After more deliberation, he eventually agreed to make a commitment to follow the directive, but since the session was nearing the end, he was told to think about it more between sessions. If he decided to follow my instructions, he was told to return the next week. If he did not decide to follow them, there would be no need to return. Johnny appeared a bit irritated when he left but said he would keep the next therapy appointment. The purpose of with- holding the delivery and having him think more about the agreement between sessions was to enhance motivation and to develop more power for the ordeal.

Upon arriving for the next session, Johnny immediately asked to hear the task and agreed to comply with it. I asked him how long it usually took before realizing a woman to whom he was talking was a potential conquest; he confidently responded, 'about five minutes.' He was smooth and proud of it. Since Johnny was receptive, I told him what to do. After speaking to a prospective woman for five minutes, he was told to recite the following litany aloud to the woman: 1)'I really don't want to have sex with you because my wife might leave me.' 2) 'I really don't want to have sex with you because I'm afraid I might get AIDS.' 3) 'I don't want to have sex with you because I'm concerned about my reputation.' 4) 'I don't want to have sex with you because I don't want to be fatigued on my job.' This litany was based on the reasons he had given for wanting to get over the problem and his admission that he wanted to be more honest with women.

Johnny was in a triple positive bind. One, if he refused to put himself in tempting situations, the problem would be resolved. Two, if he completed the ordeal and if, by some slight chance, a woman still had sex with him, I'd compliment him for improving his honesty which was one of his goals. Third, if he reneged on his agreement and continued his habit without completing the litany, I'd inform him that therapy is sometimes 'an assessment procedure for motivation' and that he was not motivated enough for change. He'd be encouraged to return to therapy when he was sufficiently motivated. We had created a no-lose situation.

During the next two therapy sessions he reported he had refrained from pursuing extramarital sex and, actually, had no desire to do so. He stated that reciting the litany was too much to go through. We talked about positive activities he was planning on his own and with his wife, and I communicated respect to him. Soon after those two sessions he said he had abstained longer than he ever had since he was married.

At a six-month follow-up, he continued to abstain, and reported his marriage was slightly more satisfactory but said he was very satisfied he'd overcome his compulsion of 38 years. Johnny said he could not explain how he was able to overcome his problem. His inability to do so was fine with me; insight never was a goal and probably contributed to the failure of his previous therapies.

The next story is one of my favorites and is an example of reframing, a strategy I described in my sixth night's note. You might recall that reframing gives new meaning to a problem by a valid and favorable description—from the client's point of view. The story is called "Cinnamon Face" and appeared in a book, My Voice Will Go With You, The Teaching Tales of Milton H. Erickson, by Sid Rosen. My audience continued to be attuned.

"A woman brought her eight-year old daughter to Erickson, reporting, 'She hates her sister; she hates me; she hates her father; she hates her teacher, her schoolmates; hates the milkman, the man in the gas station—she just plain hates everybody. She hates herself. I've tried for a long time to get her to go to Kansas for the summer to visit her grandparents. She hates them but she doesn't know them.'

When Erickson asked the reason for the hate, the woman responded, 'A mass of freckles on her face. The kids in school call her Freckles and she hates those freckles.'

Although the girl was in the car and didn't want to come in, Erickson told the mother to bring her in even if she had to use force. The girl walked on her own to the doorway, with fists clenched, jaw jutting out and scowled at Erickson sitting at his desk. She was ready for a fight.

As she stood in the doorway, he looked at her and proclaimed, 'You're a thief! You steal!'

She said she was not a thief and did not steal, knowing those accusations to be untrue.

Erickson countered, 'Oh yes, you're a thief. You steal things. I even know what you stole. I even have proof that you stole.'

Her anger mounting, she contradicted, 'You haven't got proof. I never stole nothin.'

'I even know where you were when you stoled what you stole.' The girl had gotten so angry she just stared, without saying a word.

Erickson continued, 'I'll tell you where you were and what you stole. You were in the kitchen, setting the kitchen table. You were standing at the kitchen table. You were reaching up to the cookie jar, containing cinnamon cookies, cinnamon buns, cinnamon rolls—you knocked it over and spilled some cinnamon on your face—you're a Cinnamon Face.'"

She smiled. When Erickson accused her of things that were untrue, a vacuum was created in her mind along with her increased anger. Upon hearing his explanation about the cinnamon items and her freckles described as "Cinnamon Face," she felt relieved and appreciated the fun situation and his joke.

A few years later a card was found printed in three shades of purple, the only color Erickson, who was color blind, could see. It read:

'Dear Mr. Erickson,

I was thinking about you today. I was reading those crazy letters you wrote me. How have you been doing? I will try to remember to send you a Valentine. This year I am in the sixth grade. You probably don't remember me that well but if you see my nickname you will. TURN OVER
    My name is B_____H_____(Ciniman Face). Well, I got to by now.
By
Cinnimon Face

With the note was a colored photograph of a lovely little girl with reddish-brown hair and her face covered with freckles. She was smiling."

Now, when I tell that story, I get a little choked up. Maybe it's because we eighth graders teased a sixth grader about his freckles at Milton Hershey School. Maybe it's the compassion the girl showed for Erickson by printing purple and sending the picture of her smiling face. Maybe the case reminds me of how people seen as hateful can suddenly become loving when tender feelings are touched in a particular way. Or maybe it's something else. I continued my presentation by introducing a paradoxical approach sometimes used by Erickson called symptom prescription. Frequently people complain of symptoms in the form of thoughts, feelings, behaviors, and sensations as if the symptoms have control over them. In using symptom prescription, the therapist tells the client to intentionally bring about the symptom at a certain frequency or for a specific duration, thereby giving him a sense of control over the symptom. The approach also helps the client to accept the symptom, an attitude that defuses the symptom's power. I described the following case of symptom prescription to my audience: "For clients who worry so much that it becomes more of a problem than that about which they are worrying, I sometimes prescribe 'worry sessions.' They consist of 30 to 45 minute periods, once a day, when the client is directed to worry as much as possible about the critical issues in her life. A woman in her late 20s saw me at a mental health center for panic attacks, and her most frequent symptom included incessant worrying— about her children, her own health, taking trips, her job, her husband, and other asundry issues. I instructed her to intentionally worry each night for 30 minutes and to write her worries in a notebook. As a rationale is necessary for giving such assignments, I told her the worries had taken control of her long enough and by writing them on paper, she'd be taking control of them.

During the next several weeks she brought in piles of paper containing her various worries, informing me she wrote them for 30 minutes nightly as assigned. I told her I'd keep them for her in my office, thereby 'unburdening' her of the worries. As a result of her newfound sense of control, she soon became progressively calmer and seemed more self-confident. After about six weeks, she said she felt she could discontinue therapy since she hadn't had any panic attacks. She added that she had gotten very tired of worrying so much."

Another paradoxical strategy story I presented to the audience was called "Purposeful Pooping." This was a case I treated.

"Anthony was a good looking, intelligent, seven-year old boy brought to me for treatment by his mother for encopresis that occurred on nearly a daily basis but only at school. Anthony agreed it would be a miracle if I could help him stop having 'dukeys' in his pants. After two sessions of interviewing him and his mother and using a children's story book in an attempt to gain his cooperation, he told me I was asking 'stupid questions' and began making silly statements about the story book pictures. Apparently he didn't feel I was joining him.

At the beginning of the third session I asked his mother to leave the office so that I could work alone with Anthony. As she was leaving the office, Anthony went to the corner and sat facing it, with his back toward me. Although mother began to correct him, I told her I'd handle it, and it was best for her to leave. After she did so, I went to the corner opposite Anthony and sat in a chair with my back toward him; I was mirroring him. By mirroring his behavior instead of correcting him, I was accepting it. By accepting his resistance, I joined him. He noticed me sitting in the corner by turning his head slightly and using his peripheral vision and then ran to the middle of the room, falling on the floor and somersaulting. When I joined him by doing the same things, he appeared shocked and stared at me having fun on the floor. I had his attention! Then, just as I had cooperated with him, he cooperated with me when I directed him to sit at a table where I wanted to talk with him about his dukeys.

Using his oppositional style, I told him he should not stop having dukeys in his pants at school. I told him it was important for him to keep track of the days he did and did not have them by recording marks on a piece of paper. He drew a bar that would indicate days he had a dukey and a snowflake for the days when he did not have one. I explained to his mother that she, the teacher, and the school counselor should compliment Anthony for recording the marks, regardless of whether he had a dukey. She was directed to not make any comment, neither compliment nor criticism, regarding the encopretic behavior. The school counselor and teacher were contacted and agreed to follow the procedure despite the teacher's reservations.

Three weeks later, the mother reported Anthony had not had any accidents in nearly two weeks. She said he seemed happier, and she felt more relaxed. When I talked alone with Anthony I assumed a position of mild disappointment, reminding him he'd not been told to stop having dukeys. He appeared a bit confused and replied forebodingly, 'Oohhh, Mommy is going to be mad at you!' I insisted we continue with our original plan and directed him to schedule having a dukey on a specific day and at a specific time, suggesting '1 o'clock on Thursday,' although he refused to agree to it. He was still, fortunately, oppositional.

Two weeks later, mother reported the encopresis had stopped, and Anthony asserted he was finished recording and having accidents. Mother reported he was '…a good boy. He smiles more now and plays.' He appeared considerably calmer than he had during the first few sessions and played quietly with blocks on the floor for the duration of the 45 minute session. Mother also related the teacher and school counselor told her he was paying better attention, getting better grades and using the bathroom appropriately.

A six-month telephone follow-up with the mother indicated Anthony continued to be happier and was not having accidents. I thought to myself, 'He is a good boy if the adults in charge will just use his oppositional style. It's his way of maintaining control. Of course when opposition is accepted it becomes cooperation."

While the presentation was becoming longer than most, and while the digestions of lunch would seem to be causing fatigue, the audience remained remarkably awake and absorbed.

My final case included hypnosis, and I introduced it by quoting Erickson's definition: "Hypnosis is a vital relationship in one person stimulated by the warmth of another." I explained Erickson viewed hypnosis as a cooperative interaction between the client and therapist, a view that differed from the authoritarian approach in which the therapist directs "You will do this" or "You will do that." Erickson's cooperative approach accepted whatever reactions and responses the person showed during hypnosis and utilized them. I entitled the case "Using Her Senses and Practicing 'PRACTICE,'" and was attempting to publish it in the Erickson Monographs.

Look, I've Hypnotized Santa!

"Deborah was a 35-year old, married mother of two who arrived for her first therapy session in an anxious, agitated state. She detailed how her demanding civil service job was exacerbating her feelings of anxiety and depression that had been ameliorated by Prozac and long-term therapy the previous year. She also wept, disclosing her anger toward her supervisors who expected her to perform tasks for which she had not been trained. It seems anxiety is frequently a polite way of expressing anger.

As I didn't presume how much of her history the client needed to divulge for me to help her reach her goals, as some therapies tend to do, I requested, ' Tell me as much about childhood and adolescent events that you think I need to know to be helpful to you. If you later think I need to know more details about the past, you can tell me then.'

She'd been raised by both parents who divorced when she was in college, had two brothers and one sister, made no mention of physical or sexual abuse but reported being teased frequently in the 5th or 6th grade, and she made few friends during that period. She eventually retaliated physically when a girl bullied her in school and reported her teachers took no action against her because they knew she had defended herself.

She reported that on a 10-point scale, with 10 being the most anxiety and 1 being the least, hers was usually at a 10 while she was at work. As she'd heard that I did hypnosis, she requested it, hoping it would help her most efficiently. She was clear that she did not wish to have long-term therapy again.

I taught her an Ericksonian self-hypnosis technique that I call 'See-Hear-touch 54321.' In explaining the purpose of it, I told her that since her anxiety-provoking thoughts and feelings were internal, the solution was to focus on external stimuli; she could do so using her visual, auditory, and kinesthetic senses. I instructed: 'You can get outside of yourself by connecting to the world around you with your senses. First, sit still with your feet on the floor and your hands in your lap. Look at a spot on the floor and using your frontal and peripheral vision, say five things that you see, then five things that you hear, then five things you can touch or feel with your skin, then say, either aloud or to yourself, four things you see, four things you hear, and four things you feel. I continued by specifying that she say three, then two, then one stimulus for each of those senses and that when she finished, she could just sit effortlessly and experience the peace, comfort, tranquility and calmness. Next, I demonstrated the entire process and said she could learn it by watching and hearing me do it. I ended by saying, 'Now I can experience the peace and comfort of connecting to the world with my senses in a sensible way...and any time I want to use my senses sensibly I can have the sense to do so...and it doesn't cost a cent. For now I can just continue to experience the comfort and relaxation.' She reported she felt more relaxed observing my demonstration and said she'd practice when she felt too anxious.

As an aside, I frequently teach this simple, self-hypnosis technique and nearly every client who practices it reports a relaxation benefit. One woman reported it was much simpler than the biofeedback she'd learned at a biofeedback center, and though I'd defended biofeedback in a commentary in the American Psychologist, Sept., 1986, I mused at the client's assertion. Despite the money, equipment, and academic training invested in biofeedback, she favored the simple and natural experience of using her senses to focus her awareness. Henry David Thoreau alluded to this simple experience of utilizing the senses in Walden when he wrote, "Yet I experience sometimes that the most sweet and tender, the most innocent and encouraging society may be found in any natural object... There can be no very black melancholy to him who lives in the midst of nature and has his senses still."

During her second therapy session, Deborah reported having used self-hypnosis at work and kept her anxiety to no more than a three on a 10-point scale most days, although one day she needed to practice it four times in succession to experience sufficient relaxation. Obviously she was motivated! Further discussion revealed Deborah frequently criticized herself and catastrophized situations. Her cognitive distortions were addressed in an hypnotic process that I had recently developed called PRACTICE which was conducted with her and taped during that session.

I usually describe PRACTICE as a stress management exercise that can foster confidence, relaxation, and overall self-esteem. It is an acronym with P symbolizing Pacing, the R standing for Relaxation, the A representing Assertiveness, the C meaning Confidence, the T standing for Thinking Rationally, the I symbolizing Imagery, the C representing Comic Relief, and the E standing for Empathy. It begins with an induction to focus attention, initiate relaxation, and orient the person to suggestions. The subject is directed to sit in a chair with her or his hands in their lap and both feet on the floor. Specific suggestions within the hypnotic process were tailored to fit Deborah's problems and life and PRACTICE was taped for her. She reported feeling inspired, relaxed, and peaceful after experiencing the hypnosis in the office and agreed to listen to the tape before the next session as many times as she needed to do so.

When she arrived for her third session, Deborah appeared significantly calmer and more relaxed than she presented in the first two sessions.

She reported having practiced "See-Hear-Touch 54321" self-hypnosis most days and listened to her hypnosis tape on two occasions. Another session of PRACTICE was conducted, and she said she felt satisfied and did not feel another appointment was necessary.

A therapy follow-up questionnaire was sent to her six months later, and she returned it indicating she was 'completely improved' and 'satisfied.'"

The presentation was over, and there was a feeling of satisfaction through the room. The audience completed feedback forms about the quality of the presentation and rated it "very interesting, informative, entertaining, enjoyable, and helpful." They made other favorable comments, my favorite being from Kevin, one of the psychotherapists. He wrote, " This was a well designed program that could be compiled into a book or literary device...I believe, with a small amount of adaptation, this could be presented in more of a dialogue format which would allow for the development of the topic into more personally applicable material. Thanks for the presentation, Hank!"

As Kevin wrote about personal applicability, I'm wondering which of the stories you might creatively relate to your life. How might you accept and utilize one of your faults, problems, or weaknesses? I continued to find the practical wisdom in Erickson's quote: "Happiness is the endowment with value of all the things you have." Some days it is the pearl that prompts me to get out of the bed. Of course some of "the things" we have require a little imagination to endow them with value, but recall Erickson's witty reframe, endowing even his polio with value: "I have an advantage over others. I have polio." Without his polio he probably would never have become "the master" of medical hypnosis.

Maybe we can explore and discover the value of our own "polios." Perhaps suicidal thoughts have value. They are signals that something in one's life does need to die; it's not the person who needs to die. What needs to die is often the clinging to some kind of loss or a craving for what is demanded. What also often needs to die is an intolerance of pain, including the "I can't stand it" attitude. And with those deaths, new perspectives of acceptance, peace, and tolerance can be born. Yes, suicidal thoughts can be a good thing and not a bad thing. Suicidal thoughts are gifts.

If suicidal thoughts are considered to be gifts to be appreciated, does that mean that our species could eliminate suicide as a problem?

CHAPTER 8

"Endurance Athletics: A Mind — Body Friendship

"Every man is the builder of a temple called his body ... We are all sculptors and painters, and our material is our own flesh and blood and bones."

HENRY DAVID THOREAU

THE URGE TO DIE HAS weakened even more, so much that you could describe it as lifeless. In a sense, I feel a victory, as though establishing a will to live is an achievement. Perhaps I can call my victory "the death of suicide."

I pick up a photo album and take out a picture of myself as a two year-old. I'm standing in that living room, the paragon of innocence, eyes and mouth gaping at nothing in particular, and then that two year-old in the picture speaks to me as an adult; I'm my own father. "Why did you think about killing me? Please don't kill me Daddy. I don't want to die."

"I am very sorry. I was mixed up. I will never hurt you and will always protect you. And I will always love you."

I am aware that child is still within me and is the part of me that is sensitive and innocent, wonders about the world, exudes purity and goodness and requires love.

While I've described a number of lifesaving strategies on preceding nights, this note would be incomplete without documentation of how exercise has saved and shaped my life. It has been most valuable as an effective antidepressant. If self-help books have been parents to me, swimming and running have been my siblings; our relationship has been rocky but indispensable. For what it may be worth, I will pass my relationship on to you.

The first big goal I set for myself came about in the Fall of 1980 when I faced the pressure of my first semester in graduate school in Boone, N.C. To better deal with the stress, I increased my running mileage to eight miles a day. Dr. Jack Deni, one of the psychology professors, told me that by running 50 miles a week for three months I could finish a marathon. Completing a marathon sounded about right for my athlete's ego, and the goal was set.

The aesthetic component of experiencing nature has always been one of the most potent rewards of running to me, and the Appalachian Mountains where my graduate school, ASU, was nestled, generously provided nature's sensory gifts. An invigorating autumn breeze caressing my skin stimulated my running pace; the orange-yellow blanket of trees covering the mountains was pure visual energy; refreshing scents of the Fall rested along each path and sounds from excited student laughter to the bubbling cascade of a mountain stream were musical notes giving me rhythm. A brisk run was a transcendental honor in a beautiful world of perpetual change. How could I not be happy and at peace during those romps?

I sometimes reflected back to the mid-seventies when a book by the psychotherapist William Glasser, M.D., was published titled Positive Addiction. Glasser's premise was that we all must take responsibility for our lives regardless of what our past might have been. In that book he advocated two specific activities that were both psychologically and physiologically addictive: meditation and running. Both were positively addictive in that their regular practice resulted in healthier states of mind and body that would remain so only if the practice were maintained. The more you practiced the more you wanted to. Glasser asserted we are responsible for practicing regularly, and his perspective certainly made sense to me. I'd practiced meditation enough to be addicted and was inspired that I was doing the same with running.

The Charlotte Observer Marathon was held in early January, giving me just enough time to complete three months of 50-mile weeks. In my state of blissful ignorance I continued to enjoy the aesthetics, the healthy feeling of staying trim and toning the muscles and the mounting confidence that I would conquer a 26-mile marathon. After all, Jack Deni was an accomplished Boston Marathoner. If he said 50 mile weeks, what else was there to know?

Plenty. Sophomore means a "wise fool" in its Greek origin, and I was probably more the latter half of the oxymoron than the former. Along with the handicapped division and age group divisions, I think marathon organizers should have a sophomore division for those who really don't know what they're doing.

Instead of running eight miles every day, which technically should have bored me and likely did cause undue stress to my muscles, I would've done much better to have followed a program of alternating easy-hard days. My eight miles was by far enough to be considered a hard day, and the alternate days could've consisted of two to three miles. The days for improvement are "the long runs" and speed work days which most runners do on alternate Sundays. Hearing something about the long run, I completed a 16-miler a few weeks prior to the race, certain I could complete the other 10 without much problems on race day. The longest run prior to a first marathon should be between 20 and 26 miles, the closer to 26 the better. Of course they are to be run very slow, hence the term LSD for long, slow distance. Following the intense long runs and speed work days, it is essential to have a rest day which means just that—no running. Completely unaware of these basic fundamentals, I was quite happy and proud with my daily accomplishments.

Suddenly Marathon weekend arrived. In celebration of my accomplishment prior to its occurrence, I drank beer until about midnight at the Sheraton Lounge the night before race day. Hey, I ran my 50 mile weeks—a little pre-race partying couldn't do any harm. So I told myself as I laid my tipsy head down to sleep on my friend, Leon's, couch in a small living room cluttered with everything from broken chairs to stacks of ancient newspapers. Awakening a couple hours early, I remained in my curvilinear position on that sagging sofa of must, gazing at the silhouettes of junk in the pre-dawn dark, wondering about the sleeping conditions of other aspiring marathoners. They were all probably sleeping restfully in comfortable beds with lovers who would show them undying support during the race and throughout their running careers. C'est la vie–I had a marathon to run.

My excitement mounted as I accomplished a vertical position, not noticing any effects from the pre-race celebration of the previous night. Unaware of proper marathon attire, my innocence continued to unveil itself; I slipped into a pair of green cotton scrubs you see in a hospital ER. I reasoned they were lightweight and couldn't possibly be too hot in the 65° temperature. My pre-graduate school girlfriend, Susan, gave them to me, and I hoped the sentimental value would fuel me more. I was ready!

A sense of jubilance spread through my spirited body as I quickly began passing runner after runner during the first few miles. What's wrong with these people? Didn't they train for this thing? And why do they keep slowing down to drink at the water stations? I continued to be one happy first-timer until about mile 12. Why did this bear suddenly jump on my back? I guess I didn't run the 16-miler this fast. Why were my hospital greens rubbing on the insides of my thighs so much that they were getting sore? My bubbly smile soon became contrived as I waved to the cheering onlookers, yelling with good intentions "You're halfway there! Lookin' good!" Halfway? Did that mean I was three feet in the ground with three to go? Lookin' good? Maybe they mean that 110 lb. blonde passing me.

I did feel a sense of satisfaction upon passing the 16 mile marker; I had run the farthest distance in my life. But upon reaching the 17th mile marker, my body came to a standstill. If my life depended on it, I may have been able to drag my 180 pounds, which felt like lead, to the finish. No one was holding a gun to my head, though, and the fatigue and soreness were excessive. Succumbing to defeat by the marathon, I became a passenger in a van picking up other dropout victims, sophomores, all wearing our forlorn expressions. What had gone wrong?

Several things. I never ran the long, slow distance during training that is essential for a marathon. An LSD conditions the muscles to endure repeated pounding and stress and is best done by incrementally building over a period of months. If I had run the 16 miler two months prior to the race and increased the mileage by two every other Sunday, with speed-work on alternate Sundays, I would've completed a 24 miler before race day. That would've been sufficient.

It also helps to dress appropriately. Of course sophomore Hank was unaware the hospital scrubs would chafe his inner thighs into strawberries, but ignorance is a lame excuse. My only good excuse was that I was ignorant that I was ignorant. Next time I'd wear an item known by the running elite as running shorts and would rub a little Vaseline on the thighs. Strawberries are much better for dessert than they are for wreaking pain on the inner thighs.

Another elementary fact includes pacing. In my typical showboat fashion, (you see, when one doesn't get enough attention and affection as a child, theatrics sometime become a strategy in the adult years for satisfying those unmet needs) I delighted in passing people and smiling at the pretty girls during the first eight to ten miles. I was running at close to a three-hour pace while my goal was just to break four hours, a common goal for one's first marathon. Together with my neglect of LSDs in training and ignorance about proper attire, my breakneck celerity was a part of a prescription for how to fail at the marathon.

Failure is not something about which to be depressed, though, and I've learned to view it as an experience for providing information. When the information will help me accomplish a particular goal if I follow it, I consider that information as vital and the failures become even more valuable. Failure is just a learning experience. The physical discomfort and disappointment from my first marathon experience motivated me to learn from it, avoid the same mistakes in my next one and finish it with satisfaction.

Back to the drawing board. I was soon running courses in the celestial mountains, only now the heavenly spectacle was a blanket of snow replacing the colorful splendor of Fall. The winter wonderland transformed my runs from arduous training workouts into spiritual escapades in which my body seemed to float through the white beauty. A scenery of serenity was further enhanced by the silent solitude of an early Saturday morning, legs strengthening, moving me through the quiet streets lined with lodgings where sleepers rested from the previous night's activities. These poetic encounters reminded me that the primary value of running is neither achievement nor competition but rather the transcendental experience of seeing, hearing, and touching nature while blending one's being into it. All else is icing on the cake.

On one occasion, a fellow runner trailing me hustled enough to join me for another of running's many benefits–camaraderie. Taller, lankier, and younger than me, he had no trouble accepting my eight- mile course, and I enjoyed our light talk about various college-kid issues. As we chatted about our running goals and aspirations, my partner ventured further, inquiring as to whether I'd heard of "triaflons." (That's how I heard his pronunciation, not suspecting a speech impediment). The sport of "triaflon" involved events in which participants swam, cycled and ran certain distances, he informed. There was one in Hawaii consisting of a 2½ mile ocean swim, a 112 mile cycling component, and a 26 mile running marathon. Another in Wilmington, N.C., was shorter–a 1.2 mile swim, a 26 mile bike course and an eight mile run. I'll never forget that routine run that would serve as an introduction to one of my life's most rewarding athletic experiences.

My partner's information intrigued me. I could easily, with my background, swim one or two miles. Running eight miles was by now a breeze. And cycling was easy enough; I learned to do it as a child. My sophomoric internal dialoging was transferring from marathons to "triaflons." I decided to do the one in Wilmington one day, some- time after my marathon accomplishment. First things first.

First, it often helps to know the name of the sport into which one is wanting to enter as a competitor. As I talked excitedly about "triaflon" to people, I received a few smiles and a few confused looks. I soon learned it was called triathlon.

It was during my internship at the Western Correctional Center, tucked away in the foothills of Morganton, N.C., that I began my serious training for the next Charlotte Observer Marathon. I lived in an old brick dormitory on the grounds of a state mental hospital built in the 19th century, fashioned with gothic architecture. The bland sterility of my living quarters reinforced a stoic attitude which is a stable foundation for marathon training. Similar conditions in my work environment, a prison for juveniles, sewed up my external framework as wonderfully insipid. Although nature was less exquisite than it was in Boone, the sweet smell of kudzu growing beside a long, desolate road, one of my favorite running routes, still resides in my memory bank. Funny how such seemingly inconsequential stimuli can remain for a lifetime.

My conditions could be improved with a running partner, and I was fortunate enough to meet Bob Leonard who lived on my floor in the dorm and had a personal record (PR) in the marathon of 2:32, a superb time. He occasionally did his slow runs with me as I maintained my quickest pace, attempting to converse while becoming winded but inspired by his skill. On Sundays, Bob often road his bike about 30 miles to stretch the quads and hamstrings, and in so doing, modeled one of the components of triathlons to me.

Another model was Terrance Stanley Fox, introduced to me through a Rod Stewart song, "Never Give Up On A Dream." On the jacket sleeve of his album, "Tonight I'm Yours," Mr. Stewart printed the following eulogy that I had blown up and framed and will explain the reason I utilized him as a mentor:

Terrance Stanley Fox (July 28, 1958 - June 28, 1981)
"I just wish people would realize that anything is possible if you try... dreams are made if people try."

At the age of eighteen, while attending university in Vancouver, British Columbia, Canada, Terry Fox lost his right leg to cancer. While undergoing chemotherapy he became aware of the many cancer victims who had lost all hope. He was touched by what he saw and inspired by the story of a young man who had completed the Boston Marathon with an artificial leg. Terry decided then to run across Canada to raise money for cancer research.

On April 12, 1980, he set out from the east coast of Canada and on September 1, 1980, after having run 3,339 miles battling the often harsh elements, he was once again stricken with cancer. People world- wide responded to his appeal which became known as the Marathon of Hope. Terry was a statesman, a symbol of strength and courage. Although he did not complete the run, he ignited a universal flame of love through his example and ideals.

–Never Give Up On A Dream

When I ran my LSDs of 20 or more miles and experienced soreness, fatigue, and self-doubt, I thought of this hero and then felt the truth in my heart–my pain was paltry and there was no question I'd finish the marathon. I was thankful I had both legs and didn't have cancer. My handicaps were my own demons, internal creatures still hanging around from my early years. I could utilize them as motivation and defeating them would be a victory in itself. I became happy to have them.

The 1983 Charlotte Observer Marathon was in January and coincided with the beginning of my first job as a staff psychologist at John Umstead Hospital in Butner, N.C. Two achievements happening simultaneously was a nice change of pace in my life, and I did not sleep alone on the marathon weekend like I did for my first attempt. Renee, a pretty brunette, was introduced to me by a friend from grad school and invited me to stay with her in her trailer. We enjoyed a brief intimacy, although she was unable to attend the race due to work commitments. I called my cousin, Jack, to tell him about my impending challenge, and he wished me luck. He couldn't talk long. I was not getting the social support that I wanted, but that was a reason I began running in the first place I reminded myself--to survive difficulty despite my lack of support from people.

I completed the marathon in 3 hours 27 minutes, and while satisfied with my achievement, felt an immense isolation after crossing the finish line. I walked around noticing loved ones and friends, hugging, chatting and joking with the runners they'd supported, individuals who could proudly call themselves marathoners. As I stumbled around, fatigued and sore, and occasionally making eye contact and smiling, I compared myself with Richard Gere toward the end of "An Officer and a Gentleman." As "Mayo," following his graduation ceremony from Naval training, he observed his classmates rejoicing with family and friends, looking around to see, if by some fat chance, his alcoholic father might show up. Mayo found no supporters and truly looked forlorn. The grandiosity I felt by making such a comparison gave me a little compensation for the loneliness. The actual accomplishment of finishing the marathon gave me a little more.

It's not healthy to do more than one or two marathons a year, and my sophomoric tendency showed up again by doing three in addition to my first triathlon. Subsequent to Charlotte, I completed one in Washington, D.C., creatively called the "D.C. Recreation Marathon." I was less than inspired by the course that wound through ghetto neighborhoods lined with winos who probably thought they were hallucinating with so many running figures invading their turf. My Uncle Ray, who I lived with when I was seven, came to the race and cousin Jack and uncles Bill and Charles came to the next one in Philadelphia. I discovered I did have supporters as long as I ran in locations close to their homes. Goodbye Mayo.

Qualifying for Boston

The epitome of blissful ignorance, though, manifested in my training for the 26 mile cycling component of that first triathlon in Wilmington, N.C. To economize, I bought a Sears' Free Spirit bike and reasoned that since I could ride the thing quite well, thank you, I'd have a fine race. Never mind how heavy and cumbersome it was. And forget about speed. Out of several hundred swimmers, I raced out of Banks Channel in about 14th place and excitedly mounted my anomaly. Why were all these other bikes so fancy? Soon I began to count the cyclists passing me as I strained with each pedal revolution. A couple of more sympathetic racers offered me their water bottles as they noticed I didn't have one and was slowly dehydrating. By the end of the bike segment, more than 100 had easily leaped ahead of me, and though I held my position on the run, I definitely learned something about cycling. Like number one, if you're going to race, buy a bike that costs considerably more than $100.

By 1984, I had been bitten by the marathon and triathlon bugs. I was satisfied with my improvements in the marathon and hoped to break 3 hours 15 minutes at the Shamrock Marathon in Virginia Beach in March, 1985. If I could achieve a PR at that level, I'd be on track to breaking the three-hour barrier which was the qualifying time in my age group for the Boston Marathon.

A segment of that beautiful Shamrock course included the boardwalk and as I clipped along it, I stole a few side glances at and listened to the ocean waves and then sucked in the Atlantic's majestic power all the way out to where the sky kissed the water. Becoming a part of nature allowed me to go beyond the limits of the body, to feel free, and though the experience was somewhat illusory, it was also both addictive and phenomenal. Achieving my goal of 3hrs.15mins. was momentarily mundane.

When I cruised across the Finish Line 21 miles later in 3 hours 8 minutes, the value of the accomplishment returned along with a sense of triumph. I was invited to the enjoyment of a post-race massage by Pat, a sensuous blonde, who later accompanied me in the evening's post race partying activities. Dancing, beer, conversation, and late night friendliness in my tenth story hotel room, with its scenic view of the moonlit ocean, further enhanced the reward structure of a marathon well run. I was having the happiest times of my life.

My confidence in the triathlon also improved dramatically after I ridded myself of the two-wheeled clunker from my Wilmington debut and bought a Trek 560. I complained about spending more than $40 for my first helmet, and I'll never forget the store manager insisting it was less expensive than brain surgery. A persuasive argument! And to be in vogue in this explosive sport of the 80s, I donned a tri-suit, an orange, red, white and purple one piece garb with straps over the shoulders, similar to something you'd see in the roaring 20s. The purported advantage of the hideous tri-suit was that one could wear it in all three of the triathlon events which prevented the waste of precious seconds necessary to change from swimming to cycling to running wear. As did many middle of the pack triathletes, I pretended that a few seconds made a big difference; wearing a tri-suit might help me place 181st instead of 183rd in a field of 500. Reminds me of Mick Jagger's line in *Ruby Tuesday*, "Lose your dreams and you will lose your mind." We were living our dreams.

My second triathlon was in early June, 1984, in Oxford, Maryland, a quaint fishing and boating town on the Tred Avon River, a tributary of the Chesapeake Bay. A lovely, pristine borough, rich in history, Oxford's flat topography was the only easy aspect of the course which included a 2.4 mile swim, a 20 mile run, and a 50 mile bike, a considerable jump up from the distances of my first triathlon. Training for it became demanding as I learned that one should complete twice the distance of each event weekly; swimming 5 miles, running 40 and cycling 100 became difficult with a full time job. Still, I was in a flow, both mentally and physically and my self-esteem was at an all time high.

Swim Cap Dude/Oxford

A Suicide Note of Hope

I invited relatives to it, feeling proud the bounced-around orphan from earlier years had surprisingly developed into an endurance athlete. My Aunt Marge and Uncle Ray, cousin Jack, Trisha, and their son, Brandon, my Uncle Bill and cousin Lynn all showed up while I applied Vaseline under my armpits to prevent hypothermia–the water temperature was 57º. Consequently, the race organizer, Fletcher Hanks, shortened the swim from 2.4. to 1.8 miles but nevertheless, numerous swimmers were pulled out by lifeboats for hypothermia. I don't know whether I swam off course by at least a 100 yards due to disorientation from the cold water, the numerous stings from jellyfish, or simply because it was unmarked, but I do know I was relieved when my feet eventually touched bottom near the shore. I ploughed through the shallow water toward land with alacrity. My relatives never looked more pleasant.

In the transition area from the swim to the run (most triathlons have a swim-bike-run sequence but this organizer had his own unique ideas) I bent over to put my shoes on. The chamois on the orange seat of my flamboyant tri-suit had become dirty from my many training rides, and a photographer from Triathlete magazine took advantage of my position. The full-page picture appeared in the August issue. I was less than delighted to have international notoriety for a dirty chamois. Luckily my face couldn't be seen.

During times of such embarrassment, I sometimes recall the wisdom and wit of Mark Twain who asserted, "We're all here for just a short while so have a few laughs and don't take things so seriously– especially yourself."

After beating my legs up on the run, they worked like how they felt on the bike. During the first 20 miles, the idea of completing all 50 was overwhelming. As I kept telling myself, "Push down with the right foot, pull up with the left foot, pull up with the right… Concentrate. Focus. Stay on the bike. Accept the soreness." I continued with this internal dialogue until about mile 41 when I began feeling jubilant that I'd finish the race. Suddenly the bike almost stopped despite my efforts, and it took me a few seconds to realize what had happened. The flat tire was like losing an erection during intercourse, and, ironically, it was a female triathlete who dismounted her bike and helped me with the tire change. Thank God for women's altruism.

Finishing a race of that magnitude without falling off the bike is an achievement in itself, and I was fortunate to barely make that one. I didn't place in the top half of the contestants, but my cousin, Jack, complimented me, something I'd always craved from a father figure. A picture of me with the five McGoverns who were present was unusually touching. When I look at it today, the picture reminds me that experiences of family love are possible. Rare, unlikely, but to be thankful for when they do happen.

My daily training continued to offer numerous benefits. After a day of working in a state hospital with psychiatrists, the release of tension was always a welcome relief. It was a wonderful change from the early years to be in a flow that enhanced my self-esteem. And the excitement of participating in triathlons in scenic settings such as San Diego, Ft. Lauderdale, and Gulf Breeze, Florida, added to my motivation to train and discipline myself. Of course my consistent, but slow, improvement served as another reward.

Swim to Bike @Gulf Coast

While I received a few awards for placing well in my age group, the large trophy I received in the Fayetteville Adventure Triathlon of 1985 gave me the most pride. The race consisted of a 1.8 mile swim, a 60 mile bike segment, and a 13.1 mile run. After a chilly swim, it was frustrating getting lost on the poorly marked bike course, taking a wrong turn that led to a desolate stretch of road with tall weeds on both sides. Undoubtedly I was in the middle of nowhere (I'd always wondered where that was and if I wasn't competing in a race, I may have celebrated my discovery of it). Resisting the temptation to comply with my inner voice saying "to hell with the whole thing" and just lay down on the grass for an afternoon nap, I soon found the course again and finished the bike.

Me and family/Oxford Triathlon

Well into the run, a muscular Marine (a Marine base was nearby attracting numerous contestants) stormed passed me at a pace that seemed unreasonably fast for the sixth mile. He continued at that pace until he was about 50 yards ahead, slowed down a bit, and I noticed I began gaining on him. Although I knew better than to run fast at this point lest I blow up, I pushed ever so slightly, eventually cruising by him without any acknowledgment. When I had about 20 yards on him, his excitement got the best of him as he found it necessary to zip ahead of me once again.

I said to myself "Jarhead," a term Adrian informed me he and his Green Beret buddies used in reference to Marines. The guy had to be dying so I let him continue his illusion of what it meant to stay ahead of me by 20 to 30 yards, not allowing him anymore than that distance. He could feel me breathing down his neck. With about a mile to go and a surge of energy from my mounting sense of competition, I blew passed my challenger with a confidence that our pac-man game was over. It was.

Winning that trophy for placing first in my age group of four and fourth overall of 60 taught me a lesson about not giving up. During the swim and especially the bike, I wasn't sure I'd finish the race. When I was playing leap frog with the pusher, I had no idea I was first in my age group. The hoopla about my place when I crossed the finish line was surreal. Was that really me who placed first? I discovered that persistence in the face of adversity can result in exciting surprises.

Eating, sleeping, drinking, and reading triathlon made it both a lifestyle and an addiction that, while receiving criticism from some, was one I never regretted. Baked potatoes and green beans, bananas, and Power Bars were my staples and I frustrated many a bartender by ordering orange juice or water instead of beer. I subscribed to Triathlete magazine and contributed this letter which was published in the August, 1985 issue:

"Bowser Backlash"

During several years of serious running, I always looked at dogs that chased me as obnoxious menaces and resorted to carrying some nefarious weapons. I almost fell into that trap when I took up cycling, but I have changed my perspective. Some of the faster, vicious carnivores encourage me to sprint. One dog that appears to be a mixture of boxer and bull dog causes my adrenaline and my speed to spike during training rides. He is fast. Maybe some race organizers could consider positioning a few of these creatures at strategic positions in the race.

Hank McGovern Butner, N.C.

By 1986, I was ready to tackle an Ironman-distance triathlon which consists of a 2.4 mile swim, a 112 mile bike, and a 26.2 mile run. Inspired by the Hawaii Ironman legend, Dave Scott, as well as the other three phenomenal pioneers, Scott Tinley, Mark Allen, and Scott Molina, I imagined their grueling daily regimens while constructing my training schedule for the Ironman in Cape Cod. If I could swim six miles, cycle 250 to 260 and run 40 a week for three months, I'd be on track to at least finishing the event. If I could do it in less than 12 hours, I'd be exhilarated.

Another lesson learned in the humbling experience of triathlon training is that of valuing the process more so than the goal. In the Myth of Sisyphus by Albert Camus, the protagonist is sentenced to roll a boulder up a hill and just as it is about to reach the zenith, it invariably rolls back down the hill, an event that is out of the control of the laborer. He is subjected to continue his efforts despite his inability to get the boulder to stay on the top. How does one endure such an absurd life? Eventually he learns to find satisfaction, or at least tolerance, in the moment by moment process of rolling the boulder. As John Lennon sings in "Beautiful Boy," "Life is what happens to you while you're busy making other plans." Whether I reached my goal of breaking 12 hours, I'd nevertheless develop my cardiovascular and muscular systems and mental stamina. And I could remind myself of this during any moment, during any breath or stride, while training.

My toughest enemy during that summer of '86 was not my internal dialogue with which I was improving my relationship. It was the Carolina sun which provided temperatures in the upper 90s and 100s while I managed 12- and 14- mile runs after 2-mile swims on Saturdays and 100 to 120 mile bike rides on Sundays. Although most health experts warn against exercising in such torrid conditions, the frequent imbibing of cool water was a reliable strategy. Carrying a water bottle during the runs was a minor inconvenience compared to the symptoms of heat exhaustion. Eventually my body memories of summer warmth from childhood beach days helped me make friends with the sun. And the blond streaks through my hair from the combination of chlorine and sun satisfied my vanity that was offset by modesty incurred from bike accidents and fatigue. What did not kill me was making me stronger.

To monitor my training progress and concurrent life experiences, I kept a daily journal that summer. My appreciation of nature is reflected in this note from July 11th, a typical Friday when I'd squeeze in bike and run workouts:

"a good workout day, aesthetically and physically. Slept enough Thursday night so that I could rise early Friday a.m. and bike to work. Traffic not too bad getting out of town, once on Cheek Rd. was able to appreciate nature. The trees rustled in a gentle breeze, the birds were a choir and the risen sun skimmed the lake just so smoothly. 24 miles to work. Ran 8 at lunch, cycled 24 to home after work."

At work, of course, I felt tired occasionally as revealed in this note from Friday, August 15th:

"Forgot to set alarm and consequently awoke a few minutes late. Hurried and biked to work faster than usual and still made it on time (24 miles). Ran 8 at lunch and maybe due to the faster bike pace of the a.m., was a bit tired in the p.m. Took short snooze at work (hoping to get fired so I can collect unemployment and train full time. Not really). Cycled 24 miles after work."

Suddenly my friend, William, who was also doing the race, and I were driving to Cape Cod. This entry sums up the event:

"Sept. 6 race day. Awoke early, of course. In a way, it just seemed like another triathlon, just longer. It seems the Ironman distance race has almost become sacred, though, so it really wasn't just another race. The swim was choppy and battling with the other swimmers was rough, getting kicked in the throat and the like. The length wasn't too bad (2.4 mi.) as I compared it with my 2nd Oxford when I swam 5 miles. I was the closest to being hypothermic as I've ever been during the last few hundred yards and was getting disoriented. The water was 67°. My swim time of 1 hr. 17 mins. didn't give me a thrill, but I didn't know that everyone's times were slow. Anyway, I went out fast on the bike even though I had to pee on about mile 20. I never stopped for that luxury, fighting through traffic and rain, inhaling bananas and cookies and keeping my speed up. I finished the 112 mi. bike in 5 hrs. 37 mins. averaging 19.9 (or simply 20 mph). Not bad. I went out on the run at a reasonable pace, just what I could handle and by the 13th mile, I thought there was a chance I could break 11 hours. However, by about the 16th mile my legs went to hell and I began establishing very short goals e.g. 'Let's see if I can make it to that stop sign. Now that tree.' It was a mental game and required stoic toughness. On top of everything else I had to go #2, but when I tried I only felt pain. Yes, the race had become a pain in the ass. Those last miles made me grow from a boy to a man and when I found the Finish area, in a somewhat delirious state, I felt jubilant. The crowd was great. I did the run in 4 hrs 15 min., a bit slow but my overall time was 11 hrs. 18 min., placing me in the top 1/3 of the competition. I was elevated to the sublime. The rest of the evening was spent eating, keeping warm, getting massaged, chatting and congratulating William on his courageous finish despite a debacle of flat tires and finishing on a bike that didn't fit him."

After Cape Cod, I felt a mixture of feelings. I was proud of the achievement, but there was something missing. Of course intimacy was missing, but I had always been aware of that. Fatigue lingered in my body for many weeks, accompanied by a restlessness telling me to "train, train." For what? And where was I to get the energy? Soon it became apparent that the missing element was a goal to which I could aspire. I realized I was happier when I had something to look forward to, to give my life meaning and to push me in the present. I was happiest when I could plant one foot in the future and one in the present so that I could give myself the present of a rewarding future. The Boston Marathon beckoned me, and breaking the three-hour barrier would quench my thirst for achievement. If an intimate relationship happened along the way, all the better. I should concentrate my efforts, though, on training for what was most within my control. Since relationships had so many uncertainties, I decided one wasn't necessary. Unlike most people, perhaps, approval for achievement was much more likely to me than affection through intimacy.

Both would come my way during that September of '87 when I landed a job at a mental health center close to Wrightsville Beach, NC. On my first day in this new location, I was walking by the Cape Fear River during Riverfest when Anna glanced at me with a smile that invited me to come more than halfway. After spending most of the day at the celebration by the river, we spent much of the cool night warming each other on the beach with a splendid ceiling of stars and a rhythm of crashing waves. The term "pleasant surprise" was invented for these experiences.

When Anna accompanied me to Penrod's Triathlon in Ft. Lauderdale in December, after three months of sleeping together, she complained that I was too preoccupied with the race. Apparently she expected me to conform to her perfectionistic standards as she had informed her girlfriend that I was the one she'd marry one day. Triathlons can be a jealous mistress, though, to a demanding woman, and marathons can be almost as jealous. After all, I did have my priorities.

I broke up with Anna in January '88, and we were on and off again during the next few months, the ones during which I trained for the Boston Marathon held in April. Although she didn't seem to appreciate my goal of breaking 3 hours, she did make pancakes for me on Sundays before I'd do my long runs or track intervals. It was ironic that while I had been the one to initially break up, I clung more to her during a period of uncertainty in the relationship. I suppose the uncertainty of whether I'd make permanent status from a probationary period on my job contributed to my insecurity. These experiences led me to create a truthful directive I sometimes expressed to my mental health clients " Tolerate uncertainty. After all, you can always count on it."

I have to give credit to Anna for one thing. Before driving me to the airport for my flight to Boston, she gave me an exquisite present that still hangs on my wall. She had four pictures framed of me in the Cape Cod Triathlon. I look at it now and remember that guy with a little sadness and a little wisdom.

Discovering my childhood friend from the Milton Hershey School, Mike Hughes, was living in Boston I rang him up and he asked me to stay with him. It had been 18 years since I'd said goodbye to him on the night I ran away (he'd been my roommate) and seeing each other put us in a time machine that could have had this quote on the wall by Alexandre Dumas, "Oh the good times when we were so unhappy." I was happy to see my friend who still had his unforgettable smile.

To enhance my comfort before race day, Mike let me sleep in his bed while he tolerated his sleeping bag on the parlor floor for two nights. No matter. The night before a race is a wakeful one for me, and since Boston was the ultimate challenge, its excitement produced exceptional insomnia. Still a surfeit of adrenaline, the last three months of training, and a bit of Irish anger compensated for my lack of sleep as did a cool, rainy morning that greeted more than 6,000 runners. The race start was so congested that I couldn't even jog for about 90 seconds after the gun went off. Then after about nine miles, I yielded to my bladder by taking a back alley pee break that stole another 30 seconds. How could I break three hours with all these obstacles?

According to a journal note I wrote shortly after the race:

"I got to mile 15 in 1:41 and mile 20 in 2:15. But then! I cooked going up those hills and enjoyed passing numerous runners… and felt the cool air and drizzle stimulating my bare chest–I felt powerful. The crowd was sensational, cheering constantly and shouting compliments…when there was 1 mile to go, the clocked showed 2:50:30 and I pushed. I completed the last mile in 6:45 and achieved a personal record of 2:57:15…"

While it would've been nice to enjoy an extended celebration of my Boston accomplishment, a miserable aftermath started with news from Anna upon my return. When she picked me up at the airport, she told me she wanted to end our romance. Despite my mixed feelings about our relationship, I felt hurt and angry about being the dumpee and managed those feelings by running hard for a couple of miles before I even unpacked. It was just two days since I'd exhausted my body in Boston–angry running was a stupid strategy.

The low back pain began abruptly. Since I was in too much pain to run, I visited a chiropractor who prescribed exercises and manipulated my back with his hands. He explained I had a joint syndrome and scoliosis.

He also told me I should be running in a matter of days and when that didn't happen, he recommended I forget about running for a couple of months. In other words, he didn't know what he was talking about.

I felt so out of control. If being dumped by Anna wasn't enough, I was on shaky grounds at work, making the mistake of sleeping with Terri, a female co-worker, who began badmouthing me to an administrator when I did not wish to continue sexually with her. The supervisor of the program in which I worked continued to say she was uncertain that she'd transfer me from probationary to permanent status, so I began looking for another job. My back pain got worse, even after dropping the chiropractor for a medical doctor, and as I was unable to run, I became increasingly depressed. I had no idea how much I was responsible for digging myself into that dark hole of wretchedness.

Friday nights had changed from social merry-making to seclusive doldrum. I'd usually go home after work, eat a few bites if it didn't require much energy and retire to the bed which I'd wish would turn into a casket. One such evening I awoke at about 11:30 and felt sociable enough to grocery shop at Kroger's where my transformation would begin. I bought a book <u>Mind Over Low Back Pain</u> by an orthopaedic, Dr. John Sarno, as he'd claimed an impressive success with about 80% of his patients. I was about to find my openness to knowledge would be the key that unlocked the door of confusion. My experience with low back pain and my psychology education were validated and neatly tied together by Sarno. He explained that most chiropractors and othopaedics put undue emphasis on defects in the anatomical structures as the causes of low back pain. As a consequence, many treatments are designed to treat those structures. However, Sarno asserted vasoconstriction, a tightening of the blood vessels, is the source of pain because a blood supply of nutrients and oxygen is cut off from muscles and joints that require those elements for proper functioning. Consistent with what I learned in a biofeedback course, he further explained anxiety-- and anger--producing thoughts cause much of the vasoconstriction. A light went on; the thoughts I'd been having about my job and failed relationship were causing much of my pain. The perspective explained by Dr. Sarno was consistent with the philosophy of Marcus Aurelius: "A man's life is what his thoughts make of it."

I realized I could treat myself with bibliotherapy, or reading therapy, about one's disorder, and I read another book about backache relief. I began a noncritical, accepting approach to my angry-- and anxiety--based thoughts. I also began jogging easily at first. I made myself aware of my thoughts and if I thought "when is this pain going away?! It must stop!" I'd remind myself "I can accept those sensations. I may not like them but they don't have to go away." If I thought, "those damn doctors!" or "that bitch, why is she..." I'd counter with thoughts like "I can accept those thoughts and let them pass. They and she are just fallible human beings." In addition to feeling more peaceful, I increased my running distance. Also, I experienced, at a deep level, the delicate and incredible relationship of my mind and body, which are not two separate things but one.

I'd continue to say to colleagues, friends, family and clients, "Exercise is not a luxury. It is a necessity." There's no need for marathons and tri-athlons. Twenty minutes a day is fine. Marathons and triathlons filled a vacuum in my life and running Boston in 2:57 and completing an Ironman strengthened my self-esteem. Such feats are not needed any-more, and perhaps they never were; the illusion of their necessity moti-vated me. There are times now when I need to motivate myself to run or swim just minimally. But once my feet hit the road and I'm feeling a cool breeze, enjoying a sunset, or gliding along the sand with the company of the ocean waves, I realize I want these experiences for the rest of my life.

CHAPTER 9

Higher Powers: From Mundane to Metaphysical

"If there is a sin against life, it consists perhaps not so much in despairing of life as in hoping for another life and in eluding the implacable grandeur of this life."

—ALBERT CAMUS

"If God made us in his image we have certainly returned the compliment."

--VOLTAIRE

"My religion is kindness."

--DALAI LAMA

I WAS BAPTIZED A ROMAN Catholic as an infant before I had any say so in the matter, and I have to say I don't appreciate that fact much. I mean since freedom is the most important value upon which this country was founded, shouldn't people be free to choose the religion into which they are indoctrinated? Baptisms and other such rituals don't have to be imposed on children.

Instead they can wait until adulthood, *after* enough knowledge has been acquired to make an informed choice about which religion, if any, to join.

Of course, the values of kindness and respect are best taught as early as possible since they transcend religious dogma and help us get along with each other.

It has been weeks since I've resolved to resist the urge to commit suicide, and the decision to live brings me to mankind's perpetual struggle to find meaning. Why live? To answer that question and quench our thirst for an afterlife, religion was created; as a source of control, it has been one of the most powerful regulators of human behavior. In deciding to live then, I feel the urge to come to terms with my religious past and to find a raison d'etre regardless of how different it might be from the majority.

Since the majority of people have had childhood families and since religious belief originates in those families, it only makes sense that my beliefs would be much different than the majority since I did not have a family, at least for any length of time.

While I have very few memories of being with my mother and father, a favorite is sitting in a St. Elizabeth's Church pew during Mass when suddenly so many people were walking down the aisles. My interpretation was they were leaving church, and as my two-year old patience level had reached its zenith, I urged my parents to get the hell up and let's go! C'mon! It's time to leave! I pleaded to their steadfast demeanors. That was when I first learned Holy Communion, to which the parishioners were walking, occurs toward the end of Mass. Luckily for all of us, we didn't have much longer.

St. Elizabeth's church and school would remain as my religious hangout for my first seven years, four of which were in the shadow of my mother's death. The church itself was awesome, appearing as a blend of a medieval English castle and the Alamo itself. Since I admired both Robin Hood and Davy Crockett, St. Elizabeth's suited me just fine. The interior was a phenomenal work of art, both sublime and sensual: domed ceiling to the sky, majestic organ music, Latin masses solemnly murmured, aromas from incense and candles and the stations of the cross dramatically displayed on the walls. An impressive theatric occurred at the end of mass when Father Burns awesomely pronounced in a singsongy echo "Pax domino vo biscum …et cum spiri tu tuo," phrases that for some odd reason remained in my memory bank for decades.

The nuns and priests were closer to God than the rest of us and since God was reportedly the father of Jesus who was born on the day after the night that Santa Claus came around with my presents, I remained well-behaved in Sister Mary Teresa's class and most of Father Burns' masses. After all, I heard more than once the song with the line about Santa, "he knows when you are sleeping, he knows when you're awake, he knows whether you've been bad or good so be good for goodness sake!" and based on the extent of Santa's supposed omniscience, he seemed at least as powerful as God.

The Easter bunny also seemed to have a lot of power, bringing me those delicious chocolate bunnies and eggs and baskets with colorful filling. And the Easter bunny and Santa both seemed a lot nicer than God. They didn't steal my mother.

As evidenced by the ten residences in which I was bounced around and my nineteen pseudo-parents, I was made into a roamin' Catholic as a youth, with the first church change being from St. Elizabeth's to St. Ann's in Arlington, Virginia with my Aunt Marge, Uncle Ray, and Bunny. Much smaller and with less sensory stimuli than St. Elizabeth's, the stations of the cross were more conspicuous and emphasized the emotions I was supposed to feel: <u>sadness</u> for Jesus, <u>guilt</u> that I was a sinner despite his sacrifice for me, <u>fear</u> that adults like Pontius Pilate could do such dastardly things, and <u>disbelief</u> that someone who could walk on water would let such punks do that to him. Since I attended public school during the week, Aunt Marge insisted little Henry go to catechism class after Sunday mass where the correct answers to questions like "Who am I?" were memorized in robot-like fashion. The answers didn't make sense because if I was made in the "image and likeness of God," I'd have the strength to do more of what I wanted which meant I wouldn't be sitting in this hard-wood chair memorizing catechism. Nevertheless, my obedience was often rewarded with a delicious chocolate eclair when we got home, making catechism somewhat tolerable.

A Suicide Note of Hope

The most wonderful experience occurred in the Spring of that second grade year when I received my first Holy Communion, wonderful because my father came down from Wilmington for it, sober and spiffy. After the ceremony, I succeeded in imploring Daddy to walk down to the elementary school yard with me where we shot basketball together. He really did love me after all.

Roamin' on to Charlottesville in third grade with Jason and Maria, who didn't attend church, I attended Holy Comforter Parochial School during the week and the church by that name by myself on Sundays. I learned that year church and religion can be lonely experiences, having nothing to do with family, and as my caretakers were secularized, I questioned why these adults weren't doing the right thing. Of course, the one Holy Catholic and Apostolic Church, the blessed Virgin Mary and the Father, Son, and Holy Ghost (who I sometimes associated with Casper the Friendly Ghost) constituted the right things, the truth in which to believe; I was confused about their pagan behavior. Since they weren't on the right religious track, their credibility in other areas was challenged in my eight year old mind, and sinning seemed more acceptable. And sinning as revenge became even more acceptable after Maria slapped me across the face for minor misbehavior on a few occasions. To feel safer, I asked God for forgiveness lest he kill me.

While I've mentioned a fire-setting sin in my second night's note, my favorite sin from that year involved trespassing with a couple buddies into ol' man Gentry's house, a haunted one, way out in a field in the middle of nowhere. The ol' man was dead and gone some years. A two-story with broken windows, creaking floors, and ghosts unlike Casper and the Holy One, I was most mesmerized by the broken whiskey bottles in the basement that our flashlights permitted us to see. I was reminded of Daddy.

The drama of ritual was further introduced in regard to my sins through Holy Confession at my fourth grade parish, St. Matthew's, in Wilmington, where I was transferred and existed with the cousin, Merrilee, her husband, Fred, and Aunt Gerry. This was a real deal. I could tell the worst things I did during the week to Father Kavanaugh, and he had to keep them secret! So cool. For my part, all I had to do was say about ten Our Fathers, Hail Marys and Glory Bees and all would be forgiven. The slate would be wiped clean. I could go out and start sinning all over because they would be pardoned again next week. My sins consisted mostly of silly peccadilloes, though, as I was scared shitless of the wrath of Merrilee; maybe God was showing me what hell was like through her. I was sure it was a sin for me to take off my rubbers she made me wear for punishment after leaving the house on a sunny day and leaving them under a bush where I could retrieve them after school. Better the torture of hell later than the embarrassment at school that day.

Perhaps to offset the tragedy in the lives of us orphans, religion was a big thing at the Milton Hershey School, the next place where I stayed. After a mad rush each morning to beat each other in making the bed, dressing, and teeth brushing, we deposited our little gluteus maximuses on the living room rug to hear Pop Miller read a bible story that was followed by questions from Pop to ascertain whether we paid attention to the parables. For some of us it was another example of competition that began at the moment of awakening. Who could remember the most about Cain and Abel and that fellow, "Joey," who was swallowed by the whale?

On Sunday mornings, the entire school of about 1400, from kindergartners to seniors, congregated in the majestic Hershey Theater for a nondenominational service put on by the school officials, students and glee club. Slightly less sacred than St. Elizabeth's, the celestial ceiling, colorful marble almost everywhere, thunderous organ exuding Bach, and homogeneous tie-shirt-suit costumes at least paralleled the grandeur of my first hangout. It got the message across that since God was associated with the spectacular ambience, he had to be omnipotent at least. Following the service, we boys could elect to attend a church of our own persuasion, and St. Joan of Arc was near enough for a pleasant stroll through the chocolate-scented Hershey air. These walks gave me a taste of freedom from the captivity of the orphanage, and Mass permitted me to avoid extra chores and house- parent ogres.

During my five years at Milton Hershey, my reasons for attending the optional St. Joan of Arc changed a bit. When I was ten, eleven, and twelve, I believed it was the right thing to do and after my father died I had the delusion that he, in addition to God, the saints, and the Blessed Virgin, were watching me. What might they do should I skip mass? And while I didn't recall having a relationship with my mother, she probably wouldn't look down upon me favorably either. Toward the end of twelve and thirteen, Holy Communion became more of a beauty pageant, including Becky and Ruby among other promising adolescent females walking down the aisle wearing those short skirts. I became nervous that God might notice the sinful physiological response that protruded from below my belt. Still, if anything got out of hand, I could always confess it, so the new motivators to attend mass were just fine. I could also look at Jesus up there suffering on the cross if I ever needed to calm down.

When I was twelve, I received the sacrament of Confirmation, a ritual cementing me as Catholic by choice although I didn't realize it was my choice to receive it. I did realize I could choose my confirmation name which would also serve as my middle name. My reasoning in choosing my name was truly solid. The swim team assistant coach, Paul Elofsky, who worked us in calisthenics routinely called me "Nick," a mistake he insisted was accidental. To ensure he would not continue to be mistaken and to simultaneously honor my favorite saint, Santa Claus, I christened myself Nicholas. The maturity I exercised in this choice confirmed I was mature enough to make a lifetime commitment to a religious doctrine. Didn't it?

My first experiences with self-hypnosis involved traditional prayer, and I have fond memories of my roommate, Gary, and I reminding each other to say our prayers at bedtime. We'd kneel by our beds in the dark beseeching God and the saints to make our orphanage more tolerable, to help us meet the criteria to be discharged from the sinner category and, most importantly, "if I should die before I wake, I pray the Lord my soul to take." Who knows, maybe instead of waking up to the sound of a yelling houseparent, I'd find myself flying with angel wings in heaven, playing a harp with other angels except I'd rather play the drums. The calm relaxation response elicited by our incantations was reinforcing enough to maintain our ritualistic behavior nightly without a miss.

After my runaway and escape (still a roamin' Catholic) from Milton Hershey, Aunt Gerry let me attend Mt. Pleasant, a public school, despite the protestations of my intensely Roman Catholic Uncle Bill who exhorted my aunt to send me to Salesianum, a Catholic boys school. It had done so much for my father who abandoned his son, pushed his wife down the steps to her death and choked to death on his own vomit. Yes, I sometimes forget to honor thy father. Aunt Gerry did mandate that I attend St. Helena's church on Sunday's, and attempting to establish my image as a First State gang member, I'd walk to mass in my black leather jacket. Another gang member, Dave Hunnings, didn't object to his girlfriend, Betsy, walking with me to mass, and the temptation to direct my young hormonal desires toward Betsy was foiled by the sacred purpose of our walk. Besides, Dave's house was on our way.

In an extremely unstable childhood, church at least served as an anchor for me and as a pleasantly sad reminder of something I had done with my mother and father.

When Aunt Gerry handed me over to my cousin Jack and his wife, Trisha, at the end of 10th grade, I was directed to walk to St. Ann's Roman Catholic Church on Sunday mornings. Without the company of Jack or Trisha, the antidote to my loneliness continued to be through imagining God, the Saints and angels, the Holy Trinity, and Jesus were my company, but some contradictions began to make me ask questions. If God and Roman Catholicism were valid, why was Jack lying in bed from the effects of last night's alcohol, just like my father, instead of taking me to church? After all, they were both Roman Catholics. If church and family were supposed to go together, why was I always going to the former alone? And why was my life so chaotic after I'd spent so much of it going to church, receiving the sacraments and saying the rosary beads?! God wasn't fulfilling his end of the bargain, and it was clearly unfair. He was not all good like catechism had taught because I knew for a fact he wasn't being good to me.

The high school philosophy class further stimulated my questioning about the validity of God and the alternative perspectives it offered loosened the rigidity of my belief system. I began to question the nature and existence of God. I liked Aristotle's conception of God as "the immovable mover" which suggested God as omnipresent and the first cause of the cosmos. I couldn't argue with that. Something had to cause everything else. Aristotle's ideas were precursors for me to those of Spinoza's pantheism, a perspective that led me to appreciate the beauty of nature.

While my flexibility in thinking was enhanced, I never questioned what caused God. It seemed Aristotle and St. Thomas Aquinas, who advanced the same argument, assumed God always was but does that not put God in competition with space and time? If God existed before space and time, he could not have any physical properties because if he did he would have utilized both of them. If he did not have any physical properties how could one claim that he did, in fact, exist? If there is such a thing as eternity how could there be a first anything?

Around the same time, John Lennon completed his first solo LP with the song "God" on it. The lexical line from the song "God is a concept by which we measure our pain" prompted me to consider the perspective of God as a psychological effect. Beliefs are psychological phenomena, and it is almost considered honorific in our culture to say one has a "belief in God." When a belief in God is analyzed, though, the roots of it become apparent in terms of childhood concept formation; children are given attention, approval and affection for practicing behaviors that facilitate their religious beliefs. Years of this positive reinforcement result in a "belief in God" as well as that admirable quality called faith. Another Lennon song, " The Luck of the Irish" addressed the political abuse of God, which always was and seems like it always will be, in the following lines "Why the hell are the English there anyway? As they kill with God on their side. Blame it all on the kids and the IRA...As the bastards commit genocide." How many nations worldwide kill with God on their side? These ideas made me realize how God can be politicized and used to justify anything.

Sometime during college, I read a little from a William James treatise " The Will to Believe" and he stated that a belief is true if it satisfies a group of people. In reaching criteria to establish truth, he divided people into two groups: tough-minded and tender- minded. The tough-minded were those requiring scientific evidence while the tender-minded were satisfied with believing in things because it made them happy. James' assertion was paradoxical because both propositions "God does exist" and "God does not exist" are true: both a Christian and an Atheist can be satisfied. It seems the question of whether God exists depends on what one means by God. When asked whether one believes in God, perhaps the most meaningful reply is, "What do you mean by God?" James' assertion was also pragmatic in that the value of a belief is emphasized rather than its ontological truthfulness. And, of course, his position was consistent with Lennon's perspective. Great minds think alike.

God then seemed to me to be a matter of personal definition, and I appreciated the statement of Voltaire–"If you wish to converse with me, define your terms." Before committing to any religion, it seems one should reach a personally acceptable definition of, or at least a perspective on, God. Since the existence of God seemed to be a matter of personal definition, agnosticism began to make more sense, and I decided I could be agnostic as well as anything else.

Just after my car accident in 1972, I did have a will to believe in God despite my previous skepticism. Certainly my brush with death made me want to believe, and my desire to believe suppressed the fear from visiting death I might otherwise have felt. During that period of searching, I escalated my confusion by becoming interested in the Hare Krishna movement. My interest was partly triggered by the release of George Harrison's song "My Sweet Lord." I went to a meal at a Krishna retreat in Philadelphia that was advertised as a "feast." After chanting "Hare Krishna, Hare Rama, Krishna Krishna, Rama Rama" for about an hour with people in orange garb and shaved heads, I was treated to the feast which consisted of a few small portions of gunk dumped on a paper plate. If I was going to hang out at airports for entire days, petitioning strangers for money, I'd require more than a little gunk to sustain my energy. If this was a feast, what in the name of Hare would breakfast be? Although I was attracted to the orange garb and bald heads, Hare Krishna was out.

During my convalescence, I prepared for my first college semester by reading much of Will Durant's <u>History of Philosophy</u> which included intriguing information about Spinoza and his pantheism. As it asserted that God was inherent in all of nature and was a part of all existence, it was congruent with Aristotle's description of God as "the immovable mover." After all, how could he move if he was everywhere at the same time? If he even tried to move he'd be spastic wouldn't he? As we resided on the edge of a scenic forest with trees whose huge size revealed their old age and by Brandywine Creek to which I used to walk seven years ago with my father, winding its way through the Autumn's beauty, it was easy for me to accept the proposition that God was everywhere within nature. How could anything less powerful account for the magnificent radiance of the shades of oranges, yellows, browns, and reds of the falling leaves occasionally dancing in the air, the reticent whisper of a gentle breeze, the incessant gurgle of the creek's flow, the fluffy white cumulus sprouting mushrooms, lazily floating? And here I was like Hesse's Siddhartha, meditating, contemplating, listening to the occasional silence and being one with the universe of change, indeed, being one with God. Yes, for now, pantheism was a good truth.

Ironically during those moments of appreciating change, I didn't give thought to how much truth changes. The truth of the moment was so wonderful it was natural to accept it as absolute. Like George Harrison peacefully sang "Be here now." Perhaps it is this powerful emotional and sensory experience that leads a person to conclude the one religious doctrine in which he believes is the absolute truth; the conclusions are certainly not logical or empirical. Yes, at the heart of religious faith are drama, art, music and the yearning for an eternal parent, but I don't know that religion will ever admit those are its essential substances. As the Roman writer Varro wrote before the time of Christ, "It is necessary for men to be deceived in religion." Since religion primarily consists of faith and beliefs, it seems accurate to describe it as a psychological phenomenon.

My tendency to link God with the arts was reflected by a statement I wrote on a piece of paper and taped on my dormitory door at High Point College. Inspired by Beethoven, as played on the ivories by my friend

Butch, the pianist, I wrote "Music is God's sister visiting the earth for an eternal moment." Of course when I became depressed during the Spring, the meaning of my statement lost its power and the paper found its way into the trash can. God never seemed uglier.

The insecurity, inferiority, and pressure I felt during college years screamed out for a higher power to which I could cling, and that desperation was suppressed by Transcendental Meditation and Behaviorism. Both included scientific evidence to satisfy their claims and both promised utopian-like effects if applied effectively. Just as many religious folk maintain the "holier than thou" attitude with others, TM prompted me to a "more calm than thou" attitude while behaviorism made me "more knowledgeable than thou." I escaped feeling inferior by ricocheting to superiority. The scientific bases for my belief systems made me fit into James' tough-minded group, and I felt more satisfied with the category than I did as a tender-minded Roman Catholic. And did I ever feel like I was reaching to a higher power when I called B.F. Skinner on the phone and asked him how he would conceptualize TM in his Behavioristic framework! When he said he wouldn't, though, I did take him off the pedestal and realized he was fallible after all. The statue had feet of clay.

A World Geography course I took required a term paper, and I wrote mine on the impact of Jesus Christ's teachings on certain regions where he traveled. A biography of Christ by Ernest Renan that I used conceptualized him as a human with an exceptionally elevated state of consciousness which was consistent with the notion of a higher power. Renan explained that when Jesus claimed to be the son of God, he also meant other human beings have the potential to be sons and daughters of God since they can develop their consciousness to a higher plateau through prayer and compassion. This conceptualization seemed reasonable to me and was congruent with Maharishi Mahesh Yogi's label "God consciousness," a label that led me to con- sider God as an adjective rather than a noun. Similarly to Renan's explanation of Christ's perspective, Maharishi asserted human beings can develop "God consciousness" through the regular practice of meditation, and by practicing twice a day, my consciousness was evolving to that plane, so I told myself.

My allegiance to Behaviorism can be partly explained by my reverence of knowledge, a reverence having roots in my childhood belief that God was omniscient. I learned from <u>Walden Two,</u> <u>Beyond Freedom and Dignity</u>, and <u>About Behaviorism</u> by B. F. Skinner, that behaviorism was the philosophy of the science of human behavior and was very impressed at the possibilities a technology of behavior offered our world. I decided that of all the phenomena in existence, it is human behavior that is most important in determining the quality of our lives and our environment. As Skinner asserted to me on the phone, "Everything is within the behavioral process."

A controversial premise of Behaviorism was the idea that behavior is caused by genetics, a person's history of rewards and punishments and the current conditions in the environment. This philosophical assumption, I learned, was called determinism. It contrasted with the assumption that we have a free will and since determinism had a scientific basis whereas free will had no scientific or logical support, I accepted determinism as the truth. There was no evidence that a free will was anything but a concept invented by humans to explain a lot, but, in fact, explained nothing. I got into many arguments with friends and other students who frequently held the position that there was no use making any effort to create and achieve if all your behavior was determined; humans can't get any credit if their behavior is caused. Not only that–if behavior is caused we can't control our destiny. I eventually realized they were confusing determinism with fatalism. Determinism was much more optimistic because it implied that by rearranging causal conditions in the present, we could change ("control" was the word usually used and it became quickly apparent that it was pejorative) our behavior. We can, to some degree, control our destiny. I developed a reputation as being an argumentative behaviorist, a reputation of which I was proud. Behaviorism had become my new religion.

My religious foundation as a youth evolved into the belief system of a scientist and remained that way, for the most part, to this day. My only religious claim was that of agnosticism, but I qualified it by suggesting God did exist but no more than as a concept. Atheists seemed to expend needless time and energy trying to prove a negative which any lawyer will tell you is a fallacy, so atheism had little appeal. Then a girlfriend gave me The Road Less Traveled by Scott Peck and I was intrigued by his assertion that God was our unconscious. He said our personal unconscious was God and used Carl Jung's concept of the "collective unconscious" to define the universal God. Peck, who I discovered had Quaker training, defined God such that it was similar to Maharishi's term "God consciousness." The degree of agreement between Maharishi and Peck was fascinating. Here was a definition of God that was quasi-scientific since the human brain was subject to scientific scrutiny, and the conscious and unconscious are phenomena of the brain. It seemed to support God as the eternal parent since a part of each human is parental. Those parts are found in consciousness. The phrase "God will hear your prayers" obviously referred to the unconscious mind's receptivity to the conscious mind which does the praying (the Father listening to the child) so went my reasoning.

I began putting things together a little more. My search for God became a jigsaw puzzle. In the summer of '73 when I was recovering from my depression, I read a book by the psychiatrist Thomas Harris, M.D., I'm O.K., You're O.K. It said we all have ego states in our psyches that can be labeled the "parent," the "adult" and the "child" and they affect our feelings and behavior. The parent can be critical or nurturing, the child "OK" (secure) or "not OK" (insecure). The adult was that part of us that is objective and helps us deal with everyday realities in a mature manner. The paradigm was similar to Freud in that his superego is comparable to the parent, his id to the child, and the ego to the adult. In our communications with each other and ourselves, these ego states are always operating such that one person's parent ("you should do it differently," "You can feel safe and secure with me') might trigger another person's "Not OK" child (I'll do it any way I want!) or "OK child" (It feels so good to be with you). Another person's "Not O.K. child" might trigger another person's "Critical Parent." The combination of possible interactions between the parent, adult, and child were numerous, and the approach was called Transactional Analysis (TA).

By joining Maharishi's "God consciousness," Peck's concept of God as the unconscious, Jung's collective unconscious, Jesus's concept of God as " The Father," Harris' "parent," and Freud's superego, I could define God as that part of both our individual and collective unconscious that can serve as mankind's personal and universal, eternal, ideal parent. There now. And since our consciousness is a part of nature, I can include pantheism in the definition. The term "Higher Power" that Alcoholics Anonymous use in reference to God connotes the potential that both our conscious and unconscious mind has to develop creative intelligence and a supreme level of love and forgiveness, attributes usually made to God. That Higher Power is in our unconscious which is God. Faith, belief, prayer, meditation, and ritual all help us develop the potential of our Godlike unconscious.

However, in my perpetual attempt to make things more complex, I reasoned by reading about existentialism, there's no need to make reference to God at all. We do have the responsibility to develop our potential and make our lives what we will without appeal to superstition or, in the case of God as a part of the unconscious, to a grandiose concept. We anthropomorphize. That is, the assertion that our unconscious is God is a reflection of our grandiosity. But perhaps we have a need for our grandiosity primarily because we know, honestly and deep down, that we are weak and vulnerable on a planet in a solar system that is completely outside of our control and without any inherent meaning. The Big Bang Theory of the creation of our universe need just go bang again at any given moment and we'll be lucky to be cosmic dust. And to add to our anxiety and insecurity is eternity which makes a mockery of purpose and meaning. Eternity is the ultimate existential trap that scares so many into chattering about heaven, hell, and reincarnation. Yes, excuse us for being a little grandiose and inventing God as a sedative when we have this mysterious existence upsetting our stomachs. My reasoning would leave me in an ineffable state of discomfort.

Which brings me again to suicide. The person who commits this act is, aside from having the obvious feelings of hopelessness and helplessness, being impatient. Since we will certainly discover death one day, why rush it? Have a little patience, hang around, help yourself to some curiosity about the unique drama you call your life. Usually the hopelessness is absurd enough that, with some effort, you can laugh at it. And by helping yourself to laugh you can't feel helpless. The process reminds me of one of my favorite book titles by Paul Watzlawick: <u>The Situation is Hopeless but not Serious.</u>

Another point about suicide. People commit it mainly to experience relief. Unfortunately, they are unable to experience the relief they are seeking after completing suicide, a seemingly obvious point which is not so obvious to the suicidal person. It is possible, though, to eventually achieve relief in this existential trap called life that I sometimes refer to as a terminal illness. Meditation, hypnosis, music, exercise, prayer, poetry, and our thoughts are just some ways to achieve that relief.

As a secular concept referring to our Godlike potential, Nietzsche, a rather arrogant existentialist, invented the term Superman, or Ubermensch. However, Nietzsche would never agree that his Superman was a substitute for God; in fact he detested the Christian God. One of his most well known statements is "God is dead." I mention his Superman because it connotes the power usually ascribed to God. The Superman was the ideal human who channeled his passions to cultivate power, the human need for which we all lust according to Nietzsche. I agree with him. The most conspicuous psychological human needs are both power and control. In their obsession with the afterlife, he asserted Christians become distracted from a more honest and genuine experience of life, an experience whether tragic or wonderful, the Superman welcomes in the here and now. Two of his other relevant quotes were: " Two great European narcotics, alcohol and Christianity" and "Faith means not wanting to know what is true." Although not an avowed atheist, he was disgusted with traditional religion and the common man. While Nietzsche's ideas made sense to me, I rearranged them so they could not contradict my notion of God as the source of power within the unconscious, symbolizing the ideal, eternal parent. Nietzsche might agree, I reasoned, that the maximal actualization of that power makes for the Superman. He just wouldn't call that power "God." You might say he preferred arrogance, with his Superman, to anthropomorphism.

A Suicide Note of Hope

The question of whether God exists is not as important as the incredible fact that humans attach so much significance to the issue. The notion that our species has a need to believe in something more powerful than itself does not support the premise that God exists; it just means we want mommy and daddy. In the two decades since college life, and partly as a consequence of practicing psychology, I've developed the view that one purpose of all religion is to create a state of consciousness that is characterized, in varying degrees, by peace, hope, and compassion. The recognition that it is our consciousness that we are creating, whether through prayer, ritual, or meditation makes a deity unnecessary. Peace is essential to our individual and species survival, and many atheists honor that fact. We can practice compassion for each other more by appreciating that we are all in this world together and that we were originally innocent when we were thrust into it. That innocent child is still a part of all of us. Peace and compassion for each other do not require a deity but can be compromised by the prejudice and hatred various religions show each other. Hope for an afterlife is also unnecessary, and I am reminded of Thoreau who, when asked about his belief in an afterlife, replied "One world at a time."

The various paths designed to achieve this elevated state of consciousness incorporate the illusion of an absolute, whether it be in the form of a deity as in prayer or symbolized by a mantra as in meditation, and it is this illusion, along with the promise of an afterlife, that provides us with a sense of security, with many craving that eternal mother and father rocking us to a lovely, angelic lullaby in a perfect place called heaven. The narcissistic part of us abhors the idea that we may become nothing but dust subsequent to our inevitable demise. We crave an ultimate rescuer. While Freud said it is our ego that helps us adjust to reality, paradoxically, our ego fears its temporariness.

So why should we develop an elevated state of consciousness, and in the process develop our own higher power, in this existence that has no inherent meaning or evidence of anything beyond death? It is only by confronting death that I can come up with answers, answers that give me a reason to live. It is the natural simplicity of the world that fulfills these reasons. The splendor of each season's trees, especially their rustling in a gentle breeze, or when tears hang from the leaves after a rain, the variety of the skies, from a cloudless Carolina blue to the awesomeness of thunder and lightning, the relentless pounding of ocean waves and the serene stillness of a mountain lake at sunset, the intelligence and compassion in a woman's eyes, the laughter of Mozart and the vigor of Beethoven, the innocent smile and happiness of a young child, the natural breath that nourishes and sustains our body and mind, and the possibility of love--these become my reasons to live. And the reasons for me to cultivate a state of consciousness that fosters happiness. I daydream of a Thoreauvian solitude deep within a forest where I can sit on a blanket of leaves and listen to my breath, not becoming, just being. It is by periodically transcending consciousness and simply being in the world with the senses that one paradoxically elevates consciousness.

The value of the experience of being cannot be overestimated. To sit and focus one's attention on a spot on the floor or on one's breath or a mantra for a specific period of time on a daily basis stills the nervous system and quiets the mind. This meditative experience brings peace. It is a time-out from the daily activity of becoming. By simply existing and quieting the mind, you contact what Maharishi calls, "the Being," or the underlying essence of life. This essential force can be defined as God, if you wish, as it is unifying and eternal. Perhaps you might agree with Peck that our personal unconscious is a part of it. Words do not accurately describe being. The simple, gentle, effortless experience of being transcends words and the daily activity of becoming. Faith becomes irrelevant. Once again I refer to Thoreau, asserting "Being is the great explainer."

As you might tell, I've often been confused regarding the concept of God and the truths of religion. The simplest way to describe my personal religious evolution is to say I've moved from prayer to meditation, from an allegiance to Catholicism to viewing all religion as a part of a menu to be tasted and chewed, and swallowed, only if it suits a particular palette, from God as a deity to a metaphor for the potential within us. In my quest for religious truth, I've decided truth is most accurately spelled, not with a capital "T" but with a small "t". Rather than one absolute truth, there seems to be many truths and each person's religion or spiritual truth

A Suicide Note of Hope

deserves respect. I support my claim that many truths exist in religion and spirituality by the fact that each denomination or sect has their own authoritative references to support its perspective. If one argues another's religion is not the truth, the counter argument usually includes a reference whether it be the Christians' Bible, the Jews' Torah, the Muslims' Koran, the Buddhists' Lotus Sutra, the Hare Krishnas' Bhagavad Gita or something else. Ultimately one admits their truth is based on faith, and faith does not point to absolute truth.

People arrive at their truth through their personal lifetimes of unique experiences, and the indoctrination by imposition of one religious belief upon another person seems disrespectful at least and destructive of individuality at worst. The Ten Commandments should not be posted in public places because it is representative of one, and only one, religion. If a person is confused about their spiritual orientation, that too needs to be respected and accepted. If it is felt the confused person would see the light if only they believed the way you do, then offer your beliefs and values as items on the menu of religion and do not shove them down the other's throat. Milton Erickson once said, "Into each life some confusion should come…and some enlightenment," and Fritz Perls, a psychologist, uttered "Don't push the river. It flows by itself." So let each person flow in their individual rivers of confusion as they peacefully meander into serene lakes of enlightenment. Respect the current of the river of life, and you can gracefully manage its logjams.

It seems to me the religion that is most truthful for any one person is the one that generates the most peace, compassion and happiness.

In studying some of my heroes mentioned in this note, I've come to see their wisdom as parts of a higher power or parts of a collective unconscious. I've borrowed some of this wisdom as well as ideas from Buddhism and cognitive psychology and developed a form of meditation that I've practiced for almost a year now. I referred to it in my fourth night's note but did not consider it worthwhile enough to pass on to you. I do now. While I have begun practicing Transcendental Meditation again, I also practice my Values Meditation each night before bed. If it suits your palate, maybe you will want to taste and practice it.

The nine values comprising my meditation are: optimism, flexibility, humor, mindfulness, acceptance, compassion, passion, responsibility, and cooperation. I chose these particular ones by a deliberate, rational process so as to give meaning and purpose to the experience. By meaning I mean something that can easily be perceived as truthful and valuable in the here-and-now, and by purpose I mean a constructive endeavor that enhances the quality of one's future. My purpose for practicing Values Meditation is to increase the likelihood that my everyday behavior will reflect the values. I expect that by meditating on the values each morning, I will establish them as a part of my unconscious and consequently, their establishment will generate an expression of them in my behavior. As Sharon Salzberg so eloquently states, "Each act can be expressive of our deepest values." It seems meaning and purpose can be fulfilled through the intentional, spiritual experience of focusing attention on our most important values. Integrating these values is like planting seeds. What grows may be beautiful.

I want to explain the basis for the nine values so that they may enhance your experience if you practice the meditation. By optimism, I do not refer to a pollyannish blindness in which one denies unpleasant experience to create a fictitious rosiness. I refer to the optimism mentioned in my sixth night's note, researched and written about by Martin Seligman in his book Learned Optimism. It is an adaptive style of thinking in which one sees negative events as temporary, specific to isolated circumstances, and as caused by factors helping one to avoid self-blame. Positive events, on the other hand, are seen as permanent, or at least longer-lasting, generalized to many circumstances, and caused by oneself. Optimism involves looking forward to positive possibilities. This optimism reminds me that, no matter what has happened in one's life, it's never too late to begin from wherever you are.

By flexibility I mean the ability to do or think about things differently, especially if what you are doing isn't working. It also means having the ability to see the same situation in at least two different ways. The different thing may seem illogical, weird, or crazy, as did many of the task assignments of Milton Erickson, because you are so accustomed to

A Suicide Note of Hope

your one attempted solution that you've tried for so long. The problem is your attempted solution, not because you are a failure, but because the attempted solution just doesn't work, neither for you nor for anyone else. One of the many therapy assignments I give to clients that has worked for me on occasion is: "Do something different." Flexibility, in contrast to rigidity, is a salient characteristic of good mental health.

It may seem inaccurate to call humor a value, but I'm not joking here. One of my favorite quotes, mentioned on an earlier night, is that of Mark Twain when he once said, "You're only here for a short while so have a few laughs and don't take things so seriously–especially yourself." And a girl I went out with in my mid-twenties, gave me some valuable wisdom, saying, "You have to be your own clown." Especially because life is so frequently absurd, I've come to see humor as a most invaluable value. Laughter also frees us, at least temporarily, from pain and tragedy and if you laugh a lot that's a lot of freedom. In my college years I wrote this statement in a diary that echoes the freedom of which I speak: "Laughter is to the mind as wings are to the gull."

I include mindfulness as a Buddhist concept although one philosopher, I think it was Sartre, referred to the experience as "being conscious of one's consciousness." Mindfulness means an awareness, a waking up to experience in the present moment. Experience is internal, including thoughts, feelings, intentions, and sensations, and external, including the behavior of oneself and others and the details of each situation. By practicing mindfulness, one accepts all experiences of the moment, notices and observes without judging, rejecting, clinging or craving. In explaining mindfulness in her book It's Easier Than You Think, The Buddhist Way to Happiness, Sylvia Boorstein tells this story, I may have mentioned earlier, of a Buddhist monk that has become one of my favorites:

The monk is being chased by a tiger and has to jump off a cliff. He grasps a vine that has grown over the cliff, and if it breaks and he falls, he is sure to drop to his death. The growling tiger remains above him. As the monk is hanging in midair, a mouse begins gnawing the vine above him. His peril is obvious, his end in moments if not seconds. He notices a strawberry growing out of the cliff in front of him, picks it and begins eating, saying " This strawberry is delicious."

When I have trouble sleeping, I sometimes tell myself "this strawberry is delicious" and drift off. I don't recall having any nightmares of tigers.

Perhaps the most peaceful value, acceptance, has been a key for me in unlocking the door from the room of anger and despair to the room of hope and serenity. Struggling to control the uncontrollable is a hallmark of depression, and in a futile tug of war one often fails to realize the best solution is to let go of the rope. It's no wonder that acceptance is at the heart of many 12-step programs such as Alcoholics Anonymous. "Let go and let God" is its aphorism. An important truth of Buddhism and one that seems true to me is that all human suffering involves clinging or craving. Because people cling to the things of this world which are impermanent, they often make themselves miserable when an inevitable loss occurs. Instead of clinging to that which will eventually be lost, accepting loss as a part of change brings one to appreciate the peace of the moment.

It seems important to distinguish sadness caused by loss from suffering caused by clinging. Sadness is healthy and makes us human. It is when that sadness goes on and on and intensifies that one can realize she is suffering, maybe depressed. It is time to give up clinging, to let go and flow with the universe. We can't control its flow, but we can control how much we flow with it and allow ourselves to feel at the same time. A sailor who was out at sea said once, "I can't control the wind, but I can always adjust my sails."

Whether one refers to the psychological process as acceptance or letting go or giving up control, it is this process that is the essence of a faith in God. When one says they'll "turn a problem over to God" or "If the Lord be willing," or recites the Serenity Prayer, they are saying that after doing what is within their control, they'll avoid the self-defeating attempt to control the uncontrollable. Faith in God, then, is the Christian's version of acceptance.

Compassion is the next part of my meditation, and I use the philosophical assumption of determinism to enhance it. As determinism asserts that all human behavior has causes and conditions and since I know from psychology that the causes and conditions are genetic and environmental, it is easier to have compassion, to be understanding and to love each human being. A piece of wisdom I've borrowed from the humanistic psychologists is that each person will meet his or her needs according to how they know how to meet those needs, and if they knew a better way, they would do so. This level of compassion is transcendental for one looks beyond the everyday behavior of others, behaviors that can be annoying and sometimes worse. It is this transcendental compassion that I like most about Jesus Christ. Even in his dying moments on the cross he demonstrated it by saying "Forgive them Father for they know not what they do." The purpose of life is to find happiness says the Dalai Llama who emphasizes it can be found by practicing compassion with as many sentient beings as possible. I don't believe the world will ever be as peaceful and compassionate as I would like it. The best we can be is as we would like the world to be, and if I practice that much compassion each day, I'm sure I'll be happy. My advice is to practice Transcendental Love.

I include passion as a value, not in a romantic or sexual sense, but as a way of fighting for something helpful to others. There are enough obstacles to fairness and justice in the world to necessitate a disciplined determination or what can be called a fight. I do not condone violence; the fight of which I speak is peaceful, a peaceful fight. My current fight is against suicide, not just for myself but for the species. We can choose a better way to die. As we evolve, there may come a day when our collective victory will be the "death of suicide." Of course I respect the right to end one's life for those experiencing interminable and excruciating pain. That is, I respect choice. Perhaps in the future people will study suicide as an aspect of history, something people did before the species evolved. We may learn to be more patient, just as I suggested to Lisa, the suicidal client I discussed in my presentation. To enhance one's patience, it helps to meditate on eternity for an entire moment. Try it–just eternity for 60 seconds.

Responsibility is the eighth value, and like some of the others, it involves issues that make up entire books. In my note on exercise, I referred to noted psychiatrist William Glasser, whose Reality Therapy primarily teaches responsible behavior, and a more recent favorite includes the book Taking Responsibility, Self-Reliance and the Accountable Life by psychologist, Nathaniel Branden. While emphasizing the importance of self-reliance as the proactive approach leading to happiness, Branden adds this truth that I believe is invaluable for any authority teaching responsibility to others: "People cannot be accountable for what you have asked them to do if they are not given the appropriate resources, information, and authority. Remember that there is no responsibility without power."

For responsible behavior to occur it must be taught, and the teaching and learning is not outside a deterministic framework. And here is where Branden makes a mistake. He shows a simplistic view of determinism indicating it "...says that no one can help anything." In other words, he confuses determinism with fatalism, an error that is not uncommon. Determinism does not negate responsibility; it emphasizes responsibility has causal conditions. While a role model, such as a parent, who teaches responsibility is ideal, acquisition of knowledge (through self-help books for example) is another kind of causal condition. The point is that determinism includes empowerment. A wealth of possibilities such as meditation, exercise, and learning new perspectives exist in the present as sources of empowerment making one responsible if they use those possibilities. While the past consists of causes for behavior in the present, the present of the here and now is an opportunity to construct experiences that can serve as causes for future behavior. As the future's past, the present is a source of causal gifts. As B.F. Skinner once posed, "We are all controlled by the world in which we live. The question is this: are we to be controlled by accidents, tyrants, or by ourselves?"

Cooperation concludes the Values Meditation. In a "Parade" magazine letter to Marilyn vos Savant, the person who has the highest recorded I.Q., the writer asked her opinion of humanity's greatest accomplishment. I was impressed to read Marilyn's reply that it has been cooperation. Often cooperating requires empathy, the skill of walking a mile in the other person's shoes as well as altruism or helping behavior. In addition to the fact that the survival of our species depends on cooperation, almost everyone feels good when they help someone else and, at least feel better when they understand the other's point of view.

Like many men, anger has been a difficult emotion for me to manage, and by practicing my Values Meditation I believe (an optimistic perspective) I'll manage it better. For instance, I can be flexible and reframe "anger" as "fear" or "hurt" because I know that when I feel angry, on a deeper and more tender level, I feel hurt and afraid. I can use humor by picturing myself on a movie screen when I'm angry. Not only do I usually appear funny, I look as though I should be a bit embarrassed! I think one of the reasons the Jerry Springer Show was so popular was because the rages into which the guests explode are often hilarious. When I am mindful to thoughts that trigger anger, I often notice it before it erupts. Frequently, simply being mindful of anger is enough to prevent destruction. The application of acceptance to anger softens it significantly. We often say "I shouldn't be getting angry! I can't stand getting angry!", and get angry about getting angry which only makes us angrier. Instead a healthier internal dialogue of acceptance of anger might go something like this: "Even though I don't like this anger I can stand it. When I make myself aware of the reasons for the hurt and fear, I can get to know myself better; I can use my anger this way.

I practice compassion by visualizing a picture of myself as a 2- or 3-year-old and nurture myself with the talk I'd give that child. Certainly he felt afraid and hurt and, consequently, angry at times. Loving that child within puts out the fire of anger as easily as blowing out a candle. Passion sometimes inspires me to do something constructive about what is making me angry, especially when the issue involves unfairness or an injustice by those in power against the less powerful. For instance, when I make enough money one day, I'd like to decrease homelessness. David Bowie's "Look Back In Anger" inspires my passion as the anger with which I look energizes me to action in the present. Focusing on responsibility for my anger reminds me to avoid blaming other people and becoming hostile and, instead, to decide how to deal with it. I've described my main ways to deal responsibly with anger in my fourth, fifth, and sixth night's notes, namely by meditation, assertive behavior and thinking rationally.

By practicing cooperation, I am reminded to avoid allowing anger to become an obstacle to accomplish tasks that require teamwork. In business decisions, I've begun using these metaphors to operate together with others when anger begins to rear its ugly head: "Don't throw the baby out with the bathwater," "Don't shoot yourself in the foot," "Just take it on the chin," "Don't burn any bridges."

The following is what I say in a slow, calm voice to practice "Values Meditation." The four lines immediately preceding and after the values are from a Buddhist meditation, related by Jack Kornfield in his book A Path With Heart. Each set of three dots denotes a pause, and the refrain ("breathing, letting thoughts drift, and relaxing") are derived from other meditations. You can practice with eyes focused on a spot or with eyes closed.

"And so I can sit here now, letting the chair support my body, aware of the quiet of this room, aware of the material world around me. And as I sit with my hands in my lap and my feet on the floor, I can begin to focus now on what is most important …

May I be filled with loving-kindness, May I be well,
May I be peaceful and at ease, May I be happy,
May I be consistent with my values of:
Optimism, to look forward to positive possibilities. . And to perceive life events reasonably and favorably …
(refrain) breathing (pause) letting thoughts drift (pause)
flexibility, may I think about things differently and do things differently… whenever necessary, to adapt, to change (refrain)
humor, may I laugh at the world's absurdities…and not take things so seriously, especially myself…and may I find amusement in the day to day, the hour to hour experiences that lend themselves quite easily to amusement.
(refrain)

mindfulness, may I be awake to and aware of my thoughts and feelings and intentions...and to monitor the relationship between my internal world and the world around me... of people and events...and people's and animal's feelings especially (refrain)

acceptance, may I endow all experience with a value...and to utilize experience well...and when things are outside of my control may I let go... and let it flow...or just let it be, peacefully...
(refrain)

compassion, may I have a heartfelt sense for other people, and animals, and all living things...and may my heartfelt sense manifest in acts of kindness and generosity...in acts of understanding and forgiveness...in acts of consideration and respect... in acts of transcendental love, ...and may my heartfelt manifestations spread, and go on and on and on. . (refrain)

passion, may I focus on a value or a cause or a belief that is worth fighting for ...and to then fight for it...wisely and with heart...
(refrain)

responsibility, may I be accountable for all my actions and all my words...for all that I do and say...and may I be accountable for my thoughts and feelings too...and whenever possible, to take a proactive approach to make things better... (refrain)

cooperation, may I operate together with others and join others... as we focus on life goals together... and as we focus on life experiences together...each day...continuing...and to continue on our path of meaning and purpose ...and as I continue to join others, I can help to enhance the harmony in this world...
(pause)

May I be filled with loving-kindness, May I be well,

May I be peaceful and at ease, May I be happy.

May I be blessed with the wisdom and the fortitude to carry forward my values with grace. And may I resolve to practice my values today.

And now I can reorient…as I feel refreshed, awake, alive… and I can look forward to my day when I can practice my values in so many ways…

When I practice at night, the last couple lines are "And now I can feel calm…peaceful…tranquil…at ease…as I look forward to a very restful night."

It seems to me our higher power is within, just like the Quakers and the Buddhists say. Indeed, it is our unconscious. And we can make it conscious by practicing the right kind of thinking like values meditation. It's also without in the form of wisdom, compassion, and creativity, and I've made numerous references throughout this note to authorities whose power I've respected and valued. I believe it's our responsibility to taste the wisdom passed down to us, to chew it and swallow it if it satisfies our appetites. It's also our responsibility to spit it out when it doesn't satisfy.

Determinism holds true according to the pragmatic definition of truth, and we have the potential to determine our behavior, behavior that determines the quality of our life and our world. The acceptance of determinism can help us understand and better tolerate one another. And the sooner we relinquish dogmatic aspects of religion that stir hatred and prejudice and embrace practices that stir compassion and kindness, the better our world will be. Just ask your unconscious. It talks to your heart every day.

I live for my philosophy so that my philosophy can help me live.

CHAPTER 10

Hello

"...If one advances confidently in the direction of his dreams and endeavors
to live the life he has imagined, he will meet with a success unimagined in
common hours...If you have built your castles in the air, your work need not
be lost; that is where they should be. Now put the foundations under them.."

HENRY DAVID THOREAU

"Our true home is in the present moment."

THICH NHAT HANH

I'VE TRIED TO GET A job in my profession since the charge against me was
dismissed by the Psychology Board but, as you may know, employers are
reluctant to hire someone if a charge was made, even if it was dismissed.
I did not think I'd be delivering pizza to make a living at the age of 45
when I was working hard in graduate school to earn a Masters Degree
in clinical psychology from 1980 - 1982. Nevertheless, I'm glad to get so
many deliveries tonight as each one is a potential tip, a tip that I depend
on, my main source of income. As I drive along this curvy road on the
outskirts of town at 9:00 p.m. this cool October night I have to laugh,

remembering my pizza delivery job from college when I reacted saying, "I can't wait to get that degree and get out of this shit!" Laughing is often so much better than crying.

Despite my current social and employment status, I'm glad to have the victory that I call "the death of suicide." If I did not have it I would not be appreciating the beauty of this night, featuring a bright, full moon illuminating the forest to my left, the splendor of stars all across the sky, some twinkling, some resting still, the fresh aroma of autumn's leaves, the silence of the night save my trusty car's engine as I gingerly approach the first address of my three deliveries. Yes, Mother Nature will remain my mother, always living and dying beautifully, as long as I'm alive.

"Here, just keep the change," Mrs. Ackerman directs, giving me a $20 bill for a $19.60 order. I consider anything less than .75 cents to be a stiff. I'm momentarily pissed.

"You cheap skate, " I mutter under my breath, walking back to my car. People don't know their stinginess helps me diagnose their personality. Impatient to get a better tip, I'm driving 55 in a 35 and then I remind myself, "Stiffs come with the territory, that's only my second one tonight, overall I'm making about $14 an hour, the experience gives me practice at not overreacting. I'm a psychologist and I can handle this," I tell myself, and I slow down to 50. Speeding tickets and car accidents are terrible for a pizza man's income.

When I began delivering pizza several months ago, I decided to do something creative with my employment status and write an article, or maybe even a book, titled <u>Zen and the Art of Pizza Delivery.</u> In my treatise I'd describe at length the Zen solutions to managing emotions, living in the moment, yielding gracefully to conflict, using breathing-meditation and practicing mindfulness while delivering pizza. Oh yes, I'd write some of my favorite quotes by Buddha such as "Holding onto anger is like grasping a hot coal with the intent of throwing it at someone else—you are the one who gets burned," and "all that we are arises with our thoughts - with our thoughts we make the world." I would not write another Buddha favorite, "Don't just do something, sit there" because customers might not appreciate me sitting in my car in their driveway with their pizza. I had promising aspirations for this illuminating work.

As a consequence of continual hassles including: much younger bosses giving me orders, other drivers scamming for the best deliveries, city planners screwing up neighborhood streets so badly that Einstein couldn't find some addresses, mistakes by cooks and phone people that make customers mad at me, the perpetual threat of getting mugged during a delivery, and people who believe the quality of their driving must reflect their i.q, I'm now considering the title of my work <u>The Pizza Man From Hell, A Consolation for Telemarketers.</u>

Of course the advantages of pizza delivery outweigh the disadvantages, and I especially value the hours of solitude behind the wheel. My longer deliveries give me time to dream, fantasize, and to occasionally reflect on the events since I started my suicide note. Many of these events have added a delicious flavoring to this brief lapse of time I call "my life," and I selectively withdraw them from my memory bank to make myself feel better during occasional blue periods. This I do as I drive along hoping for better tips.

<u>Sexual Hysteriament Revisited</u>

I imagine the expression on the face of Cluckland Center's Director, Dr. Stone, the man who fired me, when he was contacted by the journalist from the Washington Post, Kirstin Downey, regarding the charge of sexual harassment that Stone used to fire me. I knew what I said on two occasions, "I'm not gonna flirt with ya" did not rise to the levels of "severe" or "pervasive" that constitute sexual harassment. The title of the article written in December 23 of 1996 accurately summed up the case: "In Combating Sexual Harassment, Companies Sometimes Overreact" and the article summarized my case, beginning by saying how I loved David Letterman and how I felt like I was emulating his humor when I first told the woman I was going to flirt with her. I was happy to give Stone and company international notoriety for their hysterical, unfair behavior.

I laugh again, fully aware of the irony that I gloat while I deliver pizza for a living. Stone and company could obviously laugh at me too, and, in a way, that's ok with me. Maybe that's a sign I'm feeling more secure. I know I have learned to take myself a bit less seriously. Just as victorious as having the Washington Post article expose Brenner and company was my success with the two complaints of sexual harassment to the North Carolina Psychology Board filed by my supervisor, Dr. Stone and the woman who heard me say, "I'm gonna flirt with ya." One complaint to the Board wasn't enough; the administration had to coach the woman to file another complaint. I reasoned since the content of the complaint lacked substance and was essentially silly, their strategy was to create a pile-on as if the more people complained the more the complaint would seem credible. Initially their strategy worked, as the Board alleged I violated the law against sexual harassment, a violation that could make me lose my license.

I requested a copy of the Board investigator's report, the document they reviewed to make their charges. The Investigator, Randy Yarborough, omitted numerous findings in his report that I had submitted to him in his investigation. I wrote seven contentions in a letter to the Psychology Board and sent a copy to their attorney, the Assistant Attorney General, Robert Curran, hoping they'd retract their charges and avoid a hearing. Fortunately Mr. Curran exercised reasonable judgment and advised the Board to dismiss its charges, advice with which it complied.

This was a huge legal victory for me, and I considered going to law school.

Stone, the woman, and Yarborough remind me of another favorite quote by Nietzsche: "Distrust anyone in whom the impulse to punish is powerful." I am also aware that as I write this note, if one of the aforementioned individuals ever wanted to sue me, I would submit that the best defense to libel is the truth. Having the NC Psychology Board's dismissal, the article from the Washington Post, and a ruling from the judge of the Employment Security Commission seem to provide a solid block of truth. I hope I'm right.

I planned for a hearing with the Office of Administrative Hearings, scheduled for February, 1997, to appeal my firing. I'd represent myself and looked forward to asking questions from witnesses like the woman and Stone, questions that might embarrass them. To avoid the hearing,

Cluckland Center and its attorney offered me a settlement fee and after I persuaded them to raise it twice, I accepted. Even though I was legally bound not to publicly disclose the amount, I considered the settlement a small victory.

Sexual hysteriament, not sexual harassment, can lead to numerous victories for the alleged perpetrator, and I still had one more. When I was working at the Center, I'd been informed on numerous occasions that the administrators would not support efforts to get clinicians to complete their work in medical charts. The noncompliance with the charts had continued for so long that it constituted Medicaid fraud. While I was employed by the Center, I became familiar with the names of clients whose charts were in a state of extreme noncompliance and knew I could report them to Medicaid officials one day.

Partly as an act of revenge, an act our judicial system refers to as justice, and to see my enemies unmasked for their incompetence and corruption, I telephoned the Medicaid office in Raleigh and related the charts. Soon federal marshals paid a visit to the center, collected the charts and gave them to investigators to determine the extent of the noncompliance. Shortly after that Dr. Stone "resigned" and shortly after that another administrator "resigned." Rumor had it they were asked to do so but who am I to jump to conclusions? The mental health center was taken over by another mental health system, and I enjoyed a toast with my friend, Angela, another whistleblower.

Damn! I ran a red light. If only the city planners would extend the duration of the yellow lights to accommodate my memories and reflections of victory. And inattention. Next delivery should be in this block. Odd addresses on one side, even on the other, can't see any addresses on a few houses, what's wrong with these people, bingo! There it is. This neighborhood looks a bit shady, not with trees but with danger lurking. Getting out of my car I'm alert to the creepy surroundings. At least my house, 5701, has a light on.

"Hello sir, how're you tonight, that will be $15.04." "Keep it," the black man with kind eyes says, smiling. It's a twenty.

" Thank you very much. I appreciate it!"

Marilyn

Just a couple of miles from my next delivery, I continue to enjoy the fresh night air driving with my window down, and my thoughts drift to one of the finest rewards of resisting suicide. You may recall from my fourth night's note the birth of my daughter who we named Angela Marie before she was adopted. A beautiful, intelligent, healthy and seemingly happy woman, I met her when she was 21 while she attended Furman University. Her name was Marilyn.

Jennifer, the biological mother, telephoned me several months after I was fired and said she'd hired a detective to find our daughter. I'd told Jennifer many years ago to tell Angela I was very willing to meet her if she ever found her. When Jennifer called I was excited to hear that I could contact an adoption specialist who would screen my letter and forward it pending her inspection. A return letter was no guarantee, but I wanted to explain the reason for the adoption to my daughter as well as give a little bit of my family background and very much wanted to meet the grown up version of the 5 lb girl of whom I caught a glimpse all those years ago through the plexiglas window at the hospital. Writing the letter was more than worth the risk of not getting a return.

The delivery is once again in a lower socioeconomic section, but when I get stiffed by the woman I'm more at ease than usual, having just reoriented from my thoughts of Marilyn. I think about the disparity between the rich and the poor in our country and realize it's natural for the woman to stiff me. Understanding and forgiveness pave the way to so much more peace and compassion for me. Getting stiffed is just a part of the territory.

I was thrilled to get Marilyn's letter. She wrote that she'd been informed some years ago that she was adopted, had always wondered how she acquired her features and characteristics, became a competitive swimmer in her younger years, and a psychology major in college. I thought "she's following in my footsteps" and had a momentary fear for her. Then I reminded myself she spent her childhood in one home, with two stable adoptive parents, (to Marilyn they are her parents, to me they're her adoptive parents), and a brother and a sister, in an upper middle class Christian neighborhood. No, she's not following in my footsteps.

We exchange a few letters and phone calls, the crescendo to our introduction. When we finally meet at the residence in Charlotte where she grew up, I'm amazed at the balanced blend of Jennifer and me. I obviously gave her hair color and height, and, fortunately, Jennifer gave her voice, lips, and laughter.

A pleasant memory is a walk we take together in a forested area with a stream trailing to the base of a waterfall, close to Furman University. We are in a clearing with trees surrounding the water, clear enough to see the sandy bottom, and the perpetual waterfall's shower resounding, nature's mantra, marking time. I want to camp here for a week and get to know my only offspring. In our brief conversation she tells parts of her personality she likely acquired from my genes. She likes a good argument and embraces controversy, disclosing she wrote a term paper promoting the legalization of prostitution that she had to defend in class. Furman is a Christian University.

We go to dinner one night, and I explain a bit about my termination and the sexual harassment charge, feeling somewhat embarrassed. Of all the times to meet my daughter—I'm fired, underemployed, and feel like a bum. And sexual harassment! Nevertheless blood is thick. When I tell her of the first time I told the woman that I'd flirt with her, and the coy reply while smiling, "It's not nice to flirt with a married woman," Marilyn asserted, "She was flirting with you!" I thought so too. That's why I said it a second time.

Although a little disappointed, I'm not surprised I don't receive an invitation to her graduation. During the next couple of years, we don't grow closer which is more her choice than mine. While I'd like more contact, we see each other only occasionally and then seldom. She rarely returns my phone calls, and I remind myself to feel lucky to find her at all and discover she's healthy and happy. It's just possible she may experience a little resentment or more towards me since it was my decision to not marry Jennifer and put her up for adoption. If not resentment, surely some ambivalence. Still I want to get as close to her as she will allow.

She goes to graduate school in Chapel Hill to earn a masters degree in occupational therapy. I tell myself not to take it personally that she switched from psychology after meeting me. I also rationalize a masters degree in psychology isn't worth much anyhow since the profession is, hypocritically, quite authoritarian, with PhDs., such as Stone abusing power. She'll probably be happier in the OT field.

She gets an internship at the beach in Wilmington, NC, the scene of my Boston Marathon training eleven years ago. I visit her and we take a night walk on the beach. We discuss the idea of posting the 10 Commandments in school classrooms, with her in favor and me opposed, and she explains she's a Protestant. She encourages me to be more aggressive in meeting women, feeling sympathy and compassion that I'm journeying solo these days and I quip that I wouldn't want a woman who would want me now, being underemployed, etc. Of course I tell her I'm joking, ha! ha! I very much appreciate her concern and am so happy to be with her, even if it is for only a day and a night. I know she has a boyfriend in medical school and is busy with school but still feel hurt she doesn't return my phone calls for two months. The hurt triggers some anger. I fantasize calling her and leaving rude messages on her answering machine but I resist, reminding myself she is my daughter. This reminder gives her much more innocence in my mind and freedom to be fallible. She does not have to call me, and in fact, doesn't have to contact me at all. I become a bit more accepting and forgiving and have an inspirational insight: Every human being is the daughter or son of someone and has a part of them that is innocent and vulnerable. It seems so important to understand and forgive one another; death also reminds me of that. The concept of the "child within" us takes on a deeper meaning, and I'm more appreciative of having met Marilyn.

Finally the coup de grace. I connect with her by phone, she assures me she has no problems or issues with me and has had a horrendous semester–the reason for which she hasn't returned my calls. I tell her she means more to me than any human, and she says she feels guilty. We agree to get together when I drive up to Chapel Hill for a meeting, so I call her about a week ahead to arrange a time and place to meet. I get her answering machine and leave a message for her but after two days she doesn't return my call. I call two more times and still don't get a return. I feel demeaned. Perhaps she has become more rude than I'd like to admit.

I recall the Buddhist perspective that human misery is caused by clinging and the statement I give myself during values meditation "Instead of clinging let go, let it flow, let it be." I also recall the verse by William Blake, mentioned a couple times earlier in this note.

It is time to practice this philosophy with Marilyn. I call her and, of course, get her answering machine. I leave a message I'm disappointed I didn't hear from her, that I won't call her anymore, that I love her and for her to feel free to call me in the future if she'd like.

I call her occasionally, grasping onto a chunk of optimism. I reason that one can let go as a matter of degree and that if she ever makes it clear she wants me to stop calling, I will honor that request. Perhaps she has mixed feelings, and I decide to respect them but not give up for once in my life. I'll make myself available to her for the rest of our lives.

Chocolate Years Revisited

I usually enjoy my last hour of pizza delivery, and I do tonight. I've made about $14.00 an hour which is almost as much as I made as a psychologist at mental health centers. I have one more, but I feel good that I've done well enough that this last one doesn't matter much. Since my money is made for the night I don't feel the pressure to play Indianapolis 500 in an effort to get more deliveries.

Driving makes me feel a bit like Walter Mitty except my mental escapes are real. I drift back now to the Fall of '97, 25 years after I would have graduated from the Milton Hershey School had I not run away. Since the Boston Marathon in '88, I've had occasional contact with Mike Hughes; having met him in 1964 he's a connection to my childhood. He tells me in late September there will be a 25 year reunion for the class of '72 and why don't I go.

"I ran away in 1969 and didn't graduate with those guys," I reply. " That's alright Hank. Some guys will be glad to see ya, especially ones from the swim team."

I reserve a room for Friday and Saturday night in a motel on Rt. 322, the road on which I began my runaway in 1969. It's within a mile of the unit Cloverdale where I lived for a year with the hateful housemother, Millie Simmons. I smile as I drive passsed knowing she'd been fired for her cruelty a few years after I got out of the school. When I found out I was still in high school and felt like screaming to my relatives who saw me as a troublemaker, "See, I told you she was a mean bitch!"

After I check into my room I visit the first unit where I lived with Mr. and Mrs. Miller, or "Pop" and "Mom.," who had treated us boys kindly. One of the kids gives me a tour, and I enjoy some memories. There's the living room where we'd sit and listen to Pop's Bible stories each morning. And there's the desks where I used to write letters to my father, all furnished now with computers for the children. Milton Hershey now accepts girls into the school, a dramatic difference from my days there. I'm even a bit envious as I watch them run around and wonder how much of a difference a co-ed school would've made for me. Would I still have run away when I was 14?

Mike Hughes, and a crowd from our class meet for supper at an Italian restaurant, and it's amazing how people and places remain the same in so many ways and yet change in so many others. Jon Haines, who built a guillotine we used with a fifth grader once, was never athletic and was even a little out of shape in 1968. He even got picked on occasionally. Now he has a black belt in karate, drives an interstate truck and manages a wife and kids. He has always wondered what happened with me and has good memories and feelings about me, and I'm definitely glad he does! After platefuls of spaghetti, Mike and I take a walk in the fresh air of the sweetest town on Earth, talking about topics as meaningful as the dirty joke his brother, Rick, told him recently. It seems we have just exited a time machine when we walk through the nostalgia pouring out of the Hershey Theater where we once attended Sunday worship.

"I'm ready to check out!" I yell to Gary, the manager, who does his paperwork in the rear of Pizza Hut.

A Suicide Note of Hope

" Twenty-four deliveries in eight hours, not bad, we owe you $3," Gary monotones in his authoritarian voice.

"I should also get hazardous duty pay. I had to bark at a German Shepherd for almost five minutes before I intimidated him enough to make one delivery."

"See ya tomorrow night, Hank." Gary thinks I'm a little weird, barking at a dog, asking children who do they like better, me or Santa Claus?, and other stunts I pull to avoid boredom.

The drive home is a little more than 10 miles so I have time for my reunion again. There is a football game Saturday afternoon with a meeting in two bars scheduled afterward and if I want to get my daily run in, I'd better do it in the morning. It's near perfect Pennsylvania Fall weather, stimulating me to clip along at a refreshing pace, frequently reminding myself to reorient to the present, the here and now, no I'm not down there on that field as a 10-year old goalie for Revere's soccer team. I'm a 43-year old runner and had better avoid these cars that I used to count with Dan, Carl, and Bill sitting on that porch before supper when Pop Miller would ring that bell. I'm in a ditch. That Porsche came a little too close. I decide to run to the end of Keystone cluster where I stayed with the Akers, houseparents of Unit Stiegel, from sixth to eighth grades. Stiegel wears the same putrid green trimming as it did when Mrs. Akers senselessly lectured me in that stairwell I had to scrub, those ludicrous lectures that should have embarrassed her. When I pass Stiegel I run backwards and look at it one last time and imitate Papillon, the escaped prisoner, yelling "Hey you bastards! I'm still here!"

The victorious feeling is another reward for having resisted suicide. Three years with the Akers was the longest time in my child- hood I spent with any two pseudo-parents and though they weren't the worst, they were far from the best, or should I say least bad. But I survived all of it. You never know when it's going to feel so good to be alive!

Running passed Cloverdale initially triggers thoughts of Millie Simmons who made me scrub the ceiling of that carport on a ladder that I fell off accidentally-on-purpose to no avail. And just because I ran away. Just as quickly as she entered my memory, I cough up a mouthful of mucous and saliva in which I put her before spitting her out on 322. Dave Feese, my friend from Cloverdale who died in a car accident in college, would applaud the spitting of Millie on 322 especially since a Mack truck just ran over her. I remind myself of my Buddhist philosophy to let go of anger and find peace, and the picture Dave drew me of the Beatles inside the sleeve of the Sergeant Pepper album comes to mind. Dave would coach me to let go of anger if he were here today. Yes, I suppose I have gotten by with a little help from my friends.

Speaking of friends, I see Bill McConnell at the football game but I vividly recall how he had been my enemy about 50% of the time. He tells me he was sad that I ran away and says it was even sadder how Akers, with whom he also lived, picked on me more than most. I told him they weren't the worst and when he says that's the saddest thing he's heard yet, we both laugh after I tell him we are in English class conjugating sad, sadder, saddest. I am just as intrigued by his story as he was sad by mine as he tells me he went to India after smashing swim records and graduating from Penn State because he didn't know what else to do. It was while climbing a mountain there that it dawned on him to send some of the rugs he'd been making back to the U.S. which led to his successful rug business.

Later that night, more than a dozen of us congregate in a watering hole to reminisce and exchange autobiographies since 1972. A few of my ol' cohorts are intrigued I'm certified in hypnosis, and fortunately, I brought a few tapes of "PRACTICE," the hypnotic script I wrote, recorded, and began marketing. John Lelii, a fifth grade classmate, is a land surveyor now and becomes increasingly interested when I explain PRACTICE is an acronym for pacing, relaxation, assertiveness, confidence, thinking rationally, imagery, comic relief, and empathy. He buys a tape and a year later gives me a call at home saying he listens to it almost weekly and that it has "transformed" him. He's much more confident, especially at work. While I was the President of our fifth grade class, and didn't do much then, I've finally helped him.

Perhaps the most conspicuous topic some of us discuss that night and at breakfast the next morning is the overall improvement in the quality of Milton Hershey School since our era. Houseparents are required to receive more training, and their abuse of students is reportedly obsolete. They've done away with the dairies so the kids don't have to milk cows and clean barns like we did. To be admitted to the school, a boy or girl must only prove neediness, whether financial or emotional, an incredible change from the requirement to be an orphan in our day. There is still very little, if any, advertisement to the public about the school, and I remark there are probably thousands of kids who are abused, neglected, or poor who'd love to live in beautiful homes, receive clothing, food and education, enjoy sports, musical programs and other extracurriculars–all for free! Somebody says the school has about five billion dollars in their trust fund. Hey, you didn't hear it from me.

Grace and Siddhartha

New night, new money. I like to play a game with tips, similar to how I counted the number of foul shots out of 30 I made when I was 12 and living at Stiegel. I'm off to a good start getting seven tips for eight deliveries.

I join Mick Jagger keeping me company on tape and picture myself with the microphone on stage in front of thousands of screaming fans and begin singing "You don't know what's goin' on…You can't come back and think you are still a man…Baby, baby, baby you're out of time…", reminding myself that's kind of like me in the psychology profession. I haven't had a job in my profession for two years. Sometimes I feel like a bum. And I was feeling a bit that way last year lying on the living room floor on a Saturday night watching a t.v. show about a cat that brings tomorrow's paper to this guy wondering if I'm hallucinating as I hear a few meows from my opened porch door. They continue and I realize I am not psychotic, at least at this moment, and think how uncanny it is having this cat visit me while I watch this particular show.

"Aauugh, it'll go away if I ignore it." I've never liked cats and even made a point to avoid dating girls who owned them back in my late teens and twenties.

"Meeeooww, meeeooww," it persisted. I walked to the door and have a heartfelt experience observing a one and a half pound, gray kitten with emerald eyes pleading with me, "Please be my daddy. I'm hungry." "Somebody has abandoned this beautiful little thing", I moan, opening the door and picking it up in one hand. After almost being hypnotized by its innocent eyes, I put it back on the floor, pour a little milk in a bowl and feel honored that I've been given this experience as I watch kitty excitedly lap up her milk. She's a little more than just cute.

"You wouldn't put me back out there in the dark to be scared and all alone would you?" I read its mind after it finishes the milk fully aware that I'm anthropomorphizing by thinking kitty has a mind and I don't care because I can feel my heart growing. My dislike of cats is history. "Of course I won't put you back outside," and I take it to the store where we buy kitty food while a couple of girls pet her and look at me like I'm the kindest man in the world after I explain to them what has just happened. After she eats her supper, she crawls onto my chest to fall asleep while I watch her and "Walker, Texas Ranger", amazed how much I enjoy doing something for a life a year after almost taking mine. Grace sleeps in my bed with me that night, the first female to do so in a good while, which doesn't matter now because I love all life. They essence of all life is curled up, lying snugly against me.

Eventually Grace is twelve pounds, Maltese and brindle, and though a little rocky at times, our relationship has been more than worth the trouble involved in cleaning litter boxes, picking up things she loves knocking off counters, treating myself after her bites and scratches, and attempting the impossible task of trying to please her. I hear other cat roommates (due to a cat's attitude that she is royalty, it does not seem accurate to say we are owners) say they spoil their feline friends, and I suppose that's a fair description of my behavior with Grace. The vet's assistant, Linda, informs me she's not spoiled--she's "rotten". I buy her packs of furry mice, throw them for her to chase and retrieve and victoriously stroll back to me with her prey dangling from her mouth. Initially thinking she manages to lose the damn things, with the consequence of my continued purchases of them, I one day find them in a multitude of crevices and crannies around the apartment, realizing they are not only prey but prisoners. Since she hides them, I rarely have any to throw to her and the human who said

A Suicide Note of Hope

he'd never own a cat thinks he's buying mice toys for Grace when he's really buying them for himself. I'm sure I'll find lots of imprisoned mice when I move the furniture out one day. Until then I need to accept my responsibility of purchasing them on a regular frequency.

I look at the ticket and see there's no charge for this pizza as I get out of my car at 5401 Winslow and realize there's almost no chance of getting a tip. "I hope dis one's better n' da last!!" a haggard woman in bathrobe and slippers blabbers to me with a facial expression obviously stolen from Hitler's great grandmother.

"I hope so too ma'am," I reply forcing an ounce of politeness imagining myself grabbing the extra large pizza and decorating her face with greasy cheese, pepperoni, and mushrooms.

"We'll here's fo' yo' trouble," she surprises me and after taking the dollar I wipe the disaster off her face.

Eight tips for nine deliveries, not bad, and I return to Grace driving comfortably back to Pizza Hut. People tell me how independent cats are, that she's content alone in the apartment for eight to ten hours, but I read in a cat book confirmation of my speculation that she'd be happier with a companion. He's just five months old, a Maine coon, adorable, and unwanted by one of my pizza customers. I name him Siddhartha, birthname of the Buddha, partly to remind me to be more Buddhistic in my attitude and behavior. He has an incredibly intelligent expression in those penetrating green eyes, long dark gray and black hair with white gloves that go quarter-way up his legs. I expect Grace will love her little brother and deeply appreciate my loving gesture of bringing him home to her.

The hissing and scratching are incredible. Rather, than love him and appreciate me, Grace becomes a hostile ingrate hating us both, so I think, failing to recognize the apartment is Grace's territory, her private jungle. The achievement of developing a happy family will require baby steps, and I initially keep them separated in different rooms, amused how they get acquainted by frequently sniffing each other under the door. Sensing their curiosity is becoming stronger than their killing instinct, I put them in the same room where they display their bravery to each other through a seemingly endless series of Mexican standoffs.

Eventually they do engage in brief, lively spats that end abruptly upon my command–I fear for the declawed Grace. As a short-term solution, I have Siddhartha's nails clipped at the Cat Clinic every six weeks for a small price, but realize in less than a year I will have paid more than I would for a declawing. I had Grace declawed in self-defense as she was scratching the daylights out of my arms, but Siddhartha's a different story. He has such an innocent, lovable disposition and never appears to hurt Grace in their battles that become increasingly playful. He doesn't scratch me at all and poses only a couple of problems, one of which is his determination to use the bathtub as his toilet, and when I fail to train him to use the litter box, I realize the "intelligence" in his eyes is deceptive, like maybe it's an illusion. He also seems to think he's doing me a loving favor by jumping onto my bed, lying on my shoulder, licking and purring at about 5 a.m. almost daily. I amuse myself thinking I'm a roamin' Catholic while he's a roamin' cat-who-licks. It should be a sin to be that cute.

Time for another tape. I'll give Mick and the boys a rest after this delivery, the street for which I suddenly find myself propelling on a little too fast to identify addresses. And the damn addresses range from those numbers posted in black and white just a few feet from the road, an obvious sign of consideration for us pizza men, to those homes whose residents claim their addresses were ripped off the door by hooligans. There's no excuse. They should have had them replaced before ordering pizza. My rule applies to the current customer; I infer this must be his house by eliminating the ones to his left and right. I won't even ask what happened to his stupid address.

" That will be $19.04 for these two delicious Italian pies," I announce fully aware my theatric presentation is designed to mask my frustration.

"Keep the change," Mr. Generosity replies handing me an Andrew Jackson whose birthday was the same as mine, and I wonder if he was as frequently reminded "that's the Ides of March, Andy," by his acquaintances. At least it's more than .75 and therefore qualifies as a tip. I stick in John Lennon who's imagining there's no heaven because it isn't hard to do, and I'm off.

With mixed feelings I have Siddhartha declawed justifying it by telling myself "better safer than sorry, it will save money in the long run…" Upon his return to his castle and my home he favors his sore paw, licking it constantly and often suspending it like a levitation. My mixed feelings quickly transforms into pure guilt and sympathy, so intense I realize I'm catching a case of "I can't stand it itis." To better control these emotions I give myself a strong dose of "I don't like it but I can stand it," and take my little boy, er cat, back to the vet's office where I learn the paw's infected. I feel like a sadist strongarming my son into a position in which I can pry open his mouth to stick the dropper of medicine he detests, and my only salvation is that I'm doing it in the midst of Grace. I always spend more time on deliveries when I discover customers have cats.

Death Kisses Revisited

Driving pizza along a favorite stretch of road, I go back to the year after I got fired when I used some humility in my efforts to acquire enough money for survival. I recall sitting in a chair pumping blood from a vein to sell plasma to supplement my income as a psychiatric technician in 1977 and '78, just after college. The most conspicuous memory is the attractive, tall blonde phlebotomist flirting with me and smiling as she checks the needle sticking in my arm, commanding, "Pump, keep pumping." Wondering if a little sadism drew her to her profession, I finally discover it did not when I awaken in her arms one morning. "Having a tolerable memory of the pain of the needle to a pleasant memory of awakening with her in bed is definitely a sign of aging," I muse.

Returning to the tolerable, the medical staff informs me I am not allowed to continue selling plasma because a blood analysis indicates I may have hepatitis C. A foreign female doctor very nicely explains the disease to me, directs me to see another physician for a conclusive diagnosis, and I feel like a defendant in court facing a possible capital punishment verdict. She informs me I'll never be permitted to sell plasma again, regardless of the conclusive diagnosis. PARADE magazine indicates approximately 10,000 people die annually from hepatitis C, compelling me to begin competing with my old opponent, the Grim Reaper. I sadly say goodbye to the possibility of meeting anymore attractive phlebotomists.

Instead I say hello to Dr. Reynolds, my potential executioner, at the county health clinic. He is just as nice as the foreign female doctor when he informs me the tests are positive, that I do, in fact, have hepatitis C. I'm told it is a disease of the liver, similar to cirrhosis, and I'm reminded of the first time I was a pallbearer at age 14 for Uncle Bernard who died of cirrhosis. His last days were ones of sheer pain and agony, and I can hear him repeatedly yelling "Dear Jesus" in his hospital bed. However, I needn't worry so much because the chances of me dying are slim; effective treatment is available. Dr. Reynolds says I just have to come up with a little money, and I say "ha ha" to myself, aware that "a little money" is relative and means something entirely different to a doctor compared to a pizza guy. When I'm financially ready Dr. Reynolds will refer me to a specialist who will likely put me on interferon and ribivarin.

I feel lucky when I read an article in the Charlotte Observer about a Dr. Riddle who treats hepatitis C patients using clinical trials which means for free! He agrees to treat me, stipulating that I will have to come up with the money for the biopsy, a minor operation that will not even keep me in the hospital overnight. The doctor listens to me describe my history to ascertain how I got the disease. I've never used illegal drug needles which is a common means of transmission. Is it possible I got it from the blood plasma clinic back in my blonde phlebotomist days? On no, very unlikely. He states with certainty I acquired it when I received an intravenous blood transfusion after the car accident in 1972, 25 years ago.

During a visit to a coffee shop an earthy woman of Native American heritage named Pam tells me of a marvelous herbalist, Lisa Singing Butterfly, who treats hepatitis C patients with a healthy concoction of plant medicines. I learned about the value of alternative approaches to traditional medicine years ago when I cured myself of low back pain through reading about the treatment used by Dr. John Sarno– alternative medicine can be quite effective. I decide to explore and intuitively feel optimistic about what I will discover. There's nothing like a brush with death to get one excited.

As I pull up to Pizza Hut I'm feeling frustrated because the phone person put the wrong address on the delivery ticket for the third time tonight, and it took me almost an hour to play detective and find the right address. The customer was not pleased with the late delivery and communicated his dissatisfaction by not tipping and I wanted to tip his flower pot off his porch and onto the cement walk but resisted the urge by reminding myself to be more Buddhistic. I'm nearly as hot as the oven when I walk in the door glaring at manager Gary.

"What the hell's going on? This is the third incorrect ticket tonight Gary!"

"O.K. just calm down. You're getting upset." Gary counters in his most authoritarian vioce.

"Yeah I'm getting upset! I'm losing money! I'm getting sick of being sent out on wild goose chases!"

"Now just listen to me!" he commands, his tone becoming imperious.

"No you listen to me! I'm outta here!" I torpedo, following up with a dramatic exit.

On my drive home I wonder what I'm going to do to make money now. My behavior was immature to put it mildly, and it's not the first time I've failed to tolerate my frustration adequately. Instead of letting loose with such an aggressive outburst, I could've done better with an appropriate assertive response, the kind I wrote about earlier in this note. I also remind myself of an insight I made into my own granite statement:"It's stupid to get angry at others' stupidity."

It's not going to help to either worry about money or my frustration intolerance for now though. I take a deep, relaxing breath, inhaling slowly from my lower abdomen and through my nose and exhale even more slowly through pursed lips, just like I used to teach my clients. Feeling a bit more relaxed, I do another calming breath and say to myself, "I can accept my self even though I make mistakes. I love the essential me, the basic part of me I call my self, although I sometimes fail in my behavior. I can look forward to positive possibilities as long as I accept my self." To enhance the experience of accepting myself, I picture myself being held by my smiling mother, with my father beside her, looking lovingly at me, when I was just a few months old. I've spent hundreds of dollars on milk thistle, L-Glutathione, CoQ10, and other herbal supplements Lisa has prescribed for me over the last year and have taken about 90% of the complete protocol. Still when I go to Dr. Reynolds to evaluate the disease, my cell and enzyme count are unchanged. I find it difficult to run 5 miles and swim 1 mile, both of which I try to do several times a week. I feel tired more than normal and know fatigue is a common symptom of hepatitis C.

I've thought about seeing Dr. Riddle again, but he fails to return my three phone calls and doesn't respond to a note I took to his new clinic and left with the secretary. I wonder whether he is refusing to see me, but the administrator of his clinic tells me he will see me if I get approval from a psychiatrist to take the interferon and ribivarin; their trial protocol specifies that anyone who has ever attempted suicide must be evaluated by a psychiatrist. Never mind that the only time I ever attempted it was more than 25 years ago. Apparently interferon has the potential to provoke emotional reactions and it's understandable they don't want to take a chance with someone who has been suicidal. And are they going to charge me $108 per visit now? I've gotten several bills for $216 so they have charged me for two visits. Dr. Riddle had informed me he'd see me at the new clinic for the same fee he'd seen me at the first one where I was scheduled to receive a free clinical trial. Maybe I'll move to Canada where health care is free.

I'll just keep taking the natural stuff and appreciate that maybe it has at least prevented the hepatitis from getting worse.

I park in the driveway and see Grace and Siddhartha sitting at attention on the windowsill and all is peaceful and serene for this moment. They do it every time. I think I'll take a nap with them. Instead, I lie down with them and stay awake until passed 3. I'm a little worried about survival, money, and frazzled about employment. I've been attending the Unitarian Universalist services for more than a year now since they accept any and all people, theists, Buddhists, Jews, agnostics, atheists and even us confusionalists who feel clearly confused about religion and spirituality, who count on uncertainty, accept ignorance and feel comfortable with the existential anxiety that plagues our species. You may have guessed Confusionalism is a term coined by yours truly, and as a consequence, I will have the right to admit only those I deem worthy of admission to the religion. But that's another story.

For now I'm driving in heavy rain along I-85 from a Universalist Service. Too many people there seemed too elitist again today, as if their intelligent approach to avoid dogma and accept all religions puts them above the rest. The issue makes me think of these lines from John Lennon's song "Working Class Hero": "You think you're so clever and classless and free…but you're still fuckin' peasants as far as I can see…" Then I laugh at how Lennon gets angry and condescending towards condescending people and how I feel condescending towards elitists which makes me condescending and who is an underemployed pizza delivery guy to get condescending towards anyone anyway?

My cousin, Jack, would probably laugh at my plight. Thinking abut him, my wrists and arm muscles tense and tighten going around this rain drenched curve at 65 m.p.h. "Is this a pond?" I wonder as I hydroplane. My lovely Corolla begins spinning, I enter a calm, dream-like state, accepting this may be the end of my life and the passenger side smashes into the cement highway divider. At one time I paid for this kind of excitement on the rides at Hershey Amusement Park.

Other than some soreness in the ribs on my right side, I feel O.K.– mostly I feel lucky. The car is totaled, but I won against the Grim Reaper once again. I am Michael Jordan at the top of the key, in the last second of the final game, going up, leaning back, releasing with the wrist… and swoosh! The crowd roars! I make that "it was nothing" grin, letting everyone know victory is just natural for me.

The EMTs take my vital signs while I sit in their ambulance. They ask the usual questions, the last being "Do you want to go to the hospital!"

"Please don't take it personally but I don't think so," and one EMT manages the smile I intended.

Although the experience provided some theater, some genuine drama, as well as a prompt to philosophize more about the brevity of life and the inevitability of death, it also caused inconveniences. A totaled car, my new pizza delivery job is out, at least for tonight. Dealing with the insurance company is never fun. Getting temporary transportation until I buy another car is a hassle in it's own rite. Still, a brush with death is a valuable learning experience. In our culture death is often considered a taboo subject. To varying degrees nearly all of us fear it. Isn't it ironic that something so inevitable is, at the same time, taboo? Why can we not talk about death calmly and comfortably and even, like some cultures, celebrate its occurrence? It is certainly within our control to desensitize ourselves to it. The taboo nature of it only exacerbates our death anxiety.

Probably most of us remember the old American Indian statement of bravery from the t.v. that was often made prior to battle: " Today is a good day to die." It is a position of acceptance and saying it and meaning it brings peace, a peace that, paradoxically, helps me enjoy life more. Yes, today is also a good day to live.

Rebirth

The painful struggle of a transformation in some ways resembles our birth experience, being forced through mother's canal, for what must seem like an eternity, gasping, hurting. witless and frightened, until finally we breathe and receive nourishment and love and cry for more.

Of course the life changes one experiences from befriending death have profound differences from those of the neophyte. Instead of the nourishment from mother's milk, it is a new philosophy that serves as my food. The more I digest it, the more I become empowered. Dostoyesky said truly, "A new philosophy, a way of life, is not given for nothing. It has to be paid dearly for and only acquired with much patience and great effort." A wrestling match with death and the victory over suicide requires that "much patience and great effort." The new philosophy is a gift earned, a present to become a part of my being until my final exit from this beautiful and terrible planet.

While I usually consider myself more of a relativist than an absolutist, I have learned to use a few ideas as absolutes. I call them my "granite truths" and say them with force, sincerity and purpose in many difficult situations.

Their empowering effect moves me, inevitably, from the position of victim to that of survivor. They are valuable tidbits within my philosophy and hoping they can be helpful, I want to share my use of them with you. When bad things happen, I often say the granite truth "I don't like this situation but I can stand it." Whether the statement is true is not dependent on the situation; one constructs the truth by sincerely, forcefully, and purposefully saying it. Similarly when I experience loss, whether it be of a person, animal, or possession, I insist "Instead of clinging, I can let go and let it flow." I can love and appreciate nature more deeply when I value loss as one form of change in the river of time. When I become aware of a growing desperation from within, that is not uncommon in our competitive, capitalistic, highly materialistic society, to get something or someone for my own, I resolve, "Instead of craving, I can let go and love what I have." In the same way, if I want to make myself happier, I state my granite truth, "I can accept and use whatever I have." And that does mean all I have, including problems and flaws. These truths will remain as my anchors to life.

For these granite truths to be felt, it is necessary, especially in the more difficult times, to say them more than once so they can sink in.

I make up what I call "My Faith Prayer for Happiness" which goes: "As I continue to value all that I have and to appreciate all that I have, especially each moment,

To tolerate any difficulty by reminding myself, 'I may not like it but I can stand it and I can handle it and I can manage, gracefully and skillfully,

To let go and let it flow or just let it be, instead of clinging or craving,

And to practice lovingkindness with all sentient beings, Then I can have faith that I will be happy."

It's been more than a month since I impulsively quit the pizza delivery job, and as I finish this note, I find comfort in my resolve to live life as long as possible, to enjoy simple things and lighten up, to look forward to positive possibilities, to tolerate uncertainty and to celebrate the death of suicide. My execution of suicide eliminates it as an option. I hope humanity will consider it antiquated one day. I'm inspired that my victory results from my love of life and my love for myself. I think my mother and father would like my inspiration.

It seems an irony I began this note around 1 a.m. on a cool October night, sitting at this desk, window open, and a gentle breeze dancing with the candlelight on the wall. Although it is a later hour, the other conditions are the same tonight as is the essence of my being; it is the layers of hopelessness that have been shed. My new layers of compassion and acceptance for self and others, of tolerance and patience for external events, and especially, my internal home of peace and happiness enhance my experience of this moment. Yes, I can live in the moment now and let the past and future remain as my next door neighbors.

One of the most valuable truths I have learned in my transformation is that suicidal thoughts can be a good thing and not a bad thing. They are good in that they are powerful signals that something in one's life does need to die. What needs to die is not the person but rather a self-defeating way of thinking. Usually what needs to die is a kind of clinging or craving and an intolerance, that is, the "I can't stand it" position. What often needs to be born is a position of acceptance, tolerance, compassion, understanding and forgiveness. With the death of the self-defeating patterns and the birth of life supportive positions, beautiful transformations are possible.

While I was moved from home to home to home so often as a child that I never really had a home, I have now created my internal home of peace and happiness that I can build on anytime, anywhere, or just enjoy for as long as I want, any place I breathe. Especially here, now. This internal home cannot be taken by anyone, and I can clean it with confidence, daily. I've described my building material throughout this note, and if you want it, you can have it.

As I look out my window, dawn's rising sun speaks to me, "Look forward to what you want during your brief visit on Earth while you experience the serenity I give you this morning. Tell yourself you can stand any difficulty. Breathe in peace. Breathe out love."

I will.

Epilogue

I discovered the reason Marilyn refused to contact me is that the biological mother told her I might not be the biological father. DNA testing confirmed I am not. I am happy to practice the skills outlined in this note and am at peace with it.

Yes, I am happy to be mindful of my sadness.

Perhaps a lifesaving feature that I have offered is the reframe of suicidal thoughts from being a bad thing to being a good thing. That is, they are signals that something in one's life does need to die; it is not, however, the person who needs to die. It may be important to plant this idea in one's mind over and over again, and at deeper levels each time. It will often be important to explore exactly what does need to die. Sometimes it may seem simple. One needs to let the clinging to something or someone die, especially if that something or someone is no longer available. What needs to die may very often be the clinging to a relationship or a job. Instead of clinging, let go, let it flow or just let it be. Yes, suicidal thoughts are a gift.

While what needs to die may often be an external thing, perhaps even more often what needs to die may be a cognitive distortion, things described in Chapter 6. For example, when I have lost a job I have thought, "I must get a job by such and such a date or it will be terrible." The two distortions in this one thought are the "musts" and the catastrophizing by the word "terrible". To counter the must, I can let the "must" die and tell myself energetically and sincerely, "It's not true that I must get a job, even though it is true that I very much want a job by a certain date." Also, if I don't get a job by a certain date, it would not be terrible if I let that word "terrible" die and instead told myself that it would be difficult but tolerable. The situation may be difficult and I will be able to handle it."

To be capable of dealing with crises, instead of committing suicide, it will often be helpful to practice the skills outlined in this book including meditation, mindfulness, assertive skills, cognitive skills, acceptance and utilization, exercise, and spiritual practice. And always remember that once you have identified what needs to die, you can give birth to a new life, a beautiful and wonderful experience of growth. You can.

This life is so brief. You can be patient. You will die one day. You can remember that death can be a friend as it reminds you to enjoy life more each day.

Advance Acclaim for "A Suicide Note of Hope"

"Hank McGovern, with the schooling of a professional and the experience of a participant, has written a book about one man's decent into madness... With lyrical sentences and a powerful sense of storytelling, McGovern... gives insight into the choice between taking one's life or living it."

TIM MCLAURIN, DECEASED,

SOUTHERN AUTHOR

"A Suicide Note of Hope' will be impossible to pigeonhole. Autobiography? Self-help book? Philosophy? Psychology? Yes. And more. The reader is drawn into the story of a man who has been through amazing hardship...and yet his sense of humor keeps coming through...you have to keep turning the pages for more."

LORI VAN WALLENDAEL, PHD, PSYCHOLOGY

PROFESSOR, UNC-CHARLOTTE,

AUTHOR, "PSYCHOLOGY AND THE LAW: INSIDE

AND OUTSIDE THE COURTROOM"

"I thoroughly enjoyed reading the first three chapters...how many therapists have the courage and wisdom to allow others to benefit from what they have learned about life through the eyes of an expert while... revealing that they are Everyman...I really enjoyed the humor...There were times I laughed out loud and just couldn't put the book down."

JOHN FARRAR, PHD, PSYCHOLOGIST, RETIRED

Made in the USA
Columbia, SC
06 August 2018